ENGLISH COUNTRY SONGBOOK

Those rude old tales – man's memory augurs ill
Thus to forget the fragments of old days
Those long old songs – their sweetness haunts me still

John Clare

ENGLISH COUNTRY SONGBOOK

EDITED BY ROY PALMER

OMNIBUS PRESS
LONDON · NEW YORK · SYDNEY · COLOGNE

First published 1979 © Roy Palmer by J. M. Dent & Sons
This edition © 1986 Roy Palmer published by Omnibus Press
(Omnibus Press is a Division of Book Sales Limited)

ISBN 0.7119.0968.7
Order Nc. OP 43850

Exclusive distributors:
Book Sales Limited
78 Newman Street, London W1P 3LA, UK.

Music Sales Corporation
24 East 22nd Street, New York, NY 10010, USA.

Omnibus Press
GPO Box 3304, Sydney, NSW 2001, Australia.

To the Music Trade only:
Music Sales Limited
78 Newman Street, London W1P 3LA, UK.

Printed by Scotprint Limited, Musselburgh, Scotland.

CONTENTS

IV ONCE I LOVED A LASS: COURTSHIP

V THE CHARMING BRIDE: MARRIAGE

VI UP TO THE RIGS: SPORT AND DIVERSION

VII THE LIFE OF A MAN: SEASONS AND CEREMONIES

LIST OF ILLUSTRATIONS

Part Title Illustrations

INTRODUCTION

As a small boy in 1847 Thomas Hardy attended a harvest home celebration at which he heard 'The Outlandish Knight'. 'He could recall to old age the scene of the young women in their light gowns sitting on a bench against the wall in the barn, and leaning against each other as they warbled the Dorset version of the ballad . . .

> Lie there, lie there, thou false-hearted man,
> Lie there instead o' me;
> For six pretty maidens thou hast a-drown'd here,
> But the seventh hath drown-ed thee!'

Hardy believed that 'this harvest home was among the last at which the old traditional ballads were sung, the railway having been extended to Dorchester just then, and the orally transmitted ditties of centuries being slain at a stroke by the London comic songs that were introduced' (F. E. Hardy, *The Life of Thomas Hardy*, Macmillan, 1962, p. 20).

He was being unduly pessimistic, though many other observers looked back to the same period as the last flowering of traditional song. As early as 1858 one of Thomas Hughes's characters in *The Scouring of the White Horse* was complaining: 'We have ceased to be a singing nation. The people have lost the good old ballads, and have got nothing in their place' (ch. VII). Walter Tomlinson remembered hearing an old singer in a farmhouse in 1853:

> It is after supper; we are all merry, men and maidens alike, and the big fire in the great chimney flashes a jovial light upon our faces all round the room, when it is suggested that old Robert should be called in to sing something for us. He is not far away, only in the back kitchen with the other farm servants, and is soon forthcoming. A tall, gaunt, iron-framed old man enters, is accommodated with a seat and a mug of ale, and informed of our desires. He may feel flattered, but betrays no emotion. . . . After a time he throws back his head, closes his eyes and begins, in a low, monotonous and lugubrious tone, a song which for length and duration is perfectly fearful. Eh! that song! Did it ever get properly finished? I never forgot that singing and I never forgot the chorus . . . ('A Bunch of Street Ballads', in *Papers of the Manchester Literary Club*, vol. 12, 1886, pp. 305–16).

Whereas Hardy was very much part of the scene he described, Tomlinson viewed the singing *de haut en bas*. The singer was produced from the back kitchen much as a child might have been called on to

1

perform a party piece for the grown-ups. The length of the song was 'perfectly fearful' and the delivery 'low, monotonous and lugubrious'. Nevertheless, the writer had a genuine interest, and even admiration, though he believed song singing to be part of the past. 'Years ago', he wrote (but, by implication, not any more) 'you would always be able to find, in any remote country village or farmhouse, some old man or other, probably entirely without school education, whose head was a perfect storehouse and repository of these popular ballads; and the great time for their most brilliant bringing forth would be the sheep-shearing suppers, the harvest homes, Christmastides, or the annual "mops", when the country servants made holiday in ribbons and Sunday clothes, and went to the hiring fairs.'

Tomlinson was not alone in his view. Cecil Sharp later wrote that in the 1880s 'it was generally assumed that we had no folk songs of our own' (*English Folk Song: Some Conclusions,* 1907, introduction); and, according to J. A. Fuller Maitland the impression 'that the English had no folk music' prevailed into the 1890s (*A Door-keeper of Music,* 1929, p. 223). It is extraordinary that this was precisely the time of the beginning of a great revival of interest in folk songs, based on the discovery of thousands of examples and their publication (or the beginnings of it) in the books of W. A. Barrett, Frank Kidson, Lucy Broadwood, Sabine Baring-Gould, Cecil Sharp, and many others.

Clearly, such a large corpus of song did not disappear in the late 1840s or 1850s and reappear a couple of generations later. Like the jungle tree of the metaphysical anecdote, it continued to exist, whether the philosopher was there to observe it or not. The song, however, presupposes both a singer and an audience, and the latter was undoubtedly in decline.

The most important factor in the transmission of folk songs was the activities of the 'old singing men', as Baring-Gould called them. These were, in modern parlance, part-time professionals whose skill was in demand within their own community at all sorts of merry-makings, both private and public. Such a one was James Parsons, of Lew Down in Devon, an illiterate hedger, born in 1814. 'He enjoyed no little local celebrity as a song-man', wrote Baring-Gould, who first met him in 1888. He was the son of 'a still more famous singer called "The Singing-machine", and grandson of another of the same fame. In fact, the profession of song-man was hereditary in the family. At every country entertainment, in olden times, at the public house almost nightly, one of the men of the Parsons family had not failed to attend, to sing as required for the company. The repertoire of the grandfather had descended to old James.' This story illustrates the prowess of 'old James', both as a singer and a drinker:

At one time Parsons and a man named Voysey were working on the fringe of Dartmoor, and met in the evening at the moorland tavern.

2

have been taught and learnt, exchanged or sold, for perhaps a pint of beer.' However, for one reason or another, not every singer was keen to part with his song, much though Burstow might wish to acquire it. Lucy Broadwood tells how he was obliged to resort to a stratagem on one occasion. A ploughman was reluctant to sing a ballad which Burstow wanted, so:

> He induced a friend to lure the ploughman into the front parlour of a tavern, hiding himself in the back room. After a time Mr Burstow's accomplice challenged the ploughman to sing as long a 'ballet' as himself. A duel of songs arose; the ballads grew and grew in length. At length the ploughman, filled with the desire to 'go one better' than his opponent, burst into the very song for which the bell-ringer was patiently waiting. He learned it there and then. ('The Collecting of English Folk Songs', in *Proceedings of the Musical Association*, vol. 31, 1905, pp. 89–109).

Such assiduity in pursuit of a song was by no means unique, but one other example must suffice. It is that of John Collinson, who took three days away from his work as a blacksmith in order to wait until his father-in-law remembered a song (no. 122).

The last, and by no means unimportant element in Burstow's repertoire – and I believe it to have been typical of many, in composition if not in size – was material from 'ballad sheets I bought as they were being hawked about at the fairs, and at other times from other printed matter'. The ballad hawker was a well-nigh ubiquitous figure in English life from the seventeenth century to the nineteenth, and the ballad presses were active in a few cases until the twentieth. It would be difficult to over-estimate the importance of these presses in the transmission and preservation of traditional song. John Clare, whose own father was fond of ballads ('I have heard him make a boast of it over his horn of ale, with his merry companions, that he could sing or recite above a hundred', quoted in Edmund Blunden, *Sketches in the Life of John Clare*, 1931, p. 46), wrote that 'the common people . . . know the name of Shakespeare as one (a poet) but the ballad-mongers who supplys hawkers with their ware is poets with them & they imagine one as great as the other' (*Autobiography, 1793–1824*, quoted in J. and A. Tibble, *The Prose of John Clare*, 1951, p. 31). (To avoid the charge of selective quotation, however, I must admit that Clare also wrote, in 1828, of the 'senseless balderdash that is bawled and sung over at Country Feasts, Statutes and Fairs', quoted in J. and A. Tibble, *John Clare: His Life and Poetry*, 1956, p. 130.)

Of course, only a proportion of the output of the ballad presses consisted of traditional material. Much of it was repeated reprintings of all sorts of composed songs, martial, sentimental, music hall, parlour, by writers such as Charles Dibdin, Henry Russell, Henry Bishop, and a host of lesser lights. Yet the proportion of traditional song printed was seldom less than a third of the total, and sometimes as much as two-thirds. 'When genuine popular ballads were printed on these sheets,' wrote Mrs E. M. Leather, 'the words were taken down from tradition for the publishers; afterwards the broadsides were taken through the country districts by pedlars and ballad chanters, who sang in the streets the ballads they had for sale' (*The Folklore of Herefordshire*, 1912, p. 181). She continued:

> I have often heard of these people from those who remember them, but could never find one; they must have died out. One who came to Weobley fair every year cried, 'A song, a song, a song for a penny! As large as a barn door and not quite so thick!' The word broadside is not used by the local peasantry; they say 'ballet'. The boys never came back from the fairs without two or three 'ballets'. One singer explained that 'they rolled them up into balls in their pockets', which is probably the reason why so few survive.

Others did see the ballad sellers. References are not legion, because such hawkers were an unremarkable, and indeed disreputable, part of the everyday scene. Samuel Marshall, a Surrey farmer born in 1864, remembered the ballad sellers of the 1880s, 'who used to come round selling old ballad songs, as long as your arm' (*The Life of a Successful Farmer*, 1952, p. 8). Edwin Grey, who was brought up in Harpenden, gives an excellent description:

> Then along would come the ballad singer; he would pass slowly along the roadway by the front of the houses, singing some harrowing verses made up specially for the occasion, the singer fitting some sort of drawling tune to the words, the more harrowing and bloodcurdling he could make the sordid theme appear the better in all probability would be the sale of his papers, for many of the people would buy whether they could read it or not; the verses would be there for anybody to read who wished. These verses were printed on single sheets of cheap paper, and sold at one penny or halfpenny per sheet. The last of these ballad singers I saw and heard was a man singing and selling verses related to the murder of Miss Harriet Lane by Henry Wainright, which terrible murder took place in 1875 (*Cottage Life in a Hertfordshire Village*, St Albans, n.d., pp. 43–4).

Broadsides, then, provided vital support for the words of traditional song. Although many traditional musicians were musically literate, song tunes were passed on largely by oral means. Indeed, the essential qualities of traditional singing style – tone and delivery, decoration and variation, pace – could only be passed on this way. Such qualities are dimly seen through a curtain of incomprehension or disparagement in the comments of some observers. Walter Tomlinson spoke of the 'entire absence of inflection' ('A Bunch of Street Ballads', in *Papers of the Manchester Literary Club*, vol. 12, 1886, pp. 305–16) in the singing of a Warwickshire shepherd, by which one assumes that he means the absence of the dynamics customary in art music. M. C. F. Morris, remembering the East Riding farm lads of the 1840s, wrote that they were, generally speaking, fond of music; they 'often delighted in exercising their voices while at work in the fields, which had a very pleasing effect, for their singing was clear and tuneful'. There is a good indication here of clarity of tone, but he continues: 'it seems that their strains were commonly extemporaneous; at least one could seldom recognize any well-known air' (*The British Workman,* Oxford, 1928, pp. 43–4). Perhaps this shows that folk tunes were used which at that time were unfamiliar to the educated ear, which would not be very surprising. More important, the 'extemporaneous strains' might indicate that practice of rhythmic and melodic variation and decoration used extensively by fine singers, and to some extent by all singers. (For an example in this book, see no. 75.)

Cecil Sharp found that one of his singers, Henry Larcombe (born 1823) of Haselbury Plucknett, Somerset, whom he visited in 1905, habitually varied every phrase of his tune when singing a ballad:

> I remember that in the first song he sang to me he varied the first phrase of the second verse. I asked him to repeat the verse that I might note the variation. He at once gave me a third form of the same phrase. I soon learned that it was best not to interrupt him, but to keep him singing the same song over and over again . . . In this way I have been able to catch and note down these variations, which have recurred two or three times, but, of course, I have missed many of those which have appeared but once (op. cit., 4th ed., 1965, pp. 28 ff. Tunes and variations are given of 'Robin Hood and the Tanner' and 'Lord Bateman').

Other collectors, after their use was pioneered by Bartok, employed recording machines, and were then able to notate songs *in extenso,* variations and all, at their leisure. Percy Grainger did some outstanding work of this kind, which he published in part in the *Journal of the Folk Song Society* (vol. III, 1908). His outstanding singer, Joseph Taylor, can now be heard on the record, *Unto Brigg Fair* (Leader LEA 4050, 1972). Indeed, the art of the traditional singer can now be studied on a considerable number of records, of which *A Song for Every Season* is a good example. This is a four record set (Leader LEA 4046–9, 1971; later issued as a single album selection, LED 2067) with forty-five songs, including no. 9 from this book, from the repertoire of the Copper family of Rottingdean, Sussex, a singing dynasty like that of the Parsons of Devon. A good deal of background information, together with the texts and tunes of many songs, is given in Bob Copper's two fine books, *A Song for Every Season* (Heinemann, 1971) and *Early to Rise* (Heinemann, 1976). Recordings are available of many other traditional singers, some of which are drawn upon in this book, and listed in the Sources and Notes.

Not all singers had repertoires of forty, sixty, a hundred songs and more, nor did they have the consummate skill of the finest performers. Almost everybody, however, was a singer in a small way. 'Each and all of them knew several songs' was Henry Burstow's comment on his friends. After a list which includes 'All Jolly Fellows', 'The Foggy Dew' and 'John Barleycorn', Samuel Marshall says: 'Every boy and master . . . knew some of the songs mentioned.' The outstanding singer was at the tip of a pyramid made up of a host of other singers, who were also his audience. The decline in traditional singing in the nineteenth century – for decline there was – was because the singing man's audience gradually deserted him for novelty, commercially provided. Flora Thompson, who was born in 1876, has beautifully described the syndrome. Writing of Oxfordshire at roughly the turn of the century, she noted: 'Traditions and customs which had lasted for centuries did not die out in a moment, and men and boys still sang the old country ballads and songs, as well as the latest music-hall successes' (*Lark Rise*, 1939, ch. IV). Yet it was the last, by a reversal of the old ideas of seniority, which had the greatest prestige:

> So, when a few songs were called for at the 'Wagon and Horses', the programme was apt to be a curious mixture of old and new.
>
> While the talking was going on, the younger men, 'boy-chaps' as they were called until they were married, would not have taken a great part in it. Had they shown any inclination to do so, they would have been checked, for the age of youthful dominance was still to come . . . But, when singing began they came into their own, for they represented the novel.
>
> They usually had first innings with such songs of the day as had percolated so far. 'Over the Garden Wall', with its many parodies, 'Tommy, Make Room for Your Uncle', 'Two Lovely Black Eyes', and other 'comic' and sentimental songs of the moment.

Next came the middle-aged men, whose predilection was for what appear to have been high Victorian items, 'mournful stories in verse of thwarted lovers, children buried in snowdrifts, dead maidens and motherless homes', sometimes varied with 'songs of a high moral tone'. From time to time, 'the company would revert to old favourites' and sing 'The Barley Mow', 'When King Arthur First Did Reign', 'Nobody Coming to Marry Me' or 'I Wish, I Wish'. Only at the end of the evening would the old men have an opportunity to sing. 'Master Price' would sing 'Lord Lovell', then:

> there would be calls for old David's 'Outlandish Knight'; not because they particularly wanted to hear it – indeed, they had heard it so often they all knew it by heart – but because, as they said, 'Poor old feller be eighty-three. Let 'un sing while he can'.
>
> So David would have his turn. He only knew the one ballad, and that, he said, his grandfather had sung, and had said that he had heard his own grandfather sing it. Probably a long chain of grandfathers had sung it; but David was fated to be the last of them. It was out of date, even then, and only tolerated on account of his age.

Flora Thompson sadly concludes that 'songs and singers have all gone'. 'The singers were rude and untaught and poor beyond modern imagining', she says; 'but they deserve to be remembered, for they knew the now lost secret of being happy on little.' What one generation spurns, another seeks out and lovingly preserves. Thanks not only to the first great revival, but to a second wave of collecting since the Second World War, though much has undoubtedly been lost, a great wealth of country songs is still available. This book gives a small selection.

Country songs cover an enormous variety of subjects, but those which refer to country life, have the country as a background, or show countrymen as protagonists have been selected. Of the 147 here, two-thirds were collected this century, and half of these in the last ten years. About half the songs were printed as street ballads at some stage, but apart from this form of publication, and in some cases issue on records, two-thirds are previously unpublished, at least in the versions given here.

Thirty-two of the pre-1974 English counties are represented, from Cornwall to Northumberland and from Kent to Westmorland, together with the Gower, 'little England beyond Wales'. Norfolk is best served, with twenty songs; eight of these are from a living singer, Walter Pardon, who can be heard on three records commercially available. *A Proper Sort* (Leader LED 2063, 1975), *Our Side of the Baulk* (Leader LED 2111, 1977) and *A Country Life* (Topic 12TS 392, 1979). I do not wish to suggest, however, that these songs are somehow peculiar to Norfolk. To take one example almost at random, 'Lads of High Renown' (no. 51) has also been found in Dorset, Staffordshire and Yorkshire, and has appeared on broadsides printed in Birmingham, Manchester, London, Pocklington and Durham. Folksong was a national phenomenon, albeit with strong regional overtones, and it is precisely for this reason that the language used approximates to standard English. A. E. Green has convincingly shown that singers used standard English for reasons of mutual intelligibility in his fine paper. 'Folk Song and Dialect' (in *Transactions of the Yorkshire Dialect Society*, vol. XIII, part LXII, 1972, pp. 20–46).

As if to prove the rule, however, several items with strong dialectal colouring have been included. One, 'Wa'ney Cockfeightin' Sang' (no. 122) is a local variant of a nationally known song in which there seems to have been some recasting of the content in order to increase local reference. Another, 'Mowing Match Song' (no. 121), is a genuine local production, dealing with a local event in the local vernacular. It seems likely that, had the song travelled farther afield, it would have been cast into some semblance of standard English, while retaining some dialect colour. It remained a local anthem, however, and though very much in the folk idiom is not a folk song in the sense of a multi-versional song orally transmitted over relatively large areas. A third, 'Turnit Hoeing' (no. 10), seems to have been a regional production which became nationally accepted and was found in different versions in widely different areas.

For convenience, the songs have been divided into seven thematic groups, the first one dealing with work. Properly so called, a work song is specifically designed to accompany the particular rhythm of a given task. On their tour of the Western Islands of Scotland in 1773 Johnson and Boswell heard such songs at the harvesting on Raasay:

> The women reaped the corn, and the men bound up the sheaves. The strokes of the sickle were timed by the modulation of the harvest song, in which all their voices were united. They accompany in the Highlands every action, which can be done in equal time, with an appropriated strain, which has, they say, not much meaning; but its effects are regularity and cheerfulness (*Journey to the Western Islands,* Oxford, 1970, p. 56).

Such songs did not apparently survive in England, even into the eighteenth century, though there is a tantalizing reference which might indicate something similar: 'we worky-folk roar out the sickle songs, as we call them', a remark reported by S. J. Pratt in a book first published in 1797 (*Gleanings in England,* 4 vols, 1804; vol. I, p. 189).

However, plenty of non-specific songs were used as a general background to work, to alleviate its monotony, as well as being sung on other occasions. M. C. F. Morris wrote of labourers 'exercising their voices while at work in the fields', and Heywood Sumner of 'songs which may still be heard where ploughmen strike their furrows' (*Besom Maker,* 1888, preface). Mrs E. M. Leather mentioned the ploughmen with rolled up copies of ballads in their pockets, to be pored over and sung when the opportunity arose.

As well as at work, such songs – or at least the more presentable ones – would also be sung at leisure. W. H. Hudson tells how the father of Shepherd Caleb Bawcombe when he came home early in the evening would collect his children round him and 'talk to them, and sing old songs and ballads he had learnt in his young years – "Down in the Village", "The Days of Queen Elizabeth", "The Blacksmith" (perhaps a version of no. 6), "The Gown of Green", "The Dawning of the Day", and many others, which Caleb in the end got by heart and used to sing, too, when he was grown up' (*A Shepherd's Life,* 1910, ch. 5). In public houses and at times of celebration the songs would also be sung.

The first section, then, deals with the ploughman (nos. 2, 3 and 4), blacksmith (5, 6), shepherd and his sheep (7, 8, 11, 12), labourer (1, 10, 18), carter (16, 19), servant girl (17) and farmer (20). It follows the rural cycle of ploughing, sowing, hay-making, sheep-shearing, harvesting. The dominant impression is a celebration of the skill, strength and sturdiness of the countryman. The glow of pride which emerges might seem to be consonant with the stereotype of a contented peasant doing deeply satisfying work in a pleasant environment. There is some truth in this, and Mabel Ashby's remark on the harvest might be extended to most farm work: 'though the disinherited had no great part of the fruits, still they shared in the achievement, the deep involvement and joy of it' (quoted *note*, no. 14). Yet no farm worker (or anyone who has worked on a farm, for that matter) can be unaware of the monotony and drudgery involved. Richard Jefferies trenchantly reminds us of the realities:

> To rise at five on a summer's morning and see the azure of the sky and the glorious sun may be, perhaps, no great hardship, although there are few persons who could long remain poetical on bread and cheese. But to rise at five on a dark winter's morning is a very different affair. To put on coarse nailed boots, weighing fully seven pounds, gaiters up above the knees, a short greatcoat of some heavy material, and to step out into the driving rain and trudge wearily over field after field of wet grass, with the furrows full of water; then to sit on a three-legged stool, with mud and manure half-way up to the ankles, and milk cows with one's head leaning against their damp, smoking sides for two hours, with the rain coming steadily, drip, drip, drip – this is a very different affair ('The Labourer's Daily Life' (originally published in 1874), in *The Toilers of the Field*, 1892, pp. 93–4).

In song at least, farm labourers seem to have complained little about the hardships of their work, though they were no means silent on the shortcomings of their employers and of society in general. The second section begins by exploring the paternalistic relationship between farmer and man. How deeply this was accepted is seen from the very wide popularity of a song like 'The Jolly Thresherman' (no. 23). Some of the songs of protest looked back to an even more paternalistic era, when the man lived under the farmer's roof, and was almost part of the family (e.g. no. 27), though the theme of the golden age being in the past had been current at least since Tudor times. Those labourers who did continue to live in, as some did, right until this century, often expressed the contrary view, as we see from a song like 'Mutton Pie' (no. 34) or from the writing of Fred Kitchen in *Brother to the Ox* (Dent, 1942).

In addition to individual complaints, songs also expressed the philosophy of both Joseph Arch's Labourers' Union of the 1870s (see 'O the Roast Beef of Old England: New Version', no. 35) and George Edwards' Norfolk Union of the late 1880s (see 'An Old Man's Advice', no. 36) which eventually led to the National Union of Agricultural and Allied Workers of today. Protest sometimes took oblique forms (nos. 38–40), and the farmer was not always the target. Indeed the labourers seem to have sided with the farmers at times, both against the squire and the tithe-gathering clergyman (28). They also attacked various tradesmen whom they thought dishonest (25, 30–33), and society in general (26), if they thought that they were

11

being badly treated. The tone of their discontent varies, from wry to outraged, from bitter to mocking, but one thing is sure: they are by no means obsequious or acquiescent.

The third section is devoted to crime. Poaching, which could in some forms be regarded as yet another form of protest, bulks large. The six songs included illustrate the wide variety of moods in which a given subject can be approached. 'The Lincolnshire Poacher' (no. 49) is jolly, 'The Nottingham Poacher' (50), defiant. Bitter grief is the dominant feeling in 'Lads of High Renown' (51) and 'Van Dieman's Land' (52), while 'Hares in the Old Plantation' (53) and 'Row Dow Dow' (54) are perky and light-hearted. There was undoubtedly an affinity between poachers and outlaws or highwaymen, in addition to the mere fact that they all operated in the country. Robin Hood (41) and such cattle thieves as Georgie (42) and Gilderoy (43) long retained a place in the affections of ordinary people, as did Dick Turpin (45). When the victim of highway robbery was a humble servant girl (46), however, or even a well-to-do butcher who was badly treated (44), popular sympathy immediately flowed the other way.

Murder and its punishment were as fascinating to country dwellers as to townspeople, and examples with a rural setting have been chosen here (nos. 55–61). They range in date from the thirteenth to the nineteenth century. Perhaps surprisingly, landscape does not often play a great part in folk song, which is concerned with emotion (in lyrical pieces) or with action (in narrative ballads), and sometimes with a combination of the two. Scenes are set with great economy: 'The sun is gone down and the sky it looks red' or 'The trees they do grow high, the leaves they do grow green'. Natural references are often in almost Homeric-style set phrases: 'the small birds were a-singing'; 'I heard the birds whistle and the nightingales sing'. On some occasions, however, the landscape beautifully echoes or contrasts with the mood of the protagonists. The premeditated murder of a woman is made all the more horrible by her unsuspecting walk through 'the fields and meadows gay' (57); conversely the bleak tale of the killing of a servantman because the daughter of the house has fallen in love with him attains great intensity with this verse:

> And through the woods as they were riding
> They saw a brake of briars grow;
> They soon became and his blood they slaughtered
> And a brake of briars pulled him through. (59)

By far the greatest number of songs which survived in the oral tradition until the twentieth century dealt with the relationship between the sexes. The themes respectively of courtship and marriage have therefore been given rather more space than the rest. Within the topic of courtship (section IV) there is tremendous variety. A woman is unable to find a man (no. 62), or alternatively rejects suitors whom she considers unsatisfactory, even going so far as to humiliate them (64–66). She deserts one man for another (63), or is in her turn deserted (78 and 79, 82, 84), or bitterly laments parting from her love (81). It may be surprising to find the woman's viewpoint so extensively expressed, and it was certainly unique in Victorian and Edwardian times to find a woman shown to be finding unashamed sexual enjoyment (67, 68, 73).

Naturally, the man is also given his share of attention. He seduces, then deserts, a woman, an archetypal theme (nos. 71, 72); or he is grief-stricken at being deserted by her or separated from her (83). Yet again, there are times when a relationship achieves harmony and mutual happiness (72, 74, 76, 77). All these matters are treated frankly, directly, but by no means without delicacy, tenderness, and sometimes humour. Such songs were a form of social and sexual education long before these matters were discussed in polite society, and they still have validity today.

The same might be said of songs dealing with marriage (section V). Here again, there is a balance in the viewpoints expressed, of the woman, the man, and the couple. Women's delight in marriage is often expressed (nos. 86, 87), with a wedding often being preceded by a joyous seduction (90–93). A valiant struggle was often needed by a daughter to overcome her parents' opposition to her choice of man (94, 95). Equally common was the daughter who allowed herself to be grotesquely mis-matched, usually in age, in order to please her parents: the complaint of the *mal mariée* is one of the staples of folk song (99, 100).

Men seem to have been rather less eager for marriage (no. 88), which may explain why they were apparently so keen to take any opportunity to seduce someone else's wife. Since time immemorial, or so it seems, cuckoldry has inspired countless jokes, tales and songs (101–106). Masculine complaints frequently mention slatternly or shrewish wives (96, 97, 98), but there are also songs of deep and abiding married love (107, 108). The fertility of the male and the fruitfulness of the female were constant preoccupations, and it is ironic that the production of children should now be considered undesirable. Richard Jefferies tells of a would-be philanthropic lady who visited the wife of a labourer 'and scolded his wife as if she was a thief for having that fifteenth boy'. In the end 'his "missis" turned on her . . . and said, "Lor, miss that's all the pleasure me an' my old man got"' ('John Smith's Shanty', 1874, in *Toilers*).

If fact, there usually were at least some other diversions open to the countryman, and these are the subject of section VI. Very rarely, he might venture to a large town, such as London. There he was very much of an innocent abroad, and needed sharp wits to avoid discomfiture at best, disaster at worst (nos. 109, 110). His more normal adventure, however, was a visit to the local town for the annual fair. In many cases, he went there partly to hire himself out, a year at a time. The hiring fairs, variously called 'mops' or 'statutes', continued in some areas until 1914, and in one or two until the 1940s. There is a fine description of Doncaster Martlemas Fair by Fred Kitchen:

> The streets were crowded with farm chaps seeking new masters, and all were dressed in breeches and leggings, while most of them wore favours in their caps, such as one gets by throwing at Aunt Sallies, and, on account of the pubs being open all day, many of them had obtained a staggering gait at an early hour. There were fightings and uproars, embracings of old friends and introductions to new ones, for you must bear in mind these lads had known no holiday for a twelvemonth, and were now let loose with a purse full of golden sovereigns. . . .
>
> Music and singing belched forth from every pub round about; *Farmer's Boy, Sweet Marie, Annie Laurie,* or *Dolly Grey,* played on concertina, melodeon, mouth-piece (jew's harp?), and tin whistle, and sung by voices over-fresh with too many 'liveners'. The recruiting sergeant, too, was always in evidence at 'stattises' and 'hirings', and many a beer-befuddled farm chap fell to the gorgeous attraction of that bright-red uniform (*Brother to the Ox*, ch. VI).

His tolerant, sympathetic tone is seldom matched by other commentators. Even the sympathetic Jefferies wrote: 'The fairs are the chief cause of immorality. Many an honest, hard-working servant-girl owes her ruin to these fatal mops and fairs, when liquor to which she is unaccustomed overcomes her.' However, he added: 'Yet it seems cruel to take from them the one day or two of the year on which they can enjoy themselves fairly in their own fashion' (*Toilers,* p. 227). The labourers obstinately clung to their enjoyment of fairs, and expressed in song the attraction of the various pleasures they provided (nos. 111–114).

One of these was drinking, and more especially, beer-drinking, which was almost a philosophy and a way of life (nos. 116–118, 120). We have seen from the success of the campaign for traditional beer in recent years that the noble beverage rightly holds its place in Englishmen's affections. Although very strong views have been expressed against hare (125) and fox hunting (126, 127), the countryman continues to enjoy these sports, and even the cruel old pastime of cockfighting was nostalgically remembered at one time (122). No doubt bell ringing (123) and horse racing (124) arouse less violent passions. The old mowing matches (121) are now no more, and though ploughing contests still continue, I have unfortunately not been able to find an English ballad on the subject.

The seventh and final section covers the seasonal ceremonies of the rural year. The countryman was, and is, fully aware of the progress of the seasons (no. 128), and of the cycle of life which enfolds not only plants and beasts, but man (129). The ancient pagan rituals were intended to ensure the fruitful continuation of life. They remain, a pale shadow of their former selves, but nevertheless still in existence. Many of the formerly ritual songs are now boisterous and jolly, sung to catchy but rather simple tunes; yet beneath can still be perceived something of the old solemnity, something of a reverberation from the distant past. A number of such songs had as their central theme, sometimes reinforced by ritual or drama, the life-giving sacrifice of a magical creature, the herring (138), horse (140), ram (145), mallard (137) or wren (143).

Several of these occasions provided the opportunity for a *quête*: begging for food or alms under the seal of tradition. The giver was blessed with good luck and the receiver obtained invaluable assistance. Many other opportunities presented themselves, including on Shrove Tuesday (no. 131), at Easter (132), in May (133–35), and at Christmas and the New Year (141, 142, 144). The volume concludes with two images of the tree of life, one sacred (146) and the other profane (147).

At present there is perhaps greater interest in English country life and traditional lore than for two centuries past. Some, perhaps, are merely seeking an escape from the complexities of modern city life. If so, they are not in bad company, for people have been looking back into a rural Eden in England's past for three hundred years and more, as Raymond Williams has pointed out in *The Country and the City* (Chatto, 1973). Others, however, are genuinely forward-looking in their approach to the country, and are seeking that alternative lifestyle which may be necessary for many or all of us in the future.

These songs can be treated as an escape into nostalgia, just as some of them were a means of escape from harsh reality for the labourers and milkmaids who sang them. Alternatively, or in addition, they are a powerful communication from the past which may help us to see our way forward. We shall never again experience quite what our ancestors felt, those singers 'rude and untaught and poor beyond modern imagining', but we can try to put a finger on their pulse, through the songs, though we must try to find our own truth in them, just as each age seeks to find its own truth in other forms of the literature of the past.

Yet in the final analysis, it could be argued that the songs' final justification is aesthetic. They have a sheer beauty of language which both reflected and helped to shape the utterance of generations of Englishmen, men like Shakespeare, Crabbe, John Clare, Wordsworth, Hardy, John Arden, as well as the countless thousands of ploughmen, shepherds, blacksmiths, milkmaids and servant girls who were the backbone of the nation. Their full power emerges, however, not on the page but on the lips. I hope that they will be savoured, but above all, sung.

I
Fellows that Follow the Plough:
Work

1   The Green Grass

If ever I had to choose a single item by which to represent English country song, this would be one of the candidates. Its appeal is partly in a luscious melody, partly in a text which achieves the difficult feat of being simple and strong, but at the same time, lyrical. The song provides in miniature the cycle of a rural year.

The sun gone down and the sky it looks red, And down on my pil-low where I lay my head, I lift up mine eyes for to see those stars shine, And the thought of my true love still runs in my mind.

2 The sap is gone down and the trees they will flaw,
  We'll branch them all round, boys, and clap in the saw;
  We'll saw them asunder and tumble them down,
  And then we will flaw them all on the cold ground.

3 Now flawing is over and haying draws near,
  With our pitchforks and rakes, boys, likewise some strong
      beer,
  We'll cut down our grass, boys, and carry it away,
  We will first call it green grass and then call it hay.

4 Now haying is over and harvest draws near,
  We'll send to the alehouse to brew some strong beer;
  We'll cut down our corn, boys, and roll it along,
  We'll take it to the barn, boys, and keep it from harm.

5 Now harvest is over and winter's come on,
  We'll jump into the barn, boys, and thresh out some corn;
  Our flails we will handle and boldly we'll swing,
  Till the very next morning that's now coming in.

6 When spring it comes on, there's a maid to her cow,
  There's a boy to his whip, and a man to his plough;
  Here's a health to our shepherds and carters all round,
  Here's a health to the jolly ploughman that ploughs up the
      ground.

  flaw: strip off bark.

2   The Oxen Ploughing

An illustration of about 1340 in the Luttrell Psalter shows oxen ploughing. The use of the ox as a draught animal continued in this country until relatively modern times. In 1874 the diarist, Kilvert, made this comment: 'As I drew near Kington I fell in with a team of red oxen, harnessed, coming home from plough with chains rattling and the old ploughman riding the fore ox, reminding me vividly of the time when I used to ride the oxen home from plough at Lanhill.' Baring-Gould, who collected the song given here from Adam Landry of Trebartha, Cornwall, noted in 1895 that oxen were still employed on the Sussex Downs, and also on the Cotswold Hills, where 'one may see the driver laying under the "bank of sweet violets" eating his bread and cheese or bacon, whilst the patient oxen stand resting in the furrow, chewing the cud'.

The cries and songs of ox-drivers to encourage their beasts often aroused comment. The Rev. Richard Warner, for example, wrote in his Tour through Cornwall (1808) that 'while the hinds are . . . driving their patient slaves along the furrows, they continually cheer them with conversation, denoting approbation and pleasure. This encouragement is conveyed to them in a sort of chaunt, of very agreeable modulation, which, floating through the air from different distances, produces a striking effect both on the ear and imagination. The notes are few and simple, and when delivered by a clear, melodious voice, have something expressive of that tenderness and affection which man naturally entertains for the companions of his labours.'

Pri-thee, lend your joc-und voi-ces for to lis-ten we're a-greed; Come sing of songs the choic-est of the life we ploughboys lead. There are none that live so mer-ry as the ploughboy does in spring—When he hears the sweet birds whis-tle and the nigh-tin-gales to sing. With my hump a-long! Jump a-long! Here drives my lad a-long! Pret-ty, Spar-kle, Ber-ry, Good luck, Speedwell, Cher-ry, We are the lads that can fol-low the plough,—oh,— We are the lads that can fol-low the plough.

2 In the heat of the daytime it's but little we can do;
We lie beside our oxen for an hour or two.
On the banks of sweet violets I'll take my noon-tide rest,
And it's I can kiss a pretty girl as hearty as the rest.

3 When the sun at eve is setting and the shadows fill the vale,
Then our throttles we'll be wetting with the farmer's
    humming ale;
And the oxen home returning we will send into the stall,
When the logs and peat are burning we'll be merry
    ploughboys all.

4 Oh the farmer must have seed, sirs, or I swear he cannot sow,
And the miller with his mill-wheel is an idle man also;
And the huntsman gives up hunting and the tradesman stands
    aside,
And the poor man's bread is wanting, so 'tis we for all
    provide.

Pretty, Sparkle and the rest: names of oxen.   *linney*: open shed.
Brown Willy: highest hill in Cornwall.   *humming*: strong.

3 All Jolly Fellows that Follow the Plough

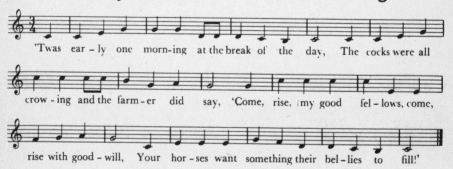

'Twas ear-ly one morn-ing at the break of the day, The cocks were all
crow-ing and the farm-er did say, 'Come, rise, my good fel-lows, come,
rise with good-will, Your hor-ses want something their bel-lies to fill!'

2 When four o'clock comes, then up we do rise,
And to our stables so merrily flies;
With rubbing and scrubbing our horses, I'll vow
That we're all jolly fellows that follow the plough.

3 When six o'clock comes, for breakfast we meet,
With bread, beef and pud, boys, we heartily eat;
With a piece in our pocket, I'll swear and I'll vow
That we're all jolly fellows that follow the plough.

4 We harness our horses and away we do go,
  We trip o'er the plains as nimbly as does;
  And when we get there so jolly and bold,
  To see which of us a straight furrow can hold.

5 Our master come to us and this he did say,
  'What have you been doings, boys, all this long day?
  If you've not ploughed your acre, I'll swear and I'll vow
  That you're damned idle fellows that follow the plough.'

6 I stepped up to him and made this reply:
  'We've all ploughed our acre, so you've told a damn' lie;
  We've all ploughed our acre, I'll swear and I'll vow,
  We're all jolly fellows that follow the plough.'

7 He turned himself round and laughed at the joke:
  'It's past two o'clock , boys, it's time to unyoke;
  Unharness your horses and rub them down well,
  And I'll give you a jug of my very best ale.'

8 So all you brave fellows whoever you be,
  Come take this advice and be ruled by me:
  Never fear your master then I'll swear and I'll vow
  That you're all jolly fellows that follow the plough.

Observing an ancient tradition, established when oxen were draught animals, the ploughman used to rise at four in the morning to bait and groom his horses. He set off to the fields at 6.30 a.m., and by 2.30 p.m. the daily stint of one acre would have been ploughed. The work of the ploughman (or horseman or waggoner, as he is known in different areas) is described in George Ewart Evans's The Horse in the Furrow *(1960).*

The song was extremely widely known – Cecil Sharp remarked that 'almost every singer knows it; the bad singers often know but little else' – and it can still be heard from time to time in country pubs. The version printed here comes from Arthur Lane, a Shropshire countryman born in 1884. He was a 'waggoner', as he called it, himself. He learned the song when he was 'living in' at a farm near Bishop's Castle: 'When we finished the horses eight o'clock or half past at night, bedded them down and all this – it was winter time – we got some straw . . . and there we'd sing till one or two o'clock. We could go in the house whenever we liked, the door was never barred.' The tune is a variant of the ubiquitous 'Villikins and his Dinah'.

4   The Ploughboy

'A trewe swynker [worker] and a good': the ploughman, both for Chaucer and for countless generations of countrymen, was a deeply respected figure. After all, on his skill as a tiller of the soil and a planter of seed the welfare of the whole community depended.

Although a form of seed-drill was popularized early in the eighteenth century by Jethro Tull, the machine did not come into widespread use until the middle of the nineteenth. Even then, broadcast sowing continued, particularly in small or awkwardly-shaped fields. Our man gives 'the corn a throw' by the old method, and in so doing seems to be more in harmony with the natural order of things. The song has a deep reverence for the fertility of the earth and for the ploughman who stimulates it.

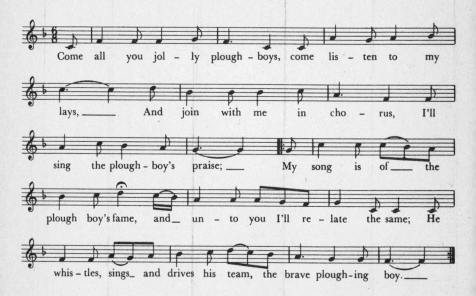

Come all you jol – ly plough – boys, come lis – ten to my lays, ___ And join with me in cho – rus, I'll sing the plough – boy's praise; ___ My song is of ___ the plough boy's fame, and ___ un – to you I'll re – late the same; He whis – tles, sings ___ and drives his team, the brave plough-ing boy. ___

2 So early in the morning, the ploughboy he is seen;
He hastens to the stable, his horses for to clean.
Their manes and tails he will comb straight, with chaff and
corn he does them bait,
Then he'll endeavour to plough straight, the brave ploughing
boy.

3 Now all things being ready, and the harness that's put to,
All with a shining countenance his work he will pursue.
The small birds sing on every tree, the cuckoo joins in
harmony
To welcome us as you may say, the brave ploughing boy.

4 So early in the morning, to harrow, plough and sow –
And with a gentle cast, my boys, we'll give the corn a throw,
Which makes the vallies thick to stand with corn to fill the
reaper's hand:
All this, you well may understand, comes from the ploughing
boy.

5 Now the corn it is a-growing, and seed time that's all o'er,
Our master he does welcome us and unlocks the cellar door;
With cake and ale we have our fill because we've done our
work so well,
There's none here can excel the skill of a brave ploughing
boy.

6 Now the corn it is a-growing, the fields look fresh and gay,
The cheerful lads come in to mow, whilst damsels make the
hay;
The ears of corn they now appear, and peace and plenty
crowns the year,
So we'll be merry whilst we are here and drink to the brave
ploughing boy.

team: until as late as 1900, most ploughing was done by a three-horse team, with a man guiding the plough and a boy walking beside the horses. In the course of ploughing their acre a day they walked eleven miles on average.

5   Twankydillo

The smith was a highly respected craftsman, who not only shod horses but made and repaired all sorts of domestic and farm implements. I am proud to be descended from one, my paternal grandfather, whom I often watched at work.

  Something of the awe originally inspired by the first workers of metal still hung about the smith in the nineteenth century. The mention in the song of 'Cole' could be a corruption of 'goat', which in turn could indicate a link with witchcraft. More prosaically, however, the 'bagpipes made of the green willow' should merely be 'blowpipes (or bellows) bound with green willow'. The reference to 'King Charlie' would appear to indicate a seventeenth century origin, which may well be the case. Country singers usually updated the royal reference, to King George or Prince Albert.

Some texts conclude with uproarious and bawdy verses celebrating the smith's sexual prowess, one of the more oblique being:

Here's a health to the pretty maid with the lily-white frock,
Who's a heart that is true and as firm as a rock.
Which makes my bright hammer to rise and to fall . . .

Here's a health to the jol-ly black-smith, the best of all fel-lows, He works at his an-vil while the boy blows the bel-lows. Which makes my bright ham-mer to rise and to fall, Here's to old Cole and to young Cole and to old Cole of all. Twan-ky dil-lo, twan-ky dil-lo, twan-ky dil-lo, dil-lo, dil-lo, dil-lo, A roar-ing pair of bag-pipes made of the green wil-low.

2 If a gentleman calls his horse for to shoe,
  He makes no denial of one pot or two.
  For it makes my bright hammer to rise and to fall,
  Here's to old Cole and to young Cole and to old Cole of all.
  Twankydillo, *etc.*
  And he that loves strong beer is a hearty good fellow.

3 Here's a health to King Charlie and likewise his queen,
  And to all the royal little ones where'er they are seen.
  Which makes my bright hammer to rise and to fall,
  Here's to old Cole and to young Cole and to old Cole of all.
  Twankydillo, *etc.*
  A roaring pair of bagpipes made of the green willow.

6   The Blacksmith

Ralph Vaughan Williams took down this song in 1905 from a King's Lynn fisherman. I have not seen it anywhere else.

2 There's Monday Tuesday, Wednesday, these are the days we
        smith,
  There's Thursday, Friday, Saturday, and welcome Saturday
        night;
  Then we receive our weekly wage and pay our alehouse score,
  On Sunday we take our repose and on Monday we work once
        more.

3 Sometimes I've money in my purse, sometimes I am without,
  But I am none the worse for that, can work for more, no
        doubt.
  For my anvil it so cheerily rings, my bellows shall swiftly
        blow,
  My fire shall heat my irons hot, and unto work we go.

7   A Lincolnshire Shepherd

The ancient, Celtic-style numerals were used by shepherds until relatively recent times. They ran as follows, in Lincolnshire at any rate, from one to twenty: yan, tan, tethera, pethera, pimp, sethera, methera, hovera, covera, dik, yan a dik, tan a dik, tethera dik, pethera dik, bumfits, yan a bumfits, tan a bumfits, tethera bumfits, pethera bumfits, figgits.

From the same county comes the true story of a practical joke involving counting sheep, or rather carrying them: 'They had all the yowes penned up and ready for shearing by hand. A chap, Fred Lack was his name, was to catch them and bring one out at a time to be shorn. They said to him, "Fred, fetch 'em from the far corner, and then when you get to the last one you won't have so far to walk." He had to struggle through the flock to get to the one in the far corner, and struggle back through them carrying an old yowe. Of course, all of the others would keep moving into the corner as one was taken from it. Fred never twigged on, and carried on struggling until they were all shorn. Then they told him of the joke they'd played.'

The words of this song were written in the 1930s by Jesse Baggaley (1906—1976), of Lincoln, and the tune was added by another Lincolnshire man, Maurice Ogg, in 1977.

26

2 From Caistor down to Spilsby from Sleaford up to Brigg,
  There's Lincoln sheep all on the chalk, all hung wi' wool and
    big.
  And I, here in Langton wi' this same old flock,
  Just as me grandad did afore they meddled with the clock.

3 We've bred our tups and gimmers for wool and length and
    girth,
  And sheep have lambed, have gone away all o'er all the earth.
  They're bred in foreign flocks to give the wool its length and
    crimp,
  Yan, tan, tethera, pethera, pimp.

4 They're like a lot of bairns, they are, like children of me own,
  They fondle round about owd Shep afore they're strong and
    grown;
  But they gets independent-like, before you know, they've
    gone,
  But yet again, next lambing time we'll 'a' more to carry on.

5 Yan, tan, tethera, tethera, pethera, pimp,
  Fifteen notches up to now and one yowe with a limp.
  You reckons I should go away, you know I'll never go,
  For lambing time's on top of us and it'll surely snow.

6 Well, one day I'll leave me yowes, I'll leave me yowes for
    good,
  And then you'll know what breeding is in flocks and human
    blood;
  For our Tom's come out o' t' army, his face as red as brick,
  Sethera, methera, hovera, and covera up to dik.

7 Now lambing time comes reg'lar-like, just as it's always been,
  And shepherds have to winter 'em and tent 'em till they're
    weaned.
  My fambly had it 'fore I came, they'll have it when I sleep,
  So we can count our lambing times as I am counting sheep.

yowe: rhymes with 'now' – ewe.
far-welted: on its back (and cannot get up).
notch: after counting to figgits (a score) the shepherd would make a notch on his stick, and start again.
meddled with the clock: the introduction of summer time or daylight saving, during the First World War.
tups and gimmers: young male and female sheep.
tent: generally to look after sheep, move them about and find suitable grazing.

8   Come All You Valiant Shepherds

Since sheep are very difficult animals to rear, the quality or otherwise of the shepherd makes or mars a flock. For many centuries the shepherd was a highly respected member of the village community, a real aristocrat of labour. His calling commanded such respect that it became a symbol for care and nurture: a phrase like 'the good shepherd' still has profound reverberations, pastoral, religious, linguistic.

I believe that the song is based on a sailors' ballad of the seventeenth century, written by Martin Parker, with the chorus of 'stormy winds do blow'. It is difficult to estimate when the shepherds' version came into existence; probably long before the first printed copy, which is in Thomas Hughes's Scouring of the White Horse *(1858). There, rather than in the vague location of 'highland hills', the shepherds are tending their flocks on White Horse Hill. Other versions have Salisbury Plain. I like to think that the song originated in the Cotswolds, for places like Blockley and Dover's Hill often occur in the song, even when it is found in other parts of the country.*

Come all you val – iant _ shep – herds that's got a val – iant
heart, That goes out on a _ storm – y night and _ nev – er feels a
smart; [Oh,] nev – er be faint - heart-ed, boys, not of rain or _ frost _ or _
snow, Nev-er yield all _ in the _ fields where the storm – y winds do blow.

2 Once I kept my flock on highland hills that were so high and
    steep;
  My ewes and lambs lapped out their tongues and up the hills
    do creep.
  I lookèd up with courage bold and after them did go,
  And drove them to their fold where the cold, stormy winds
    do blow.

3 As soon as I was foldèd down and turning back again
  Until some joyful company where I was entertained,
  In drinking of strong liquor, boys, which was my heart's
    delight.
  Never yield all in the fields where the stormy winds do blow.

4 Those shepherds are the finest fellows that ever trod English
    ground,
[When they go into an alehouse they value not a crown];
They call for liquor merrily and pay before they go.
Never yield in the fields where the stormy winds do blow.

lapped out their tongues: hung them out (a sign of thirst).

9   Pleasant Month of May

Making hay was very hard work involving many operations which, when the weather was unfavourable, could be spread over several weeks. First, cutting: originally with sickles, later with scythes, later still with horse-drawn then tractor-drawn machines. After a short period for drying, the swathes were turned with a pitchfork, then raked into small heaps called 'haycocks'. Finally the hay was loaded on to carts, a process which in itself required considerable skill and care. Then the hay would be taken into the stack-yard and built into ricks, which were thatched with straw. Despite the gruelling work, under a hot sun, there was a good deal of pleasure. Jokes would fly thick and fast and who, after once taking part, could ever forget the fragrance of the hay?

Using artistic licence, the song compresses all this into a single day. The feeling of deep satisfaction in work and delight in nature is characteristic of the repertoire of the Copper family of Rottingdean from which it comes. The first printed text appeared in 1695, and a hundred and fifty years later J. H. Dixon described the song as 'An old and favourite ditty sung in many parts of England at merry-makings, especially those which occur during the hay-harvest' (Ancient Poems, Ballads and Songs of the Peasantry of England *1846 p. 192). It continued in oral tradition until the present century.*

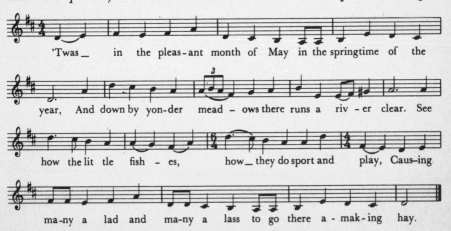

'Twas in the pleas-ant month of May in the springtime of the
year, And down by yon-der mead – ows there runs a riv – er clear. See
how the lit tle fish – es, how they do sport and play, Caus-ing
ma-ny a lad and ma-ny a lass to go there a - mak-ing hay.

2 Then in comes the scytheman that meadow to mow down,
  With his old leathered bottle and the ale that runs so brown.
  There's many a stout and labouring man comes here his skill
      to try,
  He works, he mows, he sweats and blows, and the grass cuts
      very dry.

3 Then in comes both Tom and Dick with their pitch-forks and
      their rakes,
  And likewise black-eyed Susan, the hay all for to make.
  There's a sweet, sweet, sweet and a jug, jug, jug, how the
      harmless birds did sing
  From the morning to the evening as we were a-haymaking.

4 It was just at one evening as the sun was a-going down,
  We saw the jolly piper come a-strolling through the town.
  There he pulled out his tapering pipes and he made the valley
      ring,
  So we all put down our rakes and forks and left off
      haymaking.

5 We called for a dance and we tripped it along,
  We danced all round the haycocks till the rising of the sun.
  When the sun did shine such a glorious light and the harmless
      birds did sing,
  Each lad he took his lass in hand and went back to
      haymaking.

piper: player of the pipe and tabor.
tapering pipes: garbled version of tabor and pipe.

10   Turnit Hoeing

'I have done some hoeing', wrote A. G. Street in Farmer's Glory *(1935),
'and it cured me of any desire to sing about it.' I know from my own experience that it is monotonous, back-breaking work, and would have been inclined
to suspect that the song's enthusiasm was ironic, if it were not for the gusto
with which country people sing it.*

The song is a relatively late production, but it was certainly in existence by 1881, when the tune was adopted as the official march of the 1st Battalion of the Wiltshire Regiment (though perhaps out of conservatism the former march 'The Lincolnshire Poacher', did not in fact give way to the upstart until 1932). In the meantime the song had gained widespread popularity through a gramophone record issued in the 1920s by the country comedian Albert Richardson, who was perhaps better-known for 'There was an old man and he had an old sow', complete with sound effects.

The Somerset version given here might seem impenetrable at first sight, but all (or nearly all) becomes clear if 's' is read for 'z' and 'f' for 'v'.

Oh! I be a tur-nit ho-er, from Zum-mer-zet-shire I came. My__ par-ents is hard work-ing volks, Giles Web-ster be my name. 'Twas on a zum-mer's morn-in', e'en at the break of day, When I took my hoe and off did go zum fif-ty miles a-way.

Chorus

And zum de-lights in hay mak-in' and a vew be vond of mow-in', But of all the jobs that I like best, gi'e ae the tur-nit hoe-ing. For the vlies, the vlies, the vlies be on the tur-nit, And 'tis all no use for ae to try to keep them off the tur-nits.

2 O I be a tidy sort of chap and soon got I a place.
I went to work like any Turk and I took it by the piece;
And so I hoed on cheerfully and good Varmer Glower,
Who vowed and swore and said I wore a ripping turnit hoer.

31

3 In winter I drives oxen about the vields a-ploughin',
   To keep the vurrow straight and clear all ready for turnit
      zowin'.
   And when the vrost bars up the wheels, out on the land we're
      goin',
   For without manure 'tis zertain zure, no turnits won't be
      growin'.

4 In on work about the varm yard until time brings me
      mowin',
   For I like none of it half so well as I do my turnit hoein'.
   And when the harvest now begins and the nut brown ale
      a-vlowin',
   So I merely bids them all goodbye and I'm off to turnit
      hoein'.

Ae: I.
Varmer Glower: as might be expected, the
   name varies from place to place, and
   even from farm to farm.
oxen: see note, no. 2.

11   The Rosebuds in June

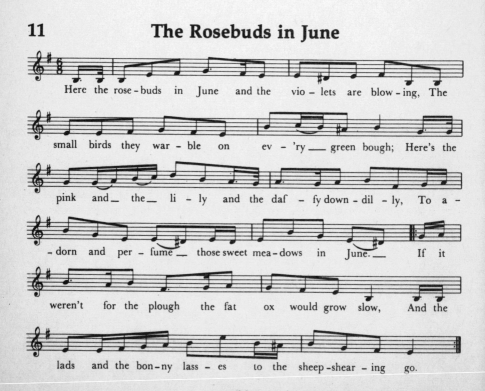

Here the rose-buds in June and the vio-lets are blow-ing, The
small birds they war-ble on ev-'ry — green bough; Here's the
pink and — the — li-ly and the daf — fy down - dil - ly, To a-
-dorn and per - fume — those sweet mea-dows in June. — If it
weren't for the plough the fat ox would grow slow, And the
lads and the bon-ny lass - es to the sheep-shear-ing go.

2 Our shepherds rejoice in their fine heavy fleeces,
And frisky young lambs which their flocks do increase;
Each lad takes his lass all on the green grass,
To adorn, *etc.*

3 Our clean milking pails they are fouled with good ale,
At the table there's plenty of cheer to be found;
We'll whistle and sing and dance in a ring,
To adorn, *etc.*

4 Now the sheep-shearing's over and harvest draws nigh,
We'll prepare for the fields, our strength for to try;
We'll reap and we'll mow, we'll plough and we'll sow,
To adorn, *etc.*

Sheep-shearing usually took place during the month of June. It was followed by a Frolic or Supper at which songs in praise of shepherds and shearers would be sung. This example, or versions of it, could be heard until recently, though it was first printed in 1716.

12   Tarry Woo'

Like 'Pleasant Month of May', this song was sung at sheep-shearings, though its popularity seems to have been confined to the north of England and Scotland. The words have a curious mixture of realism ('clothe the back and cram the wame') and sentimentality ('up you shepherds, dance and skip'; 'how happy is the shepherd's life, far from court and free from strife'). At times, we are not far from a literary Arcadia, and it is perhaps not without significance that the first printed version appeared in about 1740, in Allan Ramsay's Tea Table Miscellany. The text given here was obtained by Vaughan Williams in 1904 from a Mr John Mason of Dent, North Yorkshire, who 'only knew one verse traditionally, but supplied the rest from a version given in a local newspaper'.

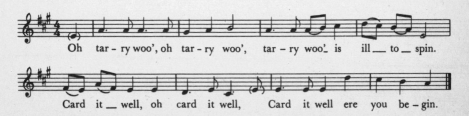

Oh tar-ry woo', oh tar-ry woo', tar-ry woo' is ill to spin.

Card it well, oh card it well, Card it well ere you be-gin.

2 When it's carded, wove and spun, then your work is nearly
      done,
   But when it's woven, dressed and clean, it will be clothing for
      a queen.

3 Up you shepherds, dance and skip, o'er the hills and valleys
      trip,
   Sing of the praise of tarry woo', and of the flock that bears it
      too.

4 Poor harmless creatures, without blame, they clothe the back
      and cram the wame,
   Keep us warm and hearty too, weel's on us our tarry woo'.

5 Sing of my bonny harmless sheep that feed upon yon
      mountains steep,
   Sweetly bleating as they go, through the weary winter's
      snow.

6 Hart and hind and fallow deer not by half so useful are,
   From kings to him that holds the plough, all are obliged to
      tarry woo'.

7 How happy is the shepherd's life, far from court and free
      from strife,
   Whilst his gimmers bleat and bay and the lambkins skip and
      play.

8 Who'd be a king, can any tell, when a shepherd lives so well,
   Lives so well and pays his due with honest heart and tarry
      woo'?

9 He lives contented, envies none, e'en not the monarch on his
      throne,
   Though he the royal sceptre sways he has no sweeter
      holidays.

10 And no such music to his ear, of thief or foe he has no fear,
   For steady Kate and Curly too will defend the tarry woo'.

tarry: Stockholm tar was used a good deal to put on the cuts or infections of sheep.
wame: belly.
plough: formerly pronounced 'ploo', as indeed it still is in some areas.
gimmers: young female sheep.

Kate and Curly: names of sheepdogs. In the Allan Ramsay version the names of breeds of sheepdog are given here: 'kent and colly' (collie).

Verse 1 can be used as a chorus.

The Rambling Comber

You com-bers all, — both great and small, Come lis-ten to— my dit-ty, — For I am he, — and on-ly he,— re-gardless of— thy pi - ty;— For I can read, write, drink and fight, And that is all my hon - our;— My fail-ing's here,— I love strong beer,— I am a ramb - ling com-ber.

2 A dozen of wool through a comb I pull,
All in a decent order;
So sleek and fine like silk shall shine,
All by my master's order;
And when 'tis done, downstairs I run,
And carry it to the owner;
I make no doubt he will soon find out
I am a rambling comber.

3 My breeches they are ragged and torn,
My stockings got no feet to;
My shoes they both have lost their soles,
My hat has got no brim to;
But yet she is always in my mind,
Let me be drunk or sober:
A pretty girl is my delight
And a glass of good October.

a dozen of wool: ? a dozen fleeces.
October: beer brewed in October from the first barley of the year's harvest.

When most people lived for long periods, even their whole lives, within one village, the itinerant excited admiration, envy, interest, and sometimes distrust. Tinker, tailor, soldier, sailor, and even the beggarman of the rhyme often appear as the 'rambling' hero of a song. In this case it is the travelling carder or comber of wool, whether tarry or otherwise, whose devil-may-care attitude gives vicarious pleasure.

14   The Reaphook and Sickle

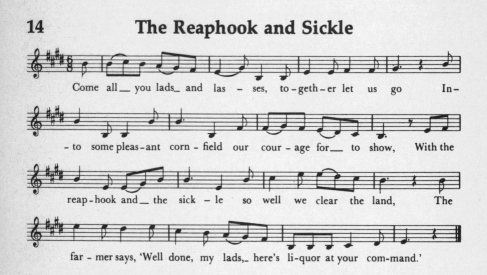

Come all — you lads — and las - ses, to - geth - er let us go In- to some pleas - ant corn - field our cour - age for — to show, With the reap - hook and — the sick - le so well we clear the land, The far - mer says, 'Well done, my lads, — here's li - quor at your com - mand.'

2 By daylight in the morning when birds so sweetly sing –
They are such charming creatures they make the valley ring –
We will reap and scrape together till Phoebus do go down,
With the good old leathern bottle and beer that is so brown.

3 Then in comes lovely Nancy the corn all for to lay,
She is my charming creature, I must begin to pray;
See how she gathers it, binds it, she folds it in her arms,
Then gives it to some waggoner to fill a farmer's barns.

4 Now harvest's done and ended, the corn secure from harm,
All for to go to market, boys, we must thresh in the barn.
Here's a health to all you farmers, likewise to all you men,
I wish you health and happiness till harvest comes again.

reaphook: heavy variety of sickle.
Phoebus: the sun.
the corn all for to lay: in some versions this
   is to 'lease' or glean; here it seems that
'lovely Nancy' is binding the corn into
sheaves.
waggoner: see no. 16.

Harvesting was both arduous and joyful. Richard Jefferies in an essay, 'Walks in the Wheatfields' (published in Field and Hedgerow, 1889), paints a harrowing picture of the reapers: 'The breast-bone was burned black, and their arms, tough as ash, seemed encased in leather. They grew visibly thinner in the harvest-field, and shrunk together – all flesh disappearing, and nothing but sinew and muscle remaining. Never was such work . . . the reaping was piece-work at so much per acre – like solid gold to men and women who had lived on dry bones, as it were, through the winter. So they worked and slaved, and tore at the wheat as if they were seized with a frenzy.' It is necessary, not to contradict this, but to complement it with Mabel Ashby's remark that 'though the disinherited had no great part of the fruits, still they shared in the achievement, the deep involvement and joy of it (Joseph Asby of Tysoe, Cambridge University Press, 1961). David H. Morgan has recently published a splendid essay, 'The Place of Harvesters in Nineteenth Century Village Life' (in Raphael Samuel (ed.), Village Life and Labour, Routledge, 1975).

15 All of a Row

The corn is all ripe and the reap-ings be-gin,— The fruits of the earth, O we ga-ther them in; At morn-ing so ear-ly the reap-hooks we .grind,— And a-way to the fields for to reap and to bind. The— fore-man goes first in the hot sum-mer glow,— And sings with a laugh, my— lads, of a— row.

Chorus

Then all of a row! Then all of a— row! And to-night we will sing,— boys, all of a row.

2 'We're in', says the Catchpole, behind and before,
  'We'll have a fresh edge and a sheaf or two more';
  The master stands back for to see us behind;
  'Well done, honest fellows, bring the sheaves to the bind.
  Well done, honest fellows, pare up your first brink
  You shall have a fresh edge and a half pint to drink.'

3 And so we go on through the heat of the day,
  Some reaping, some binding, all merry and gay,
  We'll reap and we'll bind, we will whistle and sing,
  Unflagging until the last sheaf we bring in;
  It's all our enjoyment wherever we go,
  To work and to sing, brothers, all of a row.

4 Our day's work is done, to the farmhouse we steer,
  To eat a good supper and drink humming beer;
  We wish the good farmer all the blessings in life,
  And drink to his health, and as well to his wife.
  God prosper the grain for next harvest we sow,
  And again in the arrish we'll sing, boys, hallo.

brink: stook.
humming: strong.
arrish: stubble.

hallo: possibly a reference to the custom which allowed reapers to mulct passers-by of a contribution, after crying out the ritual words 'Hello, largess'.

From very early times, sickles were used to cut the corn. Scythes were not introduced until the nineteenth century, and even then did not quickly displace the sickle. In a similar fashion, the scythe in its turn co-existed with the reaper-binder for a time: even until the 1950s it was customary to scythe round a corn field so that the binder could get in.

The reapers worked as a team, with a captain. Usually the tallest and strongest, he was chosen by the men, and given the title of Lord of the Harvest, or, as here, Catchpole. He bargained with the farmers, organized the work, shared out the wages, and presided at the celebrations after the harvest. Songs like 'The Reaphook and the Sickle' and 'All of a Row' would be among those sung at the Harvest Home.

The Jolly Waggoner

When_ first I was a wagg'ner And a wagg'ner I did go, I
filled my par-ents' hearts_ Full of sor-row, grief and woe; I

Chorus

filled my par-ents' hearts_ full of sor-row, grief and woe. __ So sing
whoa, my lads, sing whoa,_ Drive_ on, my lads, heigh-o; There is
none can lead a life__ Like we jol - ly wagg'ners do.__ So sing
whoa, my lads, sing whoa, Drive on, my lads, heigh-o; There is
none can lead a life___ Like we jol - ly wagg 'ners do.

2 It's a cold and stormy night,
   I was wet to the skin;
   I'll bear it with contentment
   Till we get to the inn,
   And then we'll get a drink
   With our landlord and our friends.

3 Now summer time is coming, boys,
   What pleasure we should see;
   The small birds are a-whistling
   On every green tree.
   The blackbirds and the thrushes O
   Are whistling in the grove.

4 Now Michaelmas is coming, boys,
   What pleasure we shall find,
   We'll make the gold and silver fly

Like chaff before the wind.
Then every lad shall take his lass
And set her on his knee.

Michaelmas: 29 September, both a quarter day and, in some parts of the country, the end of the farming year. Workers could therefore expect to receive wages due, and thus to be able (at least within rather modest limits) to 'make the gold and silver fly'.

A waggoner (the word was often pronounced with two syllables only – 'wagg'ner') could be one of two distinct trades. One was a farm worker skilled both in the care of horses and in field work with them. In Suffolk he was called a horseman, for which see George Ewart Evans's Horse in the Furrow *(1960).*

On the other hand, and this is the meaning here, he could be the driver of one of the stage waggons used to transport goods and the occasional passenger, until they were driven off the roads by the competition of railways. Indeed, some versions of this song include complaints that 'the world is topsy-turvy turned, and all things go by steam' and 'the railway it has ruined us, who badly fared before'.

Little Nell had what for her was a delightful ride in a stage waggon in The Old Curiosity Shop *(1841), and as late as 1864 W. H. Barrett's father rode in one, and described it to his son:*

Old Jacob had one of those lumbering road wagons like you see in pictures now; on the axle of one of the wheels was cut the date 1745, which is when it was made. The wagon had been on the road for over a hundred years when first I saw it, for it had been made for Jacob's grandfather. When he died, his son took it over before he left it to Jacob, and during all that time it had gone up and down the turnpike between King's Lynn and London more times than anyone could count (Tales from the Fens, *Routledge, 1963).*

The waggons travelled at about walking pace, and the waggoner often walked beside his team of up to eight horses. 'The Jolly Waggoner' is still occasionally seen as an inn sign, and it seems that the calling had a reputation for good fellowship.

17   The Country Lass

Apart from the housework, the traditional tasks of the women and girls of a farm were to look after the pigs and poultry and to manage the dairy. At haymaking and harvest, however, they were expected to turn out to help in the fields.

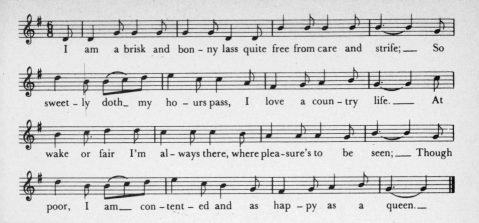

I am a brisk and bon-ny lass quite free from care and strife;— So
sweet-ly doth_ my ho-urs pass, I love a coun-try life.— At
wake or fair I'm al-ways there, where plea-sure's to be seen;— Though
poor, I am_ con-tent-ed and as hap-py as a queen.—

2 I rise up in the early morn my labour to pursue,
   And with my yoke and milking pails I trudge through
      morning dew,
   My cows to milk, and there I taste the sweets which nature
      yields;
   The lark doth sing to welcome me into the flowery fields.

3 And when the meadows they are mowed my part I freely take,
   And with the other village girls I go the hay to make.
   Such friendship, love and harmony amongst us there is seen,
   The swains invite the village girls to dance upon the green.

4 And in the time of harvest, too, how cheerfully we go,
   There are some with bottles, some with sickles, some with
      scythes to mow.
   And when the corn is free from harm we have not far to
      roam,
   So all away to celebrate and welcome Harvest Home.

5 In winter when our cattle all are fed with hay and straw,
   The cock he crows to waken me, my icy cream to thaw.
   Though western winds do whistle and the northern winds do
      blow,
   'Tis health and sweet contentment which the country lasses
      know.

6 In summer heat nor winter cold we have no cause to grieve,
   For in the time of need we all each other do relieve.
   So still I think a country life all others do surpass:
   I sit me down in sweet content, a happy country lass.

The Farmer's Boy

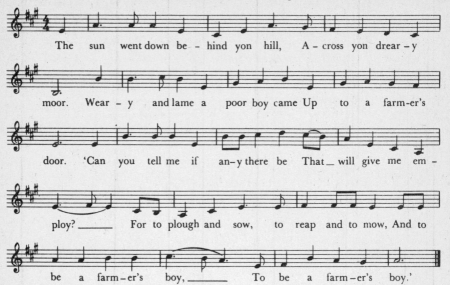

The sun went down be-hind yon hill, A-cross yon drear-y moor. Wear-y and lame a poor boy came Up to a farm-er's door. 'Can you tell me if an-y there be That will give me em-ploy? For to plough and sow, to reap and to mow, And to be a farm-er's boy, To be a farm-er's boy.'

2 'For my father's dead, and mother's left
With her five children small;
And what is worse for mother still,
I'm the eldest of them all.
Though little I be, I fear no work
If you will me employ,
For to plough and sow, to reap and to mow,
And to be a farmer's boy,
To be a farmer's boy.

3 'And if that you won't me employ
One favour I have to ask:
Will you shelter me till break of day
From this cold winter's blast?
At break of day I'll trudge away
Elsewhere to seek employ,
For to plough and to sow, to reap and to mow,
And to be a farmer's boy,
To be a farmer's boy.'

4 The farmer said, 'Pray, take the lad,
No further let him seek.'
'Oh, yes, dear father', the daughter cried,

While the tears ran down her cheek;
'For those that will work it's hard to want
And wander for employ,
To plough and sow, to reap and mow,
And to be a farmer's boy,
To be a farmer's boy.'

5 In course of time he grew a man,
And the good old farmer died;
He left the lad the farm he had,
And his daughter for his bride.
So the boy that was now farmer is;
He sits and thinks with joy
Of the lucky, lucky day he came that way,
To be a farmer's boy,
To be a farmer's boy.

An early eighteenth century origin has been suggested for this song, but I believe that it has a strong whiff of enclosure about it. The farm which is providentially inherited, lock, stock and barrel, suggests an early nineteenth century mentality – and landscape. The tune most frequently used is 'Ye Sons of Albion', which dates from the time of the Napoleonic Wars; and the earliest record of the text which I have so far seen is an entry under the title of 'The Lucky Farmer's Boy' in the 1832 catalogue of Catnach, the street ballad printer.

Be this as it may, 'The Farmer's Boy' (which should not be confused with the long poem of the same name by Robert Bloomfield, published in 1800) remained popular for a hundred years and more. It was sung as a kind of agricultural workers' anthem at the meetings called in the 1890s by George Edwards to revive the union. Even at the present time it is well-loved in country districts.

The text varies hardly at all, but many different tunes are found with the song. However, the familiar air was sung by Arthur Lane (for whom, see no. 3), whose version is given here.

19   Joe the Carrier's Lad

From early in the seventeenth century until the 1914–18 War, villages throughout the country were linked to market towns by a network of local carriers' routes. The carrier acted both as country 'bus driver and as a shopping agent for those who could not make the journey. Though the railways killed off the long-distance coach and carrying trade, local carriers were able to continue, since few villages had stations. It was only the advent of the motorbus, lorry and car which brought about the demise of the old carrier's cart. In Brother to the Ox *(1942), Fred Kitchen has an excellent chapter on a visit to Doncaster in a carrier's cart.*

My name is Joe, the car-rier's lad, a mer-ry chap am I, I al-ways am con-tent-ed, be the wea-ther wet or dry. I snap my fin-gers at the frost, I whis-tle at the rain, I've braved the storms for many a day and will do so a-gain.

Chorus

Oh, crack, crack, goes my whip, I whis-tle and I sing, I sit up-on my wag-gon, I'm as hap-py as a king, My horse is al-ways will-ing, and I am nev-er sad, There's none can lead a life more gay than Joe the car-ri-er lad.

2 My father was a carrier a twenty years ago;
  On Thursdays to the market almost regular he would go.
  Sometimes he'd take me with him, particular in the spring,
  Then there I'd sit upon the box and hear my father sing.

3 The girls they all do smile at me as I go driving past,
  My horse he is a beauty as he trots along so fast;
  And many a mile we've put behind and happy days we've
      had,
  There's none can treat a horse more kind than Joe the carrier's
      lad.

4 I never think of politics or anything so great,
  I care not for their high-bred talk about the church and state;
  But I act aright as man to man, and that's what makes me
      glad,
  You'll find there beats an honest heart in Joe the carrier's lad.

carrier's lad: in some versions, carter's lad.

20   **The Old Cock Crows**

*If the farm worker has his anthem, in the shape of 'The Farmer's Boy', then
the farmer has his in this song. Significantly, both were rewritten for town
use, one as 'The Factory Boy', and the other with this chorus:*

> *I like to hear the engine start, early in the morning,*
> *I like to sit me down at breakfast time, just as the engine's roaring;*
> *And I like to see the piecers as on the floor they lay,*
> *Hurrah for the life in the factory while we're waiting for the judgement day.*

*Ironic, for both songs may well have originated in the town for country con-
sumption in the first place.*

Be-hold in— me a jol-ly farm-er that— lives in the fields so green. I like to rise in the morn-ing when the (a) pret-ty lit-tle vi-o-lets are seen. Yes, I like to rise up ear-ly and mer-ri-ly fol-low the plough; I like to watch the dai-ry and go milk-ing the old dun cow. I like to hear the old cock crow, ear-ly in the morn-ing, I like to stroll through the bright green fields, just as the day is dawn-ing. I like to hear the lit-tle birds sing their mer-ry lay: Hur-rah for the life in the coun-try and a ram-ble in the new-mown hay.

Variant
(a) Verse 2

etc.

2 I like the life of a farmer, yes I like to live at my farm,
   And I shouldn't like the city, for a country life so charm;
   And I like to watch the girls in the dairy making butter and
        cheese,
   I like to hear my own girl, Mary, tell her tales 'neath the apple
        trees.

II
A Health to the Master:
Deference and Protest

21   Harvest Home Song

In an account of his boyhood in Leicestershire, William Gardiner described a harvest supper which took place in about 1778:

> With what glee I did mount the harvest waggon for the fun of jolting over the rugged roads to the wheat-field. From shock to shock it moved slowly to gather the rustling sheaves. . . . The day's toil over, we hastened home for the harvest supper. At the head of the board sat the worthy host, by whose side I was placed. Then came Will, Ralph, Joe and Jim, and their wives and helpers. Presently a shoulder of mutton, scorching hot, as the day had been, a plum pudding and a roasted goose were put on the table, when they soon fell to, each playing his part in good earnest. The gingered ale went merrily round. Joe, who was a good singer, was called upon to entertain the company. The jokes growing coarser as it grew late, I was taken to bed from a scene not to be imitated (Music and Friends, *vol. III, 1853*).

> One of the songs which would almost certainly have been sung, for it was universally popular, was some form of toast to the health of the master and mistress.

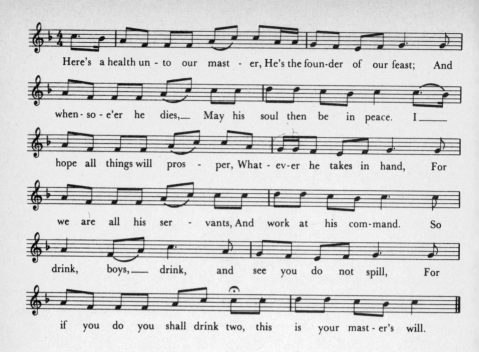

Here's a health un-to our mast-er, He's the foun-der of our feast; And
when-so-e'er he dies,— May his soul then be in peace. I——
hope all things will pros-per, What-ev-er he takes in hand, For
we are all his ser-vants, And work at his com-mand. So
drink, boys,— drink, and see you do not spill, For
if you do you shall drink two, this is your mast-er's will.

2   Our harvest now is ended,
        And supper it is past;
        Here is our mistress's good health
        In a full flowing glass.
        She is a rare good woman,
        For she prepares good cheer.
        Come one, come all, my heroes
        And bravely drink your beer.
So drink, boys, drink, until you come to me,
For the longer we do sit, boys, the merrier we shall be.

3   In yon green wood there lies an old fox,
        A-mumping of his chops;
        Close by his den you may catch him some knocks,
        So catch him, so catch him, my boys.
        Ten thousand to one you can't catch him or not,
        His beard and his brush are the same.
        I am sorry your tankard is empty, good sir,
        For it is all run adown the red lane.
Down the red lane, 'tis gone down the red lane,
For we will merrily hunt the fox adown the red lane.

22 God Speed the Plough

The old Harvest Frolic, Feast or Supper, as it was variously called, seems to have been killed off, like so many things, by the 1914–18 War, though it is still not unknown for farmers to give a special supper to their men on the last day of harvest (or it was in the 1950s, when I attended more than one). A. G. Street, who was born in 1891, remembered the older style:

> *The big barn would be cleared out sufficiently to make room for the seating of thirty or forty people. The words 'God Speed the Plough', in letters eighteen inches high, on the wall at one end, would be freshened up with whitewash; this was usually my job. A local caterer would arrive in the morning with tables, benches and provender. The menu consisted of cold meat, beef, mutton, or ham, with hot boiled potatoes for the first course, and hot figgety duff puddings with whole raisins in them for the second. They were boiled all day in the dairy copper.*
>
> *There were no windows in the barn, and the lighting was provided by oil lamps on chain plough traces. I can visualize that scene quite clearly: three tables in U-shaped formation, my father in the chair at the top table, and the foreman and myself at the ends of the others. I can see the ruddy countenances of the company, shining like burnished copper in the pool of light from the lamps overhead* (Farmer's Glory, 1935).

Here's a health to the far-mer and God speed the plough. Send him in his fields a good crop for to grow; — Send him in his fields a good crop for to grow, That all things may pros-per which he takes in hand, For the

Chorus

far-mer in-deed is a cap-i-tal man. Plough and sow, reap and mow, — Lambs to rear and sheep to shear. Health and con-tent-ment the coun-try-men wear.

2 We build up our ricks and we fill up our barn;
  It's the farmer supports all the nations with corn. *(repeat)*
  Here's the blackbird and thrush, we will join their sweet song,
  We'll be jovial together now harvest is done.

3 Where young men and maidens trip over the plain,
  Where the sweetest of pleasures all joys do maintain; *(repeat)*
  We'll walk through the valleys where the valleys look gay,
  And the innocent lambs all around us will play.

4 Now harvest is over and home we must go,
  Here's some to the threshing and some to the plough; *(repeat)*
  Wi' good beef and beer we will eat, dance and sing,
  For the farmer enjoys more his life than the king.

23   The Jolly Thresherman

*The virtue of a laborious and uxorious worker is rewarded by the massive
bounty of a noble squire: such paternalism is rather too sickly for the taste of
the late twentieth century, but it was much appreciated in Victorian times.
The deep longing at that period for security should not be under-estimated – it
underpins much of the writing of Dickens, and if ordinary people could not
find security in reality, then they could enjoy it vicariously. Accordingly, the
song was widely popular. Vaughan Williams collected this version in 1904
from a Surrey labourer, then aged sixty-one, who had learned most of his
songs from 'ballets' (ballad sheets) or from his father.*

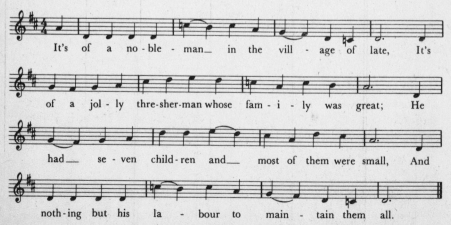

It's of a no-ble-man— in the vill-age of late, It's
of a jol-ly thre-sher-man whose fam-i-ly was great; He
had— se-ven child-ren and— most of them were small, And
noth-ing but his la-bour to main-tain them all.

2 As a noble squire rode by the highway,
  He met the jolly thresherman by the dawning of the day.
  'O thresherman, O thresherman, come tell unto me,
  How you maintain your wife and your small family.'

3 'Sometimes I do reap and sometimes I do mow,
  And sometimes a-hedging and ditching I do go.
  There's nothing comes amiss to me, to harrow and to plough,
  And so I get my living by the sweat of my brow.

4 'At night when I get home as tired as can be,
  The youngest of my family I takes upon my knee;
  The rest they flock around me with a sweet prit-prattling
       noise,
  And that's all the comfort a poor man enjoys.

5 'My wife she is willing to join in the yoke;
  We live like turtle-doves and neither do provoke,
  But still the times grow harder and I am very poor,
  And I hardly know how to keep the wolf from the door.'

6 'Now since you have spoken so well of your wife,
  It's I will make you happy all the days of your life;
  Here's sixty acres of good land I freely give to thee
  To maintain your wife and small family.'

24   The Old Farmer

*The sentiments here are very similar to those expressed by the old countryman
known as the King of the Norfolk Poachers:*

> *The Tiller of the soil is the highest and oldest workman of all. No one can do
> without him and the product of his hands. The Gold miner can[n]ot eat his gold,
> nor the Coal miner his coal, nor the Iron miner his Iron. All and every one is
> dependent upon the tiller of the Soil. He is the Father of all Workers, like the
> old saying has it:*

> > *The King he governs all,*
> > *The Parson pray for all,*
> > *The Law[y]er plead for all,*
> > *The Ploughman pay for all*
> > *And feed all*   (I Walked by Night *ed. L. R. Haggard, 1935*).

I have been tra-vell-ing twen-ty long years, I have ram-bled a-bout in the world,___ And many a brave fel-low I have seen, most gra-cious-ly to___ be-hold;___ To pick up a liv-ing all in the land, my song is all true___ I vow,___ For there's none so rare___ as can___ com-pare with the fel-lows that fol-low the plough.___

2 The farmer you know to market must go to sell both his
    barley and wheat;
His wife she rides all by his side all dressed so clean and neat,
With a basket of butter and eggs by her side so merrily they
    do go,
For there's none so rare as can compare with the fellows that
    follow the plough.

3 Then after market, home they come, which is the best
    comfort of all,
With lots of plum pudding all in the pot and lots of good beef
    as well.
Then after supper a jug of brown ale is brought to the table I
    vow,
For there's none so rare as can compare with the fellows that
    follow the plough.

4 The miller you know has a living to get, so he lives on the fat
    of the land;
By taking of toll he increases his gold, as you all can
    understand.

But this miller would fail as well as the rest, and that you
    must all allow,
For there's none so rare as can compare with the fellows that
    follow the plough.

5 The soldier you know for all he does fight, the parson for all
    he does pray,
The exciseman he rides about very grandly his spirits and
    wine to assay.
There is not a trade that ever was made in any wide country
    through,
Neither soldier nor sailor nor tinker nor tailor but what is
    upheld by the plough.

25   The Rigs of the Time

Oh, 'tis of an old but-cher, I must bring 'im in, 'E charge
two shill-in's a pound, 'e think it no sin; Clap 'is
thumb on 'is stil-yards and make 'em go down, 'E
swears it's good weight if it want half a pound. Sing-ing
hon-est-y's all out of fash-ion. These are the rigs of the
time, time, my boys, These are the rigs of the time.

2 Now the next is a baker I must bring 'im in,
  'E charge fourpence a loaf, 'e thinks it no sin;
  When he do bring it in it's no bigger'n your fist,
  And the top of the loaf is popped up in the dish.

3 Now no wonder that butter be a shillin' a pound:
  See the new farmers' daughters as they ride up and down;
  If you ask them the reason, they'll say, 'Bonny lad,
  There's a French War and our cows has no grass'.

4 Oh, the next is a publican, I must bring 'im in,
  'E charge fourpence a quart 'e think it no sin;
  When he do bring it in the measure is short,
  The top of the pot is popped up with the froth.

5 Now the very best plan that I can find
  Is to pop them all up in a high gale of wind;
  And when they get up the cloud it will bust,
  And the biggest old rascal come tumblin' down first.

stilyards: steelyards (for weighing).

'Rigs' means 'goings-on'. The song looks at the goings-on or doings of various dishonest tradesmen during the later years of the Napoleonic Wars. For the 'new farmers', whose daughters are mentioned, see 'The New-fashioned Farmer' (no. 27). The last verse may refer to the ballooning craze of 1811, thus giving a precise date to the song, which was recorded from a retired Norfolk ferryman, John ('Charger') Salmond, in 1947. When Peter Kennedy visited him in 1953 he remembered a further verse: 'Here's next to the tailor who skimps with our clothes/And next the shoemaker who pinches our toes/We've naught in our bellies, our bodies are bare/No wonder we've reason to curse and to swear' (Folk Songs of Britain, Cassell, 1975, p. 523).

26 The Labouring Man

Farm workers – or labouring men, as they were called, much more evocatively – having served their country in the French Wars, came back in 1815 to hard times and ingratitude. They were not the first veterans to do so, nor would they be the last. Their resentment smouldered for several decades, sometimes flaring into desperate violence against gamekeepers or, in the case of the revolt of 1830, into the widespread destruction of the threshing machines which were depriving them of a winter livelihood. The memory of hurt and injury lingered for generations, as in this song, which Lucy Broadwood took down at Dunsford, Surrey, in 1898.

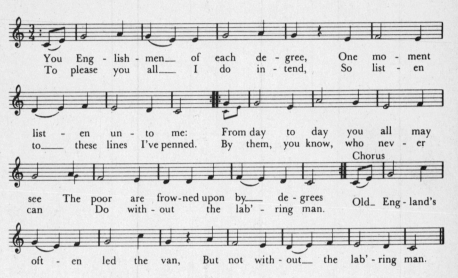

You Eng - lish - men__ of each de - gree, One mo - ment
To please you all__ I do in - tend, So list - en

list - en un - to me: From day to day you all may
to__ these lines I've penned. By them, you know, who nev - er

Chorus

see The poor are frow - ned upon by__ de - grees Old_ Eng - land's
can Do with - out the lab' - ring man.

oft - en led the van, But not with - out__ the lab' - ring man.

2 In former days you all must know,
   The poor man cheerful used to go,
   Quite neat and clean, upon my life,
   With his children and his darling wife;
   And for his wages, it is said,
   A fair day's wages he was paid;
   But now to live he hardly can –
   May God protect the labouring man.

3 There is one thing we must confess,
   If England finds they're in a mess,
   And has to face the daring foe,
   Unto the labouring man they go
   To fight their battles, understand,
   Either on sea or on the land;

Deny the truth we never can,
They call upon the labouring man.

4 Some for soldiers they will go,
And jolly sailors too, we know,
To guard old England day and night,
And for their country boldly fight;
But when they do return again
They are looked upon with great disdain;
Now in distress throughout the land
You may behold the labouring man.

5 When Bonaparte and Nelson too,
And Wellington at Waterloo,
Were fighting both by land and sea,
The poor man gained these victories.
Their hearts are cast in honour's mould,
The sailors and the soldiers bold;
And every battle, understand,
Was conquered by the labouring man.

6 The labouring man will plough the deep,
Till the ground and sow the wheat,
Fight the battles when afar,
Fear no danger or a scar;
But still they're looked upon like thieves
By them they keep at home at ease,
And every day throughout the land
They try to starve the labouring man.

7 Now if the wars should rise again
And England be in want of men,
They'll have to search the country round
For the lads that plough the ground.
Then to some foreign land they'll go,
To fight and drub the daring foe;
Do what they will, do what they can,
They can't do without the labouring man.

The New-fashioned Farmer

Good peo-ple all, I pray at-tend And list-en to my stor-y, How the farm-ers used to live In our na-tive coun-try. [When mast-ers liv'd as mast-ers ought And hap-py in their sta-tion, Un-til at length their stink-ing pride Has ruin-'d half the na-tion.]

Chorus

Fol del lol lol, fol de lol lol li-do.

2 A good old-fashion'd long grey coat
   The farmers us'd to wear, sir,
And on old Dobbin they would ride,
   To market or to fair, sir,
But now fine geldings they must mount,
   To join all in the chase, sir,
Dress'd up like any lord or 'squire,
   Before their landlord's face, sir.

3 In former times, both plain and neat,
   They'd go to church on Sunday,
And then to harrow, plough, or sow,
   They'd go upon a Monday;
But now, instead of the plough-tail,
   O'er hedges they are jumping,
And instead of sowing of their corn,
   Their delight is in fox-hunting.

4 The good old dames, God bless their names,
   Were seldom in a passion,
But strove to keep a right good house,
   And never thought on fashion;
With fine brown beer their hearts to cheer,
   But now they must drink swipes, sir,

It's enough to make a strong man weak,
    And give him the dry gripes, sir.

5 The farmers' daughters us'd to work
    All at the spinning wheel, sir,
But now such furniture as that
    Is thought quite ungenteel, sir,
Their fingers they're afraid to spoil
    With any kind of sport, sir,
Sooner than handle a mop or broom,
    They'd handle a piano-forte, sir.

6 Their dress was always plain and warm,
    When in their holyday clothes, sir,
Besides, they had such handsome cheeks,
    As red as any rose, sir,
But now they're frill'd and furbelow'd,
    Just like a dancing monkey,
Their bonnets and their great black veils
    Would almost fright a donkey.

7 When wheat it was a guinea a strike,
    The farmers bore the sway, sir,
Now with their landlords they will ride,
    Upon each hunting day, sir,
Besides, their daughters they must join
    The ladies at the ball, sir,
The landlord say, we'll double the rents,
    And then their pride must fall, sir.

8 I hope no one will think amiss,
    At what has here been penn'd, sir,
But let's hope that these hard times
    May speedily amend, sir,
It's all through such confounded pride,
    Has brought them to reflection,
It makes poor servants' wages low,
    And keeps them in subjection.

swipes: small beer.   *strike:* measure of corn varying according
                           to locality from half a bushel to four
                           bushels.

In the popular mind the post-1815 slump in agriculture was partly attributed to the extravagance of farmers. This view was shared by William Cobbett. One of his many passages on the theme was inspired by a visit to a farm in Surrey where the farmer was selling up:

> Every thing about this farm-house was formerly the scene of plain manners and plentiful living. Oak clothes-chests, oak bedsteads, oak chests of drawers, and oak tables to eat on, long, strong, and well supplied with joint stools. Some of the things were many hundreds of years old. But all appeared to be in a state of decay and nearly of disuse. There appeared to have been hardly any family in that house, where formerly there were, in all probability, from ten to fifteen men, boys, and maids: and, which was the worst of all, there was a parlour! Aye and a carpet and bell-pull too! . . . And I daresay it has been 'Squire Charington and the Miss Charingtons; and not plain Master Charington, and his son Hodge, and his daughter Betty Charington, all of whom this accursed system has, in all likelihood, transmuted into a species of mock gentlefolks, while it has ground the labourers down into real slaves (20 October 1825, Rural Rides, Penguin, 1967, pp. 226–7).

The Essex singer from whom Vaughan Williams took down the song in 1904 knew only the tune, chorus, and first four lines. The remainder has therefore been supplied from a street ballad.

28   The Tythe Pig

Tithes were a constant source of conflict between priest and people from the tenth century onwards. (They became compulsory during the reign of King Edgar, 959–975.) Resentment was not difficult to express. One Hampshire farmer is said to have notified the tithe-owner that he was about to pull his turnips. When the men and carts arrived at the field the farmer drew ten turnips, solemnly handed over one of them, and said he would let the tithe-owner know when he would draw any more. A Staffordshire pottery group shows a farmer ironically offering his tenth child to the parson.

Feeling grew particularly strong in the 1830s – from which time I date this song, or at least its publication in street ballad form – and the Tithe Commutation Act of 1836 substituted a fixed rent charge for tithes. Even the rent charges caused discontent and the acts of 1936 and 1951 commuted them into a lump sum payable by instalments until the year 2000. Thus some form of compulsory tithe will have lasted for a thousand years.

The song was taken down from a Devon miller in 1888. Not all the words were noted, so the text has been supplemented from a sheet printed by James Catnach of Seven Dials, under the title of 'The Sucking Pig'.

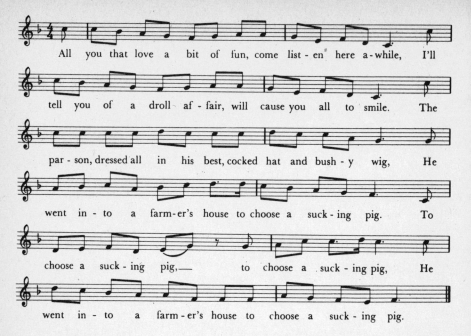

All you that love a bit of fun, come list-en here a-while, I'll
tell you of a droll af-fair, will cause you all to smile. The
par-son, dressed all in his best, cocked hat and bush-y wig, He
went in-to a farm-er's house to choose a suck-ing pig. To
choose a suck-ing pig,— to choose a suck-ing pig, He
went in-to a farm-er's house to choose a suck-ing pig.

2 'Good morning', said the parson, 'good morning, sir, to you;
I've come to choose a sucking pig, [you know it is my due.
Therefore I pray go fetch me one that is both pump and fine,
Since I have asked a friend or two along with me to dine.']

3 Then went the farmer to the sty, among the pigs so small,
He chose the very smallest pig, the smallest of them all;
But when the parson saw the choice, how he did stamp and
    roar,
He snorted loud, he shook his wig, he almost cursed and
    swore.

4 'O then', replied the farmer, 'since my offer you do refuse,
I pray, sir, walk into the sty, there you may pick and
    choose.'
Then in the sty he ventured without any more ado;
The old sow ran with open mouth and at the parson flew.

5 O then she caught him by the coat and took off both the
    skirts,
Then ran between his legs and threw him in the dirt.
The parson cursed the very hour he ventured for the pig;
You'd laugh to see the young ones, how they shook his hat
    and wig.

6 Then next she caught him by the breech while he so loud did
        cry,
  'O help me from this cursèd sow or I shall surely die.'
  The little pigs his waistcoat tore, his stockings and his shoes;
  The farmer cries, 'You're welcome, sir, I hope you'll pick
        and choose.'

7 At length he let the parson out all in a handsome trim,
  The sow and pigs so neatly in the dirt had rollèd him.
  His coat was to a spencer turned, his brogues were ripped
        behind,
  Besides his backside was all bare, and his shirt hung out
        behind.

8 He lost his stockings and his shoes which grievèd him full
        sore,
  Besides his waistcoat, hat and wig were all to pieces tore.
  Away the parson scampered home as fast as he could run;
  The farmer almost split his sides with laughing at the fun.

9 The parson's wife stood at the door awaiting his return,
  And when she saw his dirty plight she into the house did
        run.
  'My dear, what is the matter, and where have you been?' she
        said.
  'Get out you slut', the parson cried, 'for I am almost dead.

10 'Go fetch me down a suit of clothes, go fetch them down I
        say,
  And bring me my old greasy wig without any more delay;
  And for the usage I've received all in the cursèd sty,
  I ne'er shall relish sucking pig unto the day I die.'

spencer: short jacket (the pig had made his frock coat into a short jacket by tearing
of the skirts).

The clergy of the established church were often unpopular in the nineteenth century and indeed earlier, because they were identified with authority, in the shape both of central government and local magistracy. The slightest hint of wordliness or hypocrisy, let alone greater offences, would be gleefully seized upon by the villagers. Here, the form of the church service, with the clerk giving the responses to the parson, is artfully used for comic effect. The parson pronounces and the clerk duly responds, but in the words of earthy scepticism rather than of the appropriate rubric. Other songs in a similar genre include 'The Mare and the Foal', no. 30. This one comes from the grand old singer, Phil Tanner (1862–1950), of Llangennith on the Gower Peninsula.

2 'Oh, never covet thy neighbour's goods',
   The parson he said, 'nor his maid.
   Don't rob a man of that what's his,
   Why a fellow should be afraid.
   Nor covet ye not, thou man of sin –
   I would venture this matter to mark –
   They neighbour's wife', said the parson.
   'The slavey for me', said the clerk.
   Amen. 'The slavey for me', said the clerk.

3 'Oh, never sigh for that dross called gold,
For blessed's the man that is poor.
Nor cast ye the loaves
Nor the fishes from the poor.
For I grieve to say it is my fate
To drive a carriage and pair in the park,
With a thousand a year', said the parson.
'Oh, give it to me', said the clerk.
Amen. 'Oh, give it to me', said the clerk.

4 'My Christian friends and brethren,
You should ever be humble and meek;
And never strike a sinful man,
When he strike you one o' the cheek,
But turn, my friend, to the erring one,
Yes, turn to the sinner so dark
Thy other cheek', said the parson.
'I'd break his nose', said the clerk.
Amen. 'Yes, land him at once', said the clerk.

5 'Oh, the boys are awfully tribulous',
The parson he said with a groan.
'And the boys too oft at Sunday School
Won't let the young hussies alone.
I've watched them grin behind their book,
And I've seen the boys, their lark:
They was kissing that girl', said the parson.
'I've done it myself', said the clerk.
Amen. 'And they're fond of it, too', said the clerk.

6 'Well now my sermon, friends, is done,
I bid you go work and pray;
And don't do as the parson does,
But do as your parson say.
And ere I depart a worldly care
I'll venture this matter to mark:
Never drink', said the parson.
'I'm awfully dry', said the clerk.
Amen. 'And you're awful wet', said the clerk.
Amen.

tribulous: Phil Tanner's word, compounded from frivolous, troublesome and tribulation.

The Mare and the Foal

The old clerk in the par - ish I know ve - ry well, He
oft - en do toll___ the eight o' clock bell; He__ went to the
ale - house and got a full pot, And for - got the old
church for to lock - a - lock - lock. *Chorus* Ri - lo ri - lid - dle
la - lid - dle,___ La did - dle la did - dle - i - day.

2 A mare and a foal they ran in great speed,
The mare from the Bible began for to read.
'Stay', said the foal, 'before you begin,
Whatever you pray for I'll answer Amen.'

3 'We'll pray for the millers who grind us our corn,
For they are the biggest rogues that ever were born;
Instead of one sackful they'll take two for toll,
May the devil take millers!' 'Amen', said the foal.

4 'We'll pray for the bakers who bake us our bread,
They'll take a small loaf and then hurl at your head;
They'll rip it and squeeze it at every roll,
May the devil take bakers!' 'Amen', said the foal.

5 'We'll pray for the tailors, for they are no men,
They'll buy an old coat and they'll sell it again;
They'll rub it and scrub it and darn up a hole,
May the devil take tailors!' 'Amen', said the foal.

6 'We'll pray for the publicans who draw us our liquor,
Small measure they like, they can fill us the quicker.
If you ask them for best beer they'll draw you the small,
May the devil take publicans!' 'Amen', said the foal.

7 'We'll pray for the butchers, for they are great cheats,
They'll buy an old cow and they'll sell it young meat.
May their fingers be burnt into cinders of coal,
May the devil take butchers!' 'Amen', said the foal.

eight o'clock bell: the old curfew bell, which was rung in some villages until the last quarter of the nineteenth century.

they are no men: sewing and garment-making was considered to be women's work; for doing it the tailors were thought unmasculine. On the other hand, they were also disliked and distrusted because their trade gave them opportunities for sexual adventures as they travelled from house to house and from farm to farm in the absence of the menfolk.

Bakers, butchers and publicans come under attack in 'The Rigs of the Time'. The same trades are the target here, with the addition of tailors and millers, both perennial subjects for satire. Although in some versions cobblers and blacksmiths come in for praise, there are no heroes, save perhaps for the mare and foal, in this song. Like 'The Rigs' it was collected in East Anglia by the composer, E. J. Moeran.

31   Good King Arthur

When good king Ar - thur reigned, He was a good - ly king, Three sons out of four he turned out of door Be - cause they could not sing.

> 2 Now the first he was a miller,
> The next he was a weaver,
> And the third he was a little tailòr,
> With the broadcloth under his arm.

> 3 Now the miller he stole corn,
> And the weaver he stole yarn,
> And the little tailòr he stole broadcloth,
> To keep these three rogues warm.

65

4 Now the miller was drowned in his dam,
   And the weaver was hanged in his yarn,
   And Old Nick flew away with the little tailòr
   With the broadcloth under his arm.

tailòr: 'Please to observe that the accent always falls on the second syllable' (note in original manuscript). Thomas Hardy makes exactly the same observation about his version, both in his letter and in *Under the Greenwood Tree* (part IV, chapter 2).

It seems unlikely on the face of it that King Arthur's sons should be respectively a miller, a weaver and a tailor. Other versions of the song provide an explanation: King Arthur is less good than he might appear, and his sons are illegitimate:

> *King Arthur he had three sons,*
> *Big rogues as ever did swing,*
> *He had three sons of whores*
> *And he kicked them all three out-of-doors*
> *Because they could not sing.*

Thomas Hardy, who quoted these lines in a letter of 1889, made this comment: 'The song, as sung in this neighbourhood (of Dorchester), has always been a coarsely humorous one – and as far as I know – orally transmitted only. . . . The tune was rather a monotonous one' (C. J. Weber (ed.), The Letters of Thomas Hardy, *Waterville, Maine, 1954, p. 30).*

The version printed here, which comes from Worcestershire, is almost exactly paralleled in French, except that the tailor is replaced by his assistant:

> *Dans l'éclus' le meunier s'noya, ha, ha, ha!*
> *A son fil le tiss'rand s'pendit, hi, hi, hi!*
> *Et le diabl' mis en furie*
> *Emporta le p'tit commis,*
> *Un rouleau de drap sous son bras,*
> *Pour n'avoir pas voulu chanter, ohé.*

32   The Miller and His Three Sons

As far back as there are records, in the shape of songs and stories, millers have been a by-word for rapacity, both financial and sexual. Chaucer is thought to have based 'The Miller's Tale' on fabliaux in existence long before the fourteenth century. One has to remember that in medieval times peasants were often forced to take grain only to their lord's mill. The resulting monopoly gave the miller endless opportunities for exaction.
'The Miller's Advice to his three Sons on the Taking of Toll' dates from

the seventeenth century. *When Vaughan Williams collected this version from a Yorkshire schoolmaster in 1904, few people had any longer cause to complain of millers. However, the atavistic detestation lingered. In some versions the father replies to the first two sons in turn, in this way: 'Thou art a fool', the old man said,/'Thou hast not well learned thy trade;/This mill to thee I ne'er will give,/For by such toll no man can live'.*

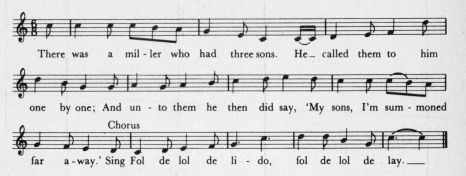

There was a mil - ler who had three sons. He _ called them to him one by one; And un - to them he then did say, 'My sons, I'm sum - moned far a - way.' Sing Fol de lol de li - do, fol de lol de lay. _

Chorus

2 Then he called to him his eldest son;
'Son', says he, 'my race is done,
And if to thee this mill I give
I would like to know how thou mean'st to live.'

3 'O father', says he, 'my name is Jack,
Out of every load I shall steal one sack;
Out of every load one stack I'll steal,
And I should never want for meal.'

4 Then he called to him his second son,
Etc.

5 'O father', says he, 'my name is Ralph,
Out of every load I shall steal one half;
Out of every load one half I'll steal,
And I should never want for meal.'

6 Then he called to him his youngest son,
Etc.

7 'O father', he says, 'I'm your youngest boy,
And stealing corn's my only joy,
And before that good meal I'd lack
I'd steal all the corn and burn the sack.'

8 'O son', he says, 'thou'rt my youngest boy,
  Thou art indeed my treasure and joy,
  And unto thee this mill I'll give,
  I'm content to die for I see thou'lt live.'

9 Now this miller's dead and in his grave,
  And hungry worms his body have;
  But where he's gone to I can't tell,
  But I leave it to you to judge for yoursel'.

33   We Poor Labouring Men

Expressions of pride and self-confidence such as this must have helped labouring men through many a dark day. The song was taken down from a Hampshire singer, early this century. Unusually, it does not seem to have appeared on street ballads.

Some says the wheel-er's best, but I sha'nt say so,___ What would the wheel-ers do if 'tweren't for we poor lab-our-ing men?___ We buys up all their carts and wheels, and so their gain comes in. There's not a trade in old En-ge-land like we poor lab-our-ing men.___

2 Some says the butcher's best but I sha'n't say so.
  What would the butchers do if 'tweren't for we poor
    labouring men?
  We buys up all their odds and ends, and so their gain comes
    in.
  There's not a trade in old Engeland like we poor labouring
    men.

3 Some says the blacksmith's best but I sha'n't say so.
What would *etc.*
We wears out all their cutters and shares, and so their gain
    comes in.
There's not *etc.*

4 Some says the tailor's best but I sha'n't say so.
What would *etc.*
We wears out all their breeches and gaiters, and so their gain
    comes in.
There's not *etc.*

5 Some says the shoemaker's best but I sha'n't say no.
What would *etc.*
We wears out all their boots and shoes, and so their trade
    come in,
There's not *etc.*

6 Some says the baker's best but I sha'n't say so.
What would *etc.*
We buys up all their stale bread, and so their trade comes in.
There's not *etc.*

7 Some says the brewer's best but I sha'n't say so.
What would *etc.*
We buys up all their fourpenny beer, and so their grain comes
    in.
There's not *etc.*

wheeler: wheelwright.
cutters and shares: coulters and ploughshares.

34   **Mutton Pie**

If there are still those who regard the agricultural labourer of the nineteenth century as having been cowed, subservient, obsequious, let them listen to this song. In Scotland it would be known as a 'corn kister', for such were the songs critical of conditions on the land sung by the single farm workers who lived on the premises, while sitting on the great corn chest. (See John Ord's Bothy Songs and Ballads, *Paisley, 1930). The practice of living in, though less* common in England, continued in remote areas such as *Cumbria* and, as *Arthur Lane's statement (quoted note, no. 3) indicates, Shropshire*, until the late years of the nineteenth, and even the early years of the present, century.

Songs critical of farmers were also sung at hiring fairs where, humorously or in earnest, they could warn a man about his future master. 'Mutton Pie', or 'Stringy Pie' as it was sometimes called, was known, with the farmer's name suitably altered, in parts of Yorkshire and Lincolnshire until a generation ago.

Come all you jol-ly lads if you want to learn to plough,
Go to Yor-kie Wat-son, he'll show you how; He's
got four 'os-ses and they're all ve-ry thin 'Cause he
Chorus
does-n't put much hay in the bin. To me whack fol the
did-dle ol the day, To me whack fol the did-dle ol the day.

2 Now our owd mester he went to the fair,
  Bought four 'osses and yan were a mare;
  Yan were blin' and t'other couldn't see,
  And t'other 'ad 'is 'ead where 'is arse ought to be.

3 Now our owd missis thinks she's giving you a treat,
  Bakes such pies aren't fit to eat;
  There's pies made of iron and cakes made o' clay,
  Rattlin' in your belly for a month and a day.

4 Our owd missis 'as a mate called Alice,
  Thowt she were fit to live in a palace,
  Live in a palace and be like a queen:
  I'm damned if she were fit to be seen.

5 Well, our owd mester to us did say:
  'There's a yowe been dead for a month and a day;

70

Fetch 'er up, Bullocky, fetch 'er up, Sly,
We'll mek our lads some rare mutton pie.'

6 So they fetched th'owd yowe and laid her on t' table
To mek 'em a pie as fast as they were able;
There was maggots by the hundreds, thousands, millions
thick,
Bullocky were wallockin' 'em off wi' a stick.

7 So come all you jolly fellows if you want to learn to plough,
Go to Yorkie Watson, he'll show you how;
He'll show you how, me boys, I've heard say,
Wants you to plough four acre a day.

blin': blind, but pronounced to rhyme   *yowe*: ewe.
with 'tin'.   *four acre a day*: the normal stint was one
                                           acre.

35 O the Roast Beef of Old England: New Version

I'll sing you a song it shall not be too long, If you
go for your rights, you will not think it wrong, So
give us a chor-us, both hear-ty and strong; O the roast beef of Old
Eng - land,   O   the old Eng-lish roast beef.____

2 Time was when our ancestors farmed their own land;
Contented and happy, no foe could withstand
Those bold, sturdy yeoman – a glorious band
Well fed with the beef of Old England,
The jolly Old English roast beef!

71

3 But somehow or other the lord and the squire
 Have got all the lands that their hearts can desire,
 And we are poor wretches just let out for hire,
  And have lost the roast beef of Old England,
  We don't get a smell of the beef.

4 A mite of fat bacon, a bit of hard bread,
 Our wages will much about give us instead,
 Yet we think those who work have a right to be fed,
  Aye, even with beef of Old England,
  With jolly old English roast beef.

5 The lord and the squire may open their eyes,
 The parson's next sermon be wonderful wise.
 We hope their fine feelings we shall not surprise,
  But we want the roast beef of old England,
  The jolly Old English roast beef.

6 So pull all together and work with a will,
 For something our wives and our children to fill,
 Much better than crusts and their tea-kettle swill,
  For jolly roast beef of Old England,
  For glorious Old English roast beef.

7 So stand by the Union, the winter's gone through,
 Neither hunger nor cold would our courage subdue,
 For there's one thing we want, and mean having it too,
  The jolly roast beef of Old England,
  The glorious Old English roast beef.

Starting in Warwickshire in 1872, the National Agricultural Labourers' Union grew to a membership of 100,000 within twelve months, under the leadership of Joseph Arch. A whole series of struggles in 1872 and 1873 culminated in the great lock out of 1874, a year in which the average wage of labourers was fourteen shillings (70p) a week. The NALU was effectively broken, though it lingered until 1896.

During the hectic early years songs played an important part at meetings and demonstrations. They were often parodies of hymns or well-known songs. One such was written by a man called Benjamin Britten, to a tune which was used for at least one other country song, 'The Hard Times of Old England' (Copper, A Song for Every Season, Heinemann, 1971, p. 204).

36   An Old Man's Advice

Joseph Arch's election to Parliament in 1885 did not arrest the decline of the NALU. Indeed, he was only an MP for a year, and when he was re-elected, in 1892, a new union was already in being. It was started in 1889, when some Norfolk men asked George Edwards to lead them. His and their efforts eventually resulted in the formation of the National Union of Agricultural Workers (which still exists, under a slightly different name). Like the earlier body, the new union made extensive use of songs at its meetings, including 'The Farmer's Boy' (George Edwards, From Crow Scaring to Westminster, 1922, p. 59). One of the new songs, based on 'The Grandfather's Clock', was sung to me as recently as 1978 by a Norfolk man, Walter Pardon, who, as a boy, had met Edwards. I have not seen it in print before.

2 My grandfather said in the noontide of life,
    Poverty was a grief and a curse;
    For it brought to his home sorrow, discord and strife,
    And kept him poor, with empty purse.

So he took a bold stand and joined the union band,
To help his fellow men he tried;
A union man he vowed he'd stand
Till the day he died.

3 My grandfather's dead; as we gathered round his bed,
These last words to us he did say:
'Don't let your union drop nor the agitation stop,
Or else you will soon rue the day.
Get united to a man for it's your only plan,
Make the union your care and your pride.
Help on reform in every way you can.'
Then the old man died.

37   I've Livèd in Service

Indoor servants were very much a part of the country scene. Here a manser-
vant falls in love with a maid. His fears that her beauty will attract the
attentions of the master prove to be well grounded. It was customary for a
maid seduced or (as here) made pregnant to be married off to some male
retainer, usually with a suitable financial inducement. In this case the man
receives the money, then decamps, leaving his master with the baby on his
hands. Behind the rather laconic text of the song one senses poignancy and
also bitterness.

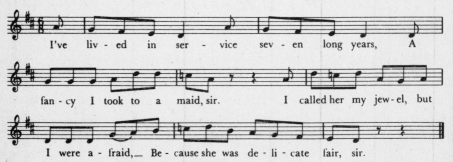

I've liv-ed in ser - vice sev - en long years, A
fan-cy I took to a maid, sir. I called her my jew-el, but
I were a-fraid,— Be-cause she was de-li-cate fair, sir.

2 I loved this maid as I loved my life,
I freely could make her my bride, sir;
As I was going upstairs one night,
I saw the young master lie with her.

3 When Sunday morning comes, to his master Jack goes,
saying, 'Master, I must have some money.'
'Some money, John boy, you are going to be wed,
But I fear you'll pay dear for your honey.

4 'How much money, John boy?' 'Ten guineas', John said,
'Ten guineas all in money.'
'And when you are married I'll lie down
A thousand bright guineas for your honey.'

5 Upstairs Jack goes, his clothes to tie up,
He tied it all up in a wallet;
And out of the window he threw it so high,
But the deuce of a bit could he follow.

6 When he got down he gazed all around,
His wallet threw over his shoulder;
He tripped along to fair Norwich town
And left the young babe to his master.

38   The Brisk Young Butcher

*Turning the tables was a deeply satisfying theme, especially when the weaker
party did the turning. The song is often called 'The Leicester Chambermaid',
for she is very much the heroine of the story. This version comes from Jack
Beeforth, who was born near Whitby in 1891. The tune is more usually
associated with 'The Banks of Sweet Dundee'.*

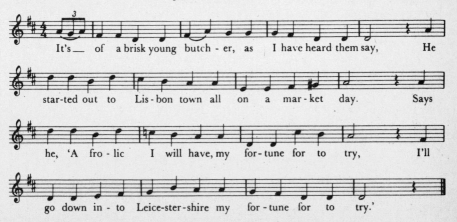

It's— of a brisk young butch-er, as I have heard them say, He
star-ted out to Lis-bon town all on a mar-ket day. Says
he, 'A fro-lic I will have, my for-tune for to try, I'll
go down in-to Leice-ster-shire my for-tune for to try.'

2 When he arrived in Leicestershire he called at an inn,
  He called for an ostler and so boldly walked in;
  He called for liquors of the best and his reckoning left unpaid,
  And presently he fixed his eyes upon the chambermaid.

3 She then took a candle to light him up to bed,
  And when they came into the room these words to her he
      said:
  'One sovereign I will give to you to enjoy your charms',
  And so this buxom chambermaid slept in the butcher's arms.

4 He arose next morning and prepared to go away.
  The landlord said, 'Your reckoning, sir, you have forgot to
      pay.'
  'Oh, no', the butcher did reply, 'pray do not think it strange,
  For I brought a sovereign to your maid and she never brought
      the change.'

5 He straightway withdrew the chambermaid and he charged
      her with the same,
  The sovereign then she did lie down fearing to get the blame;
  The butcher he rode off with glee, well pleased with what was
      passed,
  But soon this buxom chambermaid grew thick below the
      waist.

6 And twelve months after he came to town again,
  And just as he had done before he called at the inn.
  It was there this buxom chambermaid she chanced him to see;
  She fetched a baby just three months old and placed it on his
      knee.

7 The butcher he was so amazed, at the child did stare,
  But when the joke he did find out how he did curse and
      swear.
  She says, 'Kind sir, it is your own, please do not think it
      strange,
  For the sovereign that you gave to me I've now brought you
      the change.'

to Lisbon town: usually, 'from London town'.

Rap-a-tap

Trade union activity was by no means the only way in which a labourer could score over a farmer. The singer of this song was Bob Hart, born near South-wold in Suffolk in 1892. He was a farm worker before going to sea, first in sailing trawlers out of Lowestoft, then in steam. He can be heard singing it on a Topic record, Flash Company *(12TS243). I believe that it dates back to the late eighteenth century.*

When I was an old farm-er's ser-vant, well, I used to have some fun,— Mind-ing my mast-er's busi-ness when he was not— at home;— For if my mast-er should go out to view the fields so gay,— I was up at the door with my rap-a-tap, Ei-ther by night or day,— ei-ther by night or day.—

2 Now it happened to be on a Thursday, my master to market
    did go,
  He asked me to mind his business as servants ought to do;
  So as soon as my master's back was turned I went blundering
    out of the barn
  And up to the door with my rap-a-tap,
  And sure I meant no harm, and sure I meant no harm.

3 Well, who should come but my mistress, she asked me to
    walk in;
  When I complained of the belly-ache she ordered me some
    gin,
  She ordered me some gin, my boys, but never a word to say
  That I'd been there with my rap-a-tap,
  And to bed we went straight way, and to bed we went
    straight way.

4 And there us two lay sporting for two long hours or more,
　The missis she liked the sport so well I thought she'd never
　　give o'er.
　'You've won my heart for ever,' she cried, 'no more your
　　master for me,
　For he can't come with his rap-a-tap,
　Not half so well as thee, not half so well as thee.'

5 Now the master he came from market and he asked me how
　　I'd got on:
　I told him I'd mind his business the same as if he were at
　　home.
　He ordered me some ale, my boys, but little did he know
　That I'd been there with my rap-a-tap,
　If 'e 'ad 'e'd a never done so, if 'e 'ad 'e'd a never done so.

rap-a-tap: it was usual for a singer to rap in rhythm on a convenient table or chair, whenever he came to these words.

40　　The Rest of the Day's Own

As well as being witty, this cheerful look at farming life has more than a grain of truth in it. The farmer in this song irresistibly reminds me of John Stewart Collis's farmer, ''E': 'A farmer is called by his men either 'the boss' or 'the guvnor' or 'the master' (now out of date), or 'the old man' (regardless of age), or more often simply 'he'. . . . On this farm . . . on the whole he was designated simply as "'E" — "'E's coming!" . . . You could recognize him a long way off by his walk. He took huge strides, head bent slightly down, like a man measuring a cricket pitch. That walk was very characteristic. . . . Having adopted a certain pace — a terrific pace — he meant to keep it up. He neither would nor could slow down a bit. "'E'll break up one of these days", they would say at intervals. He did not intend to lose a minute — for time was money to him as certainly as to any business man' (The Worm Forgives the Plough, Penguin, 1975, pp. 62–3). The song first appeared in a collection published in 1915.

78

One day when I was out of work a job I went to seek, To
be a farm-er's boy.___ At last I found an ea-sy job at
half-a-crown a week, To be a farm-er's boy.___ The
farm-er said, I, think I've got the ve-ry job for you; Your
dut-ies will be light, for this is all you've got to do.

Rise at three ev'-ry morn, Milk the cow with the
Plough the fields, mow the hay, Help the cocks and the

crum-pled horn, Feed the pigs, clean the sty,
hens to lay, Sow the seed, tend the crops,

1
Teach the pig-eons the way to fly;
2
Chase the flies from the

tur-nip tops, Clean the knives, black the shoes,
Help the wife, wash the pots,

1
Scrub the kit-chen and sweep the flues,
2
Grow the cab-bag-es

and car-*rots*, Make the beds, dust the coals,

Mend the gram-o-phone,___ And then if there's no more

work to do The rest of the day's your own.'___

79

2 I scratched my head and thought it would be absolutely prime
  To be a farmer's boy.
  The farmer said, 'Of course you'll have to do some overtime,
  When you're a farmer's boy.'
  Said he, 'The duties that I've given you, you'll be quickly
      through,
  So I've been thinking of a few more things that you can do
  Skim the milk, make the cheese, chop the meat for the
      sausagees,
  Bath the kids, mend their clothes, use your dial to scare the
      crows.

3 In the milk, put the chalk, shave the knobs off the pickled
      pork,
  Shoe the horse, break the coal, take the cat for his midnight
      stroll,
  Cook the food, scrub the stairs, teach the parrot to say his
      prayers,
  Roast the joint, bake the bread, shake the feathers up in the
      bed,
  When the wife's got the gout, rub her funny bone
  And then if there's no more work to do, the rest of the day's
      your own.'

4 I thought it was a shame to take the money, you can bet
  To be a farmer's boy
  And so I wrote my duties down in case I should forget
  I was a farmer's boy.
  It took all night to write 'em down, didn't go to bed,
  But somehow I got all mixed up, and this is how they read:
  Rise at three, every morn, milk the hen with the crumpled
      horn,
  Scrub the wife every day, teach the nanny goat how to lay,
  Shave the cat, mend the cheese, fit the tights on the sausagees,
  Bath the pigs, break the pots, boil the kids with a few carrots,
  Roast the horse, dust the bread, put the cocks and hens to bed,
  Boots and shoes, black with chalk, shave the hair on the
      pickled pork,
  All the rest I forgot, somehow it had flown,
  But I got the sack this morning, so the rest of my life's my
      own.

III
The High Gallows Tree: Crime and Punishment

41   Robin Wood and the Pedlar

It's of a ped - lar both stout and bold, As fine a ped - lar as ev - er you see; He takes his pack all_ at his back, And a - way goes ped - lar right o - ver the lea. He takes his pack all_ at his back, And a - way goes ped - lar right o - ver the lea.

2 The first he met was two troublesome men,
  Two troublesome men all on the lea;
  And one of them was bold Robin Wood,
  And the other was Little John so free.

3. 'What have you in your pack', cried bold Robin Wood;
  'What have you in your pack, come tell to me.'
  'I've several silks [suits] of the gay green silk,
  And bow strings, by one, two, three.'

4 'If you've several silks of the gay green silk,
  And bow strings, by one, two, three,
  One of your packs shall belong to me
  Before you go one step from me.'

5 Then Robin Wood he drew his sword,
  And the pedlar unto his pack did stand;
  They heaved about till the blood did flow,
  Till he cried, 'Pedlar, pray hold thy hand.'

6 So they heaved about till they both did sweat,
  Till he cried, 'Pedlar, pray hold they hand;
  I'll find a man of a taller stand
  That can whop the pedlar, likewise thee.'

7 'Now, I'll go, master', cried Little John,
  'Now I'll go master, and try my hand.'
  They heaved about till the blood did flow,
  Till he cried, 'Pedlar, pray hold thy hand.'

8 'What is your name', cried bold Robin Wood,
  What is your name, come tell to me.'
  'My name unto you I never will tell
  Until both your names you have told to me.'

9 'My name it is bold Robin Wood,
  And the other is Little John so free.'
  'Now it still lies at my good will
  Whether I'll tell you my name or no.

10 'Now my name it is Gamble Gold,
   And Gamble Gold from the merry green wood,

And Gamble Gold from the foreign countery;
For killing a man in my father's land,
And from my father's countery I'm forced to flee.'

11 'Now if your name it is Gamble Gold,
And Gamble Gold from the merry green wood,
And Gamble Gold from the foreign countery;
Then you and I are two sisters' sons,
What nearer cousins could ever be?'

12 Then up to the tavern they all did dine,
Where they tapped their bottles and drank their wine.

Gamble Gold: probably Gamelyn, hero of the manuscript *Tale of Gamelyn* (1340).

After a long career of robbing the rich (who else?) to give to the poor, Robin Hood died in 1247. Or so one tradition would have us believe, but another story holds that he was still alive in 1265, when he helped to defeat Simon de Montfort at the Battle of Evesham. Whatever the truth may be — and Professor Child believed that Robin was 'absolutely a creation of the ballad-muse', the great outlaw is still a household name, seven hundred years later.

Robin Hood ballads were very widely sung. As early as 1363, for example, a slothful friar admits in William Langland's Piers Plowman *that, while his knowledge of the Lord's Prayer is less than perfect, 'I kan rymes of Robyn Hose, and Randolf, Earl of Chester'. (For the latter, see no. 55). William Thackeray's ballad catalogue of 1689 lists twenty-one Robin Hood titles. However, it does not include 'The Bold Pedlar and Robin Hood', which seems to have been printed for the first time early in the nineteenth century, by Catnach, having 'escaped the attention of Ritson, Percy, and other collectors of Robin Hood ballads' (as Dixon remarked). The version given here was obtained by Mike Yates as recently as 1964 from a Sussex singer.*

42   Spare Me the Life of Georgie

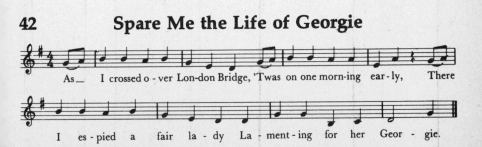

As— I crossed o-ver Lon-don Bridge, 'Twas on one morn-ing ear-ly, There
I es-pied a fair la-dy La-ment-ing for her Geor-gie.

2 'Come fetch to me some little boy
   That can go on an errand quickly,
   That can run ten miles in an hour
   With a letter for a lady.

3 'Come, saddle me my milk-white steed,
   And bridle it most rarely;
   That I may go to Newcastle Gaol
   And beg for the life of Georgie.'

4 When she got to Newcastle Gaol
   She bowed her head so lowly;
   Three times on her bended knees did fall,
   Saying, 'Spare me the life of Georgie.

5 'It is no murder George have done,
   Nor have he killèd any;
   But he stole sixteen of the king's fat deer,
   And sold them in the army.'

6 The judge looked over his right shoulder,
   And, seeming very sorry,
   He says, 'My dear, you are now too late,
   He is condemned already.'

7 'Oh, six babies I have got with me,
   And I love them most dearly;
   I would freely part with them every one
   If you spare me the life of Georgie.'

8 The judge looked over his left shoulder,
   And seeming very hard-hearted,
   He says, 'My dear, you are too late,
   There is no pardon granted.'

9 'Oh George shall hang in a chain of gold,
   Which a few there are, not many,
   Because he became by a noble bride,
   And beloved by a vict'rous lady.'

in the army: normally, in 'Bohenny' (Bohemia) or 'Germanie'.

The judge looked over his right shoulder . . . his left shoulder: the first action was a good sign, since the right is associated with good, and therefore with mercy. Since this was not possible, the judge turned to the (literally and figuratively) sinister side, and confirmed the sentence.

Because he became . . .: the last two lines are probably a garbled version of: 'Because he came of a noble line/And was loved by a virtuous lady.'

While some songs accurately reflect historical conditions and events, others are more concerned with emotional than with factual truth. A ballad called 'Georgie' or 'Geordie', very widely known until recent times in both Britain and America, is really two separate narratives, albeit with a number of similarities, both in substance and in terminology. The Scottish ballad tells of Geordie's being saved from the scaffold in Edinburgh on the payment by his wife of a ransom. It is said to refer to George, Earl of Huntly, who, after failing on a mission for the Queen Regent of Scotland in 1554, was imprisoned and subjected to the forfeiture of his estates, but afterwards restored to favour.

The English variety also tells of a wife's travelling on an errand of mercy, this time to Newcastle. However, her intercession fails, and her husband is executed. George Stoole, alias Skelton, alias Stowell, who is said to have inspired this ballad, was executed at Newcastle in 1610 for stealing horses and cattle. Street ballads on the event appeared almost immediately afterwards, passed into oral circulation, and continued to be sung for some three centuries. The version given here was learned from the singing of a Worcestershire dairy-maid in 1851.

43   Gilderoy

Unlike Robin Hood, freebooters such as Gilderoy were heartily disliked by the common people because of their ruthlessness and rapacity. Indeed, Gilderoy was apprehended by the Perthshire citizenry in a sort of levée en masse, in response to the placing on his head of a price of £1,000. Shortly after this, in July, 1636, he was executed at Edinburgh. Despite his ill fame (or perhaps because of it), Gilderoy's name was well known in England by 1650, thanks to street ballads (though the earliest copy at present extant was published in 1685). William Stenhouse, writing in 1839, tells us that the best-known of the ballads was composed not long after Gilderoy's death by Peg Cumminghame, 'a young woman of no mean talent, who unfortunately became attached to this daring robber, and had cohabited with him for some time'. The same prim commentator goes on to complain that although some stanzas had 'real poetical merit', there were 'many indelicate luxuriances that required the aid of the pruning-hook'. When Lucy Broadwood printed Henry

Burstow's version in 1907 she felt constrained to prune one luxuriant stanza (the third), which is now printed in full for the first time.

Some similarities between 'Gilderoy' and 'Georgie' will be seen. As Cecil Sharp commented, 'This habit of describing in the same words incidents of a similar nature that occur in different ballads has often been noticed, and is one of the surest indications of the genuine traditional ballad.'

Now_ Gil - der - oy_ was a bon - ny boy, and he would not _ the rib - bons wear; He pul - led off_ his_ scar - let coat, he gar - ter - ed_ be - low his knee. He was be - loved by the lad - ies so fair, he was such a _ rak - ish _ boy; _____ He _ was my sov - er - eign, my heart's de - light, my char - ming young_ Gil - der - oy.

2 Young Gilderoy and I were born all in one town together,
And at the age of sixteen years we courted one another.
Our dads and mothers both did agree and crowned with
      mirth and joy,
To think upon our wedding day, with me and my Gilderoy.

3 Now Gilderoy and I walked out all in the fields together,
He took me round the waist so small, and down we went
      together;
And after he done all a man could do he rose and kissed his
      joy,
He was my sovereign, my heart's delight, my charming
      young Gilderoy.

4 What a pity it is that a man should be hanged for stealing
      woman,
Where he neither robbed house or land, he stole neither horse
      nor mare.

He was beloved by the old and young, he was such a rakish
    boy,
He was my sovereign, my heart's delight, my charming
    young Gilderoy.

5 Now Gilderoy for some time has been dead and a funeral we
    must have,
With a brace of pistols by his side to guard him to his grave;
For he was beloved by the old and the young, he was such a
    rakish boy,
He was my sovereign, my heart's delight, my charming
    young Gilderoy.

Gilderoy: gille roy, the red-haired lad.
would not the ribbons wear: perhaps this should be 'would knots of ribbons wear'.

he neither robbed . . .: in fact, he was hanged for cattle-stealing.

44   The Three Butchers

The robbery and murder of a luckless butcher by thieves with a naked woman as decoy and accomplice, is a stirring story. It has exercised its fascination for at least three hundred years, the earliest extant version being a black-letter broadside, 'The Three Worthy Butchers of the North', written by one Paul Burges, and printed between about 1672 and 1679. The scene was originally set in Norfolk, but many of the later versions changed it to Northumberland. Vaughan Williams took down the first verse from an Essex singer in 1904, adding the note: 'For rest of the words see book of ballad sheets.' They have been duly supplied from the composer's own collection of broadsides, in the shape of a sheet printed by J. Catnach.

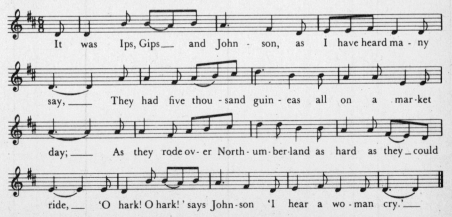

It was Ips, Gips and John-son, as I have heard ma-ny say, They had five thou-sand guin-eas all on a mar-ket day; As they rode ov-er North-um-ber-land as hard as they could ride, 'O hark! O hark!' says John-son 'I hear a wo-man cry.'

2 Then Johnson being a valiant man, a man of courage bold,
He ranged the woods all over till this woman he did behold.
'How came you here?' said Johnson, 'How came you here, I
    pray?
I am come here to relieve you if you will not me betray.'

3 'There has been ten swaggering blades has hand and foot me
    bound,
And stripped me stark naked with my hair pinned to the
    ground.'
Then Johnson being a valiant man, a man of courage bold,
He took his coat from off his back to keep her from the cold.

4 As they rode over Northumberland as hard as they could ride,
She put her fingers in her ear and gave a dismal cry.
Then up starts ten swaggering blades with weapons in their
    hands,
And, riding up to Johnson, they bid him for to stand.

5 It's 'I'll not stand', says Gibson, then, 'No, indeed, not I;
Nor I'll not stand', says Gibson, 'I'll sooner live than die'.
'Then I will stand', says Johnson, 'I'll stand the while I can;
I never yet was daunted nor afraid of any man.'

6 Then Johnson drew his glittering sword with all his might
    and main,
So well he laid about him till eight of them was slain.
As he was fighting the other two this woman he did not
    mind,
So she took the knife all from his side and ripped him up
    behind.

7 'Now I must fall', says Johnson, 'I must fall unto the ground;
For relieving this wicked woman she gave me my death
    wound.
O base woman! O base woman! Woman, what has thou
    done?
Thou has killed the finest butcher that ever the sun shone on.'

8 This happened on a market day as people were riding by,
To see this cruel murder they gave a hue and cry.
So now the woman's taken, and bound in fetters strong,
For killing the finest butcher that ever the sun shone on.

45   Bold Turpin

*Dick Turpin was a cattle-thief, smuggler, deer-stealer, housebreaker, high-
wayman and murderer. He was a complete ruffian, utterly lacking the quixo-
tic qualities which were later attributed to him. He did not even accomplish
the feat of riding to York in a day: this was done in fact by another highway-
man, William Nevison, in 1676. Turpin did make his way to Yorkshire in
1737 when the hunt for him in his native Essex grew too hot. He lived
undetected under his wife's name of Palmer, until a characteristically ill-
tempered dispute with an inkeeper whose gamecock he had shot led to his
arrest, eventual unmasking, and execution at York, in 1739.*

*Despite all this, tradition has made him into a figure of wit, dash and
daring. Songs and chapbooks (not to speak of novels and plays) told and
retold his story, apparently tirelessly. Richard Jefferies reported in 1874 that
the favourite set of prints on the walls of even the poorest cottage showed
Turpin's ride to York on Black Bess ('The Labourer's Daily Life'). This
song was collected from an Essex man in 1904 by Vaughan Williams.*

Bold Turpin was riding one day on the moor, He
saw a noble law-yer a-riding before; Tur-
-pin he rode and to him he did say, 'How
of-ten do you see bold Turpin pass this way?'

Chorus
O aye, Turpin he-ro, I am your val-iant Turpin bold.

2 'Now', says Turpin, 'for to be after, [acute]
   My money I have hid all in my boot.'
   'And now', says the lawyer, 'a man can't find,
   I have hid my money in my cape coat behind.'

3 And they rode together and came to a hill;
   Turpin bid the lawyer for to stand still:
   'Take off your coat, sir, it must come off,
   My horse is want of a new saddle cloth.'

4 Now Turpin has robbed him of all his store,
  And when that is gone he knows where to get more;
  'And the very first town that you come in,
  Tell him you've been robbed by bold Turpin.'

5 Now Turpin is caught [, in prison he was cast,]
  And for a gamecock he was hung at last;
  A hundred pounds there he laid aside,
  All for Jack Ketch his legacy.

Jack Ketch: public hangman.

46   The Box Upon Her Head

In country districts at one time a common sight must have been the servant girl trudging home at the end of her engagement with her box of clothes on her head. Poor as they were, such girls nevertheless ran the risk of being robbed, for footpads and highwaymen seldom had any scruples about stealing from the humble.

The song is sometimes called 'The Staffordshire Maid', because in some versions the girl is travelling home to see her parents who live in Staffordshire. In the earliest text which I know, a 22-verse street ballad of the eighteenth century (Douce Collection, Bodleian Library), the parents live at Hurley (which is in Warwickshire, though not far from Staffordshire).

References to servants in eighteenth and nineteenth-century literature are legion, though seldom do we see the strength of character shown here. A further variant title is 'The Undaunted Female'.

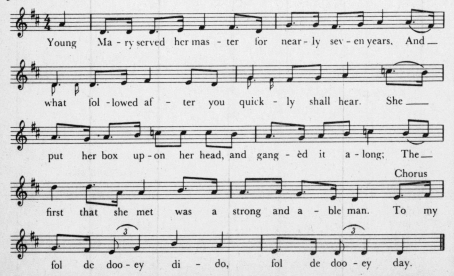

Young Mary served her master for nearly seven years, And what followed after you quickly shall hear. She put her box upon her head, and gangèd it along; The first that she met was a strong and able man. To my *Chorus* fol de doo-ey di-do, fol de doo-ey day.

2 He says, 'My pretty fair maid, where are you going this way?
   And I will show you a nigher way across the country.'
   He took her by the hand and led her to a lane;
   He says, 'My pretty fair maid, I tell you plump and plain.

3 'Deliver up your money without one word or strife,
   Or else this very moment I will take away your life.'
   When tears from her eyes like fountains did flow;
   Saying, 'Where shall I wander or where shall I go?'

4 And while this able fellow was feeling for his knife,
   This fair young damsel she took away his life.
   She put her box upon her head and gangèd it along,
   The next that she met was a noble gentleman.

5 He says, 'My pretty fair maid, where are you going so late?
   And what noise was it that I heard at yonder gate?
   That box that is upon your head to yourself does not belong,
   To your mistress or your master you have done something
        wrong.

6 'To your mistress or master you have done something ill,
   For one moment without trembling you cannot stand still.'
   'The box that is upon my head, to myself it does belong,
   To my mistress or my master I have done nothing wrong.

7 'To my mistress or my master I have done nothing ill,
   But I fear in my own heart that it is the man I have just
        killed.'
   She took him by the hand and led him to the place
   Where this able fellow lie bleeding on his face.

8 He jumped from off his horse to see what he had got:
   He had got three loaded pistols, some powder and some shot.
   He had got three loaded pistols, some powder and some ball,
   And a whistle in his pocket the robbers for to call.

9 He put the whistle to his mouth and blew it loud and shrill,
   And four young able fellows came tripping o'er the hill.
   This gentleman shot one of them so easy and so free,
   And his pretty fair maid shot the other three.

10 He put the box upon his **horse and** walkèd by her side,
He says, 'My pretty fair maid, I'll make you my bonny
bride.
I will make you my loving bride before it's very long,
For taking of your own part and firing of your gun.'

gangèd it: went. The same archaism occurs in a number of versions.

she took away his: the street ballad version mentioned above makes it clear that the girl struck the man with his own staff, while he was bending over to box the try to open it.

He put the whistle to his mouth: in the street ballad the gentleman makes a plan of action before blowing the whistle.

47   Salisbury Plain

As I rode o-ver Salis-bu-ry Plain, O— there I met a scamp-ing— young blade. He— kissed— and en-tic-ed me so, — That a-long with him I was forced for to go.

Variant

verse 5

92

2 Till we came unto a public house at last,
And there for man and wife we did pass.
He called for ale and wine and strong beer,
Then at length we to bed did repair.

3 'Undress yourself, my darling', says he,
'Undress yourself and come to bed with me.'
'Oh yes, that I will', then said she,
'If those flash girls you will keep away.'

4 'Those flash girls you need not fear
For you shall be safe-guarded, my dear;
I'll maintain you as a lady so gay
If I go robbing on the highway.'

5 Early the next morning my love [he a]rose
And instantly he put on his clothes;
And straightway to the highway did sail
Where he robbed from coaches to mail.

6 So now my love in Newgate cell do lay,
Expecting every moment to die.
The Lord have mercy on his poor soul,
I think I hear his death bell now toll.

7 So now young men a warning take by me,
And never keep those flash girls company,
For if that you do you will rue,
And you will die upon the high drop at last.

from coaches . . . .: perhaps, 'from the coaches of the mail'.

The last farewell or goodnight to the world, ostensibly delivered from the gallows by a condemned criminal about to die, has produced a whole genre of ballads. Within it, a valediction from the man's wife or sweetheart is an interesting variation (cf. 'Georgie' (no. 42) and 'Gilderoy' (no. 43).) 'Salisbury Plain' has an eighteenth-century ring, though I have not seen it on street ballads. Vaughan Williams collected this version, with its fine Aeolian tune, in 1904.

Australia

Come all ye young fel-lows, where so-'er you may be, Come
lis-ten a-while to my sto-ry._____ When I was a
(a)
young man, my age sev-en-teen, I ought-n't'a' been serv-ing Vic-
-tor-ia, our queen, But those hard heart-ed judg-es, oh how
(b)
cru-el they be, To send us poor lads to Aus-tra-lia._____
Variant
(a)   (b)

*Verses 2—4 begin here.

2 I fell in with a damsel, she was handsome and gay,
   I neglected my work more and more every day;
   And to keep her like a lady I went on the highway,
   And for that I was sent to Australia.

3 Now the judges they stand with the whips in their hand,
   They drive us like horses to plough up the land;
   You should see us poor fellows, working in that jail yard,
   How hard is our fate in Australia.

4 Australia, Australia, I would ne'er see no more,
   Worn out with the fever, cast down to death's door;
   But should I live to see, say, seven years more,
   I would then say adieu to Australia.

The loss of the American Colonies deprived the British Government of a place of exile for convicts. As an alternative, transportation to Australia was started in 1787. It was successively abolished by New South Wales (1840), Van Dieman's Land, which changed its name to Tasmania at the same time (1852), and finally by Western Australia (1868).

Historians differ as to whether transportation was a severe punishment for convicts, or a favourable opportunity for them to begin a new life, but the popular tradition is unequivocal: for many generations after its abolition, songs and stories continued to express the people's fear and loathing. Some songs remain in oral circulation to this day: 'Van Dieman's Land' (see no. 52) can still be heard, and 'Australia' (based on an older ballad of transportation to Virginia) is from the repertoire of a traditional singer, Bob Hart of Suffolk (1892–1978).

49 The Lincolnshire Poacher

Instead of 'Bad luck to every magistrate' in the last verse, some versions have 'Success to every gentleman'. No doubt the prudent singer would have suited his words to his audience. George IV had a particular liking for the song, and slighting references to his Justices of the Peace would hardly have been well received at Windsor.

George IV enjoyed the tune which is still well known, thanks to the National Song Book, but the melody much earlier associated with the song was 'The Manchester Angel'. This continued in oral circulation, and a recently collected version is given here.

The singer, a traveller called Joe Saunders, remarked: 'I'll sing you one they larns 'em in the schools — only they don't larn it 'em right.'

Although other counties — Leicestershire, Northamptonshire, and even Somersetshire — are sometimes introduced, it seems that Lincolnshire was originally intended, at least from the evidence of the earliest printed version, which appeared in 1776.

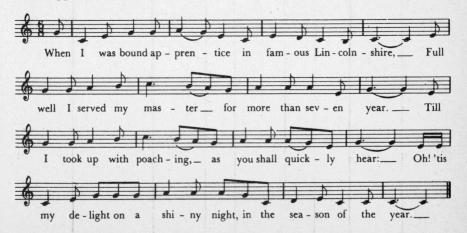

When I was bound ap-pren-tice in fam-ous Lin-coln-shire,___ Full
well I served my mas-ter___ for more than sev-en year.___ Till
I took up with poach-ing,___ as you shall quick-ly hear:___ Oh! 'tis
my de-light on a shi-ny night, in the sea-son of the year.___

2 As me and my comrades were setting of a snare,
  'Twas then we seed the gamekeeper – for him we did not
      care,
  For we can wrestle and fight, my boys, and jump o'er
      anywhere,
  Oh! 'tis my delight, *etc.*

3 As me and my comrades were setting four or five,
  And taking on him up again, we caught the hare alive;
  We caught the hare alive, my boys, and through the woods
      did steer:
  Oh! 'tis my delight, *etc.*

4 I threw him on my shoulder, and then we trudged home,
  We took him to a neighbour's house and sold him for a
      crown;
  We sold him for a crown, my boys, but I did not tell you
      where,
  Oh! 'tis my delight, *etc.*

5 Bad luck to every magistrate that lives in Lincolnshire,
  Success to every poacher that wants to sell a hare;
  Bad luck to every gamekeeper that will not sell his deer:
  Oh! 'tis my delight, *etc.*

shiny night: moonlit night.

50   The Nottingham Poacher

*Enclosure aroused a great deal of resentment among countrymen, and poaching
provided one way of protesting. The Thorney Moor Woods of the song could
possibly be Thorney Wood Chase, near Nottingham, part of the ancient
Sherwood Forest, which was enclosed in 1792. However, the deforestation
which followed, and the consequent disappearance of the deer, would have left
little scope for poaching. It seems much more likely that the reference is to the
village of Thornehagh (pronounced 'Thorney'), near Newark, where the
800-acre common called Moor Fields was enclosed in 1797, and known there-
after as Thornehagh Moor Woods. The new enclosure seems to have been
stocked with game and provided with gamekeepers.*

    *One can postulate a not uncommon life-history for the song. Starting as a
home-made production (Dixon darkly suggests that it 'was written by a*

gentleman of rank and education'), it would circulate locally, then gradually spread further afield. It might then come to the notice of a ballad-printer: certainly a copy appeared under the imprint of Thomas Ford of Chesterfield, in about 1840. Others would then reprint the ballad, and it would achieve national circulation. This in fact happened, and it remained popular until our own times. The version given here is from the traditional Staffordshire singer, George Dunn, who died as recently as 1975. The song is normally entitled 'Thorney Moor Woods'.

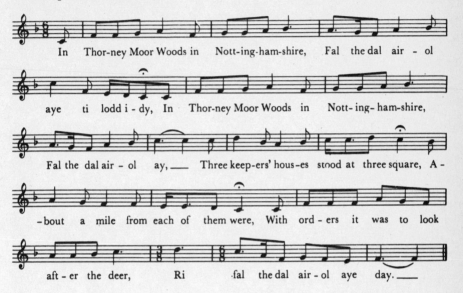

In Thor-ney Moor Woods in Nott-ing-ham-shire, Fal the dal air - ol aye ti lodd i - dy, In Thor-ney Moor Woods in Nott- ing- ham-shire, Fal the dal air - ol ay, ___ Three keep-ers' hous-es stood at three square, A- -bout a mile from each of them were, With ord - ers it was to look aft - er the deer, Ri fal the dal air - ol aye day. ___

2 When me and my mates went out at night
  With my two dogs close on my heels,
  When me and my mates went out at night
  With my two dogs close on my heels,
  'Twas to catch a fat buck in Nottingham Fields.

3 The very first night we had bad luck:
  Jack, my very best dog got stuck;
  He came to me both bloody and lame,
  And sorry was I to see him the same,
  He was not able to follow the game.

4 I searched his wounds and found them slight:
  I know some keeper's done this for spite,
  But I'll take my pike-staff in my hand,
  I'll search the wood till I find the man,
  Then I'll tan his hide right well if I can.

5 The very first thing that we found
Was a big fat buck nearly dead on the ground,
The very first thing that we found
Was a big fat buck nearly dead on the ground;
I know my dogs gid him his best wound.

6 I pulled out my knife and I cut the buck's throat,
I pulled out my knife and I cut the buck's throat,
And now you would have laughed to see limping Jack
Go hopping along with the buck on his back;
He carried him like some Yorkshireman's pack.

7 We ordered a butcher to skin the game,
Likewise another to sell the same.
The very first joint they offered for sale
Was to an old woman who brewed bad ale,
And it causèd we poor lads in jail.

8 The assizes are opened and we're all here,
The assizes all over and we're all clear:
The gentlemen felt a sorrowful scorn
That such an old woman should be forsworn,
And all to pieces she ought to be torn.

gid: gave.

51   Lads of High Renown

*During the reign of George III (1760–1820) thirty-two new Game Laws
were passed. The increasingly repressive legislation was bitterly resented, and
eventually led to bloody battles between gamekeepers and poachers. There was
no shortage of incidents of the kind described in 'Lads of High Renown',
though it is not known whether a particular event inspired the song. Certainly, it must have been in existence by 1811 or 1812, when its first verse
inspired a Luddite anthem in Yorkshire, 'The Croppers' Song'. Numerous
street ballad printings followed in the 1830s and 1840s, under a profusion of
titles, including 'The Poacher's Fate', 'The Gallant Poachers' and 'The Gallant Poacher' (the last two also serving at times for quite different songs). A
number of oral versions turned up later in the nineteenth and in the twentieth
century. This one is from Walter Pardon of Knapton, Norfolk, who was born*

in 1914. He tells me that this was the first song he learnt, at the age of about seven. It came from his uncle, Billy Gee (born 1863), who learnt it from his father (Walter's grandfather), Tom Gee.

1. Come all you lads of high re-nown Who love to drink strong ale that's brown, And pull a loft-y phea-sant down With pow-der, shot and gun. 3. The moon shone bright, not a cloud in sight, The keep-er heard us fire a gun And to the spot did quick-ly run; He swore be-fore the ris-ing sun That one of us must die.

Tune A for verses 1, 2, 4, 5, 7, 8, 10, 11, 12. Tune B for remainder.

2 I and five more a-poaching went,
To kill some game was our intent;
Our money gone and all was spent,
We'd nothing else to try.

3 The moon shone bright, not a cloud in sight;
The keeper heard us fire a gun
And to the spot did quickly run:
He swore before the rising sun
That one of us must die.

4 'Twas the bravest youth among the lot,
'Twas his misfortune to be shot;
In memory he'll ne'er be forgot
By all his friends below.

5 In memory he ever shall be blest,
He rose again to stand the test,
Whilst down upon his gallant breast
The crimson blood did flow.

6 For help he cried but was denied;
   It was the wound the keeper gave,
   No mortal man his life could save;
   He now lies sleeping in the grave
   Until the judgment day.

7 That youth he fell upon the ground
   Within his breast a mortal wound,
   Whilst from the woods a gun did sound
   Which took his life away.

8 The murderous man that did him kill,
   All on the ground his blood did spill,
   Shall wander far against his will
   And find no resting place.

9 Destructive things his conscience stings;
   He must wander through this world forlorn
   And always feel the smarting thorn
   That pointed out with finger's scorn,
   And die in sad disgrace.

10 To prison then we all were sent,
   We called for aid but none was lent;
   Our enemies they were full bent
   That there we should remain.

11 But fickle fortune on us shine
   And unto us did change her mind;
   With heart-felt thanks for liberty
   We were let out again.

12 No more locked up in those midnight cells
   To hear the turnkeys ring the bells;
   Those cruckling doors I bid farewell,
   The rattling of the chain.

Van Dieman's Land

So strong was official feeling against poachers in the decades after Waterloo, that in 1828 it was enacted that if three men were found in a wood after dark, and one of them carried a gun or bludgeon, all were liable to be transported for fourteen years. It is my theory (set out in some detail in the Folk Music Journal, 1976, pp. 161–4) that the ballad was written in 1829 or 1830 in direct response to the first cases brought under the new act. It was enormously successful, was reprinted on street ballads dozens of times, and even inspired what I take to be a sequel, 'Young Henry the Poacher'. Although convicts were not transported to Van Dieman's Land after its change of name to Tasmania in 1852, the shock and horror of the memory was such that the song continued in widespread oral circulation almost to the present day.

Come all you gal-lant poach - ers that — ram-ble void of care, While — walk-ing out — one moon - light night — with — gun and dog — and snare, With your hares and lof - ty phea - sants — you — have at your — com - mand, Not think - ing of the last ca - reer up - on Van Die-man's Land.

2 It's poor Tom Brown from Nottingham, Jack Williams and
    poor Joe,
There were three daring poachers the country did well know;
At night they were trepanned by the keepers hid in sand:
Fourteen years transported, boys, upon Van Dieman's Land.

3 The very day we landed upon that fateful shore,
The planters they stood round us full twenty score and more;
They ranked us up like horses and sold us out of hand,
They roped us to the plough, brave boys, to plough Van
    Dieman's Land.

4 The cottage that we lived in was built of clods and clay,
And rotten straw for bed, and we dare not say nay;
Our cots were fenced with fire, to slumber when we can,
To drive away wolves and tigers come by Van Dieman's
Land.

5 There was a poor girl from Birmingham, Susan Simmons was
her name,
Fourteen years transported, you all have heard the same.
Our planter bought her freedom, he married her out of hand;
She gave to us good usage upon Van Dieman's Land.

6 It's oft-times when I slumber I have a pleasant dream:
With my pretty girl I have been roving down by a sparkling
stream;
In England I've been roving with her at my command,
But I wake broken-hearted upon Van Dieman's Land.

7 Come all you daring poachers, give hearing to my song:
It is a bit of good advice although it is not long.
Lay aside your dogs and snares, to you I must speak plain,
For if you knew our hardships you'd never poach again.

trepanned: trapped.
wolves and tigers: not normally found in Tasmania.

53   Hares in the Old Plantation

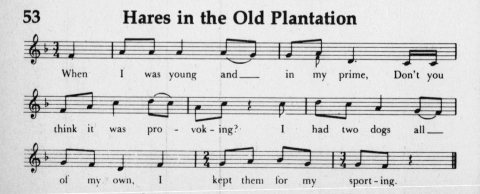

When I was young and in my prime, Don't you
think it was pro - vok - ing? I had two dogs all
of my own, I kept them for my sport - ing.

2 When I had two dogs and an airgun too,
  I kept them for my keeping,
  For to kill some game at night .
  When the keepers they were sleeping.

3 I and my dogs went out one night
  To view a habitation,
  What started one, right away she ran,
  Right away into my plantation.

4 Before I could get half a field or more,
  Or very little further,
  Up jumped another old hare and away dogs went,
  Made hare shriek murder.

5 Up she jumped and followed out aunt,
  When the dogs stopped her running.
  'O, pray, poor puss, do lay still,
  For your uncle [is] a-coming.'

6 I picked her up and I broke her neck
  And into my pocket put her;
  [Thinks I to myself I had better be going
  Before I meets the looker.

7 I went into a neighbour's house
  And I asked him what he'd give me.
  He said he'd give me a crown a brace
  If I would bring him fifty.

8 I went into a public house
  And there I gets quite mellow;
  I spent a crown, another one throwed down,
  Wasn't I a good-hearted fellow?]

aunt, puss: names for female hares. The female of the species was prized by poachers
because it was considered better eating.

*Not all poaching songs have the sombre colour of 'Van Dieman's Land' or
'Lads of High Renown'. Later in the nineteenth century when the Game
Laws, if still irksome, were much less draconian, there were jaunty, cheeky
songs like this one.*

54   Row Dow Dow

Just before the Great War, Fred Holman of Tatsfield in Surrey went out poaching on a large estate at Addington, owned by C. H. Goschen (1839–1915), a one-time director of the Bank of England. Holman was caught and imprisoned. He later made a jocular song about his experiences, of which he would apparently supply hand-written copies for the price of a pint in his local, The Old Ship. As a consequence, the song became fairly well known in the area. Stephen Sedley collected this version at nearby Biggin Hill, Kent, in 1967, from a traveller known as 'Sharper's Joe'.

If you come and lis - ten for a while a
sto - ry I will tell you, And if you don't pay at-ten-tion I'm
sure I can't com-pel you; And as you've asked me_for to sing I'd
bet - ter start at once,_ And tell you how I got six weeks and

Chorus

my mate got six months_ With my row dow dow,
fol rid - dle lad - dy, With my row dow dow.

2 It happened on one Monday night, two more, myself and
    Clarkie,
We went a–pheasant shooting in a place we knowed was
    narkery.
Five keepers rushed upon us and the guns began to rattle,
And 'course my mate he did a bunk and left me to the battle.

3 Me and Clark got captured, boys, was taken to the lock-up;
I was charged by the magistrate, I was shooting Goschen's
    cocks up.
But if we had run away we never would have been taken,
And all we got to think about are wives and little children.

4 Now marching up to Wandsworth Gaol our minds was
    always wandering,
We were thinking of the prospects of our wives and little
    children.
When they got us to the stir they set us grinding flour,
Likewise pumping water, boys, unto some lofty tower.

5 [Now the twenty-fourth of December my time it did expire;
    When I got out I had some scran, that's what I did require.]
And since I've had this glass of beer it's making me feel
    merry;
My mate don't come out of Wandsworth Gaol till the middle
    of January.

Goschen: see above.
grinding flour . . . pumping water: the
    reference seem to be to the treadmill,
which was phased out as a result of the
Prison Act of 1898.
scran: food.

55   Henry, My Son

Randolf, Earl of Chester (see note, no. 41, for his mention in Piers Plowman) *died in 1232. The wife of his nephew and successor, John, is supposed
to have tried to poison her husband. Such is the possible origin of the story of
a huge corpus of ballads, usually entitled 'Lord Randal', and often, especially
in England, 'Henry, My Son'. In all the ballads a man, having been
poisoned by a woman, is questioned by his mother and makes a verbal testament. To his murderess he bequeaths a rope (or some other symbol of retribu-
tion). Over the centuries there have been all sorts of changes – the murderess
can be wife, sweetheart, or even sister, but the basic plot seems remarkably
tenacious.*

'Where have you been all day, Hen - ry, my son?
Where have you been all day, my be - lov - èd one?'
'In the mead-ows, in the mead-ows. Make my bed, there's a
pain in my head, And I want to lie down and die.'

105

2 'What have you had to eat, Henry, my son?
What have you had to eat, my beloved one?'
'Poisoned berries, poisoned berries.
Make my bed, ther's a pain in my head,
And I want to lie down and die.'

3 'Who gave you poisoned berries? . . .'
'My sister . . .'

4 'What will you leave your father? . . .'
'Gold and silver . . .'

5 'What will you leave your mother? . . .'
'Love and kisses . . .'

6 'What will you leave your sister? . . .'
'A rope to hang her . . .'

7 'How shall I make your bed? . . .'
'Long and narrow . . .'

56 The Babes in the Wood

My friends, you must know, a long time a-go, There were
two lit-tle child-ren whose names I don't know. They were
sto-len a-way on a bright sum-mer's day And
left in a wood, so I've heard folks say.
Chorus
Pret-ty babes in the wood, pret-ty babes in the wood, Oh,
don't you re-mem-ber the babes in the wood?

[2 And when it came night, oh, sad was their plight.
The moon did not shine and the stars gave no light.
They cried and they cried, and they bitterly sighed.
Poor babes in the wood, they lay down and died.

3 And when they were dead the robins so red
Brought strawberry leaves and over them spread,
And sang them a song the whole night long.
Poor babes in the wood, poor babes in the wood.]

'The Norfolk gent his will and Testament and howe he Commytted the keepinge of his Children to his owne brother who delte moste wickedly with them and howe God plagued him for it' was registered for publication as a street ballad on 15 October 1595. Ever since then the story had been well-known, not perhaps from ballads, but from nursery stories and pantomimes The original of this version was written by William Gardiner (1770–1853) of Leicester, to words by a Mr Combe.

57   Hangèd I Shall Be

As I was bound ap - prent - ice, I was
bound un - to a mill. I served my mas - ter
tru - ly for sev - en years or more.

2 Until I took up courting with a girl with a rolling eye,
I told that girl I'd marry her, if she would be my bride.

3 I asked her if she'd take a walk through the fields and
meadows gay,
And there we told the tales of love and fixed the wedding
day.

4 As we were a-walking, and talking of things that grew
around,
I took a stick all out of the hedge and knocked that pretty
maid down.

5 Down on her bended knees she fell and loud for mercy cried:
   'O, come spare the life of an innocent girl, for I am not fit to
   die.'

6 Then I took her by her curly locks and dragged her on the
   ground
   Until I came to the river-side that flowed to Ekefield town.

7 That ran so long in distance, that ran so deep and wide,
   And there I plunged that pretty fair maid that should have
   been my bride.

8 When I went home to my parents' house, about ten o'clock
   that night,
   My mother she jumped out of bed, all for to light the light.

9 She asked me and she questioned me, 'What stains your
   hands and clothes?'
   And the answer I gave back to her, 'I been bleeding at the
   nose.'

10 No rest, no rest, all that long night, no rest could I find,
    For the sparks of fire and brimstone all round my head did
    shine.

11 And it was about two days after, this fair young maid was
    found
    A-floating by the river-side that flows to Ekefield town.

12 The judges and the jurymen, on me they did agree,
    For murdering of this pretty fair maid; so hangèd I shall be.

   Ekefield town: does not exist; but this could be a garbled version of Hocstow, the
original location.

*Samuel Pepys, well known for his love of music and singing, assembled a
large collection of street ballads, which includes 'The bloody Miller Being a
true and just Account of one* Francis Cooper *of* Hocstow *near Shrewsbury, who was a Millers Servant, and kept company with one* Anne Nicols
*for the space of two years, who then proved to be with Child by him, and
being urged by her Father to marry her he most wickedly and barbarously
murdered her, as you shall hear by the sequel.' This was the ancestor of a
great family of songs on the same theme, widely known in Britain and*

America until recently, under such titles as 'The Cruel Miller', 'The 'Prentice Boy', 'The Wexford Murder', 'The Berkshire Tragedy' and 'The Wittam Miller'. One motif which invariably appears is that of the guilty bloodstains, explained as a 'bleeding at the nose'. H. E. Rollins, the American ballad scholar, found a reference in a contemporary diary which authenticates and dates the original murder: 'I heard of a murther near Salop on Sabb. day ẙ 10. instant, a woman fathering a conception on a Milner was Kild by him in a feild, her Body lay there many dayes by reason of ẙ Coroner's absence' (Philip Henry's Diaries and Letters, 20 February 1684, ed. M. H. Lee, 1882, p. 323). The composer, E. J. Moeran, took down this version from a Norfolk man in 1921.

58   The False-hearted Knight

A man, or a demon in human guise, murders several women, but is eventually killed by a potential victim who is too clever for him. The theme can be simply stated, but it has held the popular imagination for centuries. Gradually, the original supernatural elements have been rationalized, apparently without reducing the story's appeal. Scores of versions of the ballad, which Professor Child called 'Lady Isabel and the Elf Knight', have been found, all over Europe. Several books have been written on the subject, including H. O. Nygard's The Ballad of 'Heer Halewijn' *(Folklore Fellows, Helsinki, 1958). The earliest known English text is a street ballad of about 1710; the version given here is from 'Jumbo' Brightwell, a Suffolk railwayman, born in 1900. The song is often known in England as 'The Outlandish Knight'.*

Now 'twas of a false knight who came from the north land, He came a-court-ing me;⸺ He had prom-ised to take me down to the north land, And there his bride⸺ make me.⸺

2 'So come give me some of your mother's gold
    And some of your father's fee;
    And two of the best horses out of the stable,
    Where there stand by thirty and three.'

3 So she mounted up on her milk-white steed,
   And he on his dapple and grey;
   And away they did ride to the great water side,
   So early before it was day.

4 'Jump you off, jump you off that milk-white steed
   And deliver it unto me;
   For six pretty fair maids I have drownded here
   And the seventh one you shall be.

5 'And take off, take off that silken gownd
   And lay it upon yon stone;
   For I think it's too rich and I think it's too rare
   For to rot all in the salt sea.'

6 'If I must take off my silken gownd,
   Then turn your back upon me;
   For I don't think it's fit that a villain like you
   A naked woman should see.

7 'And stoop you down and cut that briar
   That hangs so near that brim,
   In case it should tangle my golden hair
   And tear my lily-white skin.'

8 Then she gave him a push and a hearty push
   And she pushed that false knight in,
   Crying, 'Lay in there, you false-hearted knight,
   Lay in there instead of me,
   For it's six pretty fair maids you have drownded in here,
   The seventh one have drownded thee.'

9 So she mounted up on her milk-white steed
   And she led his dapple and grey,
   And away she did ride to her own father's hall,
   Two hours before it was day.

10 The old parrot was up in the window so high
   And he cried aloud and did say,
   'I'm afraid that some villain came here last night
   And have carried my lady away.'

11 Her father he was not so sound asleep
   That he heard but that bird did say;
   And he cried, 'What waggeth, my pretty, polly,
   Two hours before it is day?'

12 'Why the old cat was up in that window high,
   And that cat he would me slay;
   So loud did I cry that help should be nigh
   To drive that cat away.'

13 'Well done, well done, my pretty polly,
   No tales will you tell of me;
   Thy cage shall be made of that bright glittering gold,
   And the door of white ivory.'

Well done . . .: the last verse is uttered by the woman. In some versions, she urges the
parrot not to betray her, in a verse such as this: 'Don't prittle, don't prattle, my pretty
Polly/Oh, and tell no tales on me,/And thy cage shall be made of the glittering gold-
/And the door of the best ivory.'

59   It's of a Farmer

*Two brothers find out that their sister is in love with a servant. They per-
suade him to go hunting with them, kill him, and hide his body. He appears
to the girl in dreams, and she discovers his body. The story has the ring of
ancient grief and savagery, as well it might, for the theme dates back at least
to the fourteenth century. Boccacio used it in his* Pot of Basil *(Decameron,
IV, 5), with the added embellishment that the girl placed her lover's head in a
pot and planted over it the herb, basil, which she watered with her tears.
There were further reworkings of the story by Hans Sachs (between 1515 and
1548) and by John Keats (1820).*

*This is not to suggest that the ballad was derived from any of these sources,
it seems more likely that both Boccacio and the unknown ballad writer were
drawing on popular tradition. Professor H. M. Belden ('Boccacio, Hans
Sachs and* The Bramble Briar', *in* Publications of the Modern
Languages Association of America, *vol. 33, 1918) dates the ballad in its
present form from the early eighteenth century, though no printed text sur-
vives from that time. Indeed, the first printing seems to have been in 1904,
when Cecil Sharp published a version, entitled 'Bruton Town', which he had
collected in Somerset. Others, invariably from oral tradition, have turned up
in the south and west of England and in North America. This one was
collected by Vaughan Williams in Herefordshire in 1913.*

111

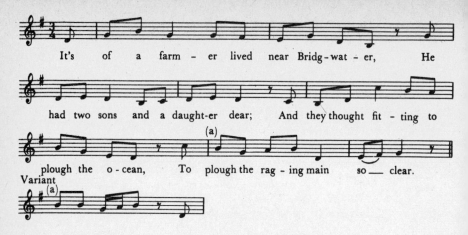

It's of a farm-er lived near Bridg-wat-er, He had two sons and a daught-er dear; And they thought fit-ting to plough the o-cean, To plough the rag-ing main so__ clear.

Variant (a)

2 'Our servantman's going to wed our sister,
   Our sister she has a man to wed;
   But their courtship shall soon be ended,
   I send him to his silent bed.'

3 One hunting day it was appointed,
   To take this young man's life away;
   They did this young man over flatter
   To hunting unto go with them.

4 And through the woods as they were riding
   They saw a brake of briars grow;
   They soon became and his blood they slaughtered,
   And a brake of briars pulled him through.

5 'O welcome home', then said the sister,
   'But where is our young servant man?
   I only ask because you whispered,
   Dear brothers tell me if you can.'

6 'Now through the woods as we was riding,
   There we lost him and never him found;
   But I tell you we are affronted
   You do hard and examine we.'

7 Three days and nights she lay lamenting,
   She dreamed, she dreamed her love she saw;
   By her bedside the tears lamenting,
   All over and over with gore.

8 'Lay still, lay still, my patient jewel,
   It's all in vain for to complain;
   Her brothers killed me, now weren't they cruel,
   In such a place that you may find.'

9 Then through the woods as she was riding
   She heard such fearful, dismal groans:
   'Surely that is my own true love
   In a brake of briars killed and thrown.'

10 She kissed his lips that was all dry-ed,
   His tears as salt as any brine;
   She kissed his lips and oft times sighed:
   'O here lays a bold young friend of mine.'

No version of this ballad has been found without corruptions in its text. The words
given here are exactly those found by Vaughan Williams. One might try to rationalize
some phrases as follows. *To huntin unto go:* a-hunting for to go. *They soon became:*
They soon came there. *You do hard:* you look so hard. *All over and over with gore:* all
covered over with blood and gore. *Her brothers:* your brothers.

60   The Prickle Holly Bush

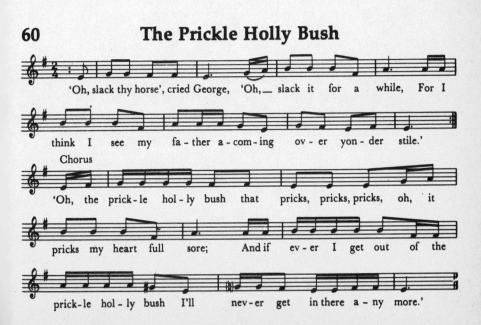

'Oh, slack thy horse', cried George, 'Oh,— slack it for a while, For I
think I see my fa-ther a-com-ing ov-er yon-der stile.'

Chorus

'Oh, the prick-le hol-ly bush that pricks, pricks, pricks, oh, it
pricks my heart full sore; And if ev-er I get out of the
prick-le hol-ly bush I'll nev-er get in there a-ny more.'

2 'Oh father have you brought me any gold, or silver to set me
   free,
   And to keep my body from the cold gaol wall and my neck
   from the high gallows tree?'

3 'No, I've not brought any gold nor silver to set you free,
   But I have come for to see you hang, oh, hang upon the high
   gallows tree.'

Similarly, with mother, sister, brother.
Final verses:

13 'Oh, slack thy horse', cried George, 'oh, slack it for a while,
   For I think I see my sweetheart a-coming over yonder stile.'

14 'Oh, sweetheart, have you brought me any gold or silver to
   set me free,
   And to keep my body from the cold goal wall and my neck
   from the high gallows tree?'

15 'Yes, I have brought you gold and silver to set you free,
   And I've not come for to see you hang, oh, hang upon the
   high gallows tree.'

*A girl is given a golden ball and told that she will be hanged if she loses it.
Not surprisingly, perhaps, she does lose it, and then pleads with various
relatives to save her by providing the necessary ransom. Such a story, with the
golden ball symbolizing the maiden's virginity, may well have provided the
basis for this ballad, which Child called 'The Maid Freed from the Gallows'.
I believe that country singers have been attracted simply by the exercise in
clemency which is rehearsed in the song, rather than by the notion of a ritual
expiation of the loss of virginity, especially as the protagonist is often a man.
The earliest English texts date from about 1770, but this version was collected
in Berkshire two centuries later, by Mike Yates. With each 'scene', so to
speak, three verses are sung to the same tune, then the chorus follows.*

Maria Marten

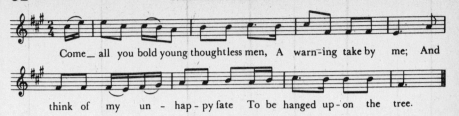

Come_ all you bold young thoughtless men, A warn-ing take by me; And

think of my un - hap-py fate To be hanged up-on the tree.

2 My name is William Corder,
  The truth I do declare;
  I courted Maria Marten,
  Most beautiful and fair.

3 I promised her I'd marry her,
  All on one certain day;
  Instead of that I was resolved
  To take her life away.

4 I went unto her father's house
  Upon the eighteenth day of May,
  'O come my dearest Ria,
  And we'll fix the wedding day.

5 'If you will meet me at the Red Barn,
  As sure as I have life,
  I will take you down to Ipswich Town
  And there make you my wife.'

6 He straight went home and fetched his gun,
  His pick-axe and his spade;
  He went unto the Red Barn,
  And there he dug her grave.

7 With heart so light she thought no harm,
  To meet him she did go;
  He murdered her all in the barn,
  And he laid her body low.

8 And all things being silent,
  They could not take no rest,
  Which appearèd in her mother's house
  When suckled at her breast.

9 Her mother had a dreadful dream,
  She dreamed it three nights o'er,
  She dreamed that her dear daughter
  Lay beneath the Red Barn floor.

10 They sent her father to the barn,
   And in the ground he thrust;
   And there he found his daughter dear
   Lay mingling with the dust.

11 Come all you young thoughtless men,
   Some pity look on me;
   On Monday next will be my last,
   To be hanged upon the tree.

*By the age of 26, Maria Marten, who was born at Polstead, Suffolk, in
1801, had produced three illegitimate children, all by different fathers. The
last, which lived for only six weeks, was the child of William Corder, also of
Polstead. He was two years the junior of Maria, the son of a farmer, and a
sort of confidence man, 'with an ungovernable propensity for forming intimate
connexions with females.' Shortly after the child's death, the couple left
Polstead, ostensibly to go to Ipswich to be married so that Maria could avoid
being charged with having had a bastard child. In fact, Corder took her to the
Red Barn, murdered her, and buried her beneath the floor. He later said that
Maria was staying at Yarmouth, and absented himself from Polstead for prog-
ressively longer intervals. In November, 1827, having married a lady whom
he had obtained by advertising in the* Morning Herald *(he did not bother to
collect the 45 replies to a further advertisement in the* Sunday Times*), he
moved to Brentford, Essex, where his wife set up a 'school for young ladies'.
In April, 1828, after a long period of anxiety as to her fate, Maria's father
dug up the floor of the Red Barn and found the corpse of his daughter. His
action was at the suggestion of his wife, Anne (who was Maria's step-mother,
and not her natural mother, as the song suggests), who claimed that she had
repeatedly dreamed that the girl had been murdered at that spot. (Recent commentators have suggested the possibility of her complicity with Corder as the
source of her information, rather than dreams). Corder was arrested, tried, and
found guilty of murder. He was hanged outside Bury St Edmund's Gaol on
11 August 1828. The song, originally published as a street ballad by Catnach, purported to have been written by William Corder, whose 'last goodnight' or 'farewell to the world' it was. The sheet sold well over one-and-a-
half million copies, and the story, in the form of song, novelette and melod-
rama, enjoyed a vogue lasting for a hundred years or so. Corder's skeleton is
still preserved in the museum of the College of Surgeons.*

IV
Once I Loved a Lass: Courtship

62   As I Was A-walking

As I was a-walk-ing one morn-ing by chance, I heard a maid mak-ing her moan;___ I asked what was the mat-ter, she said in a flut-ter,___ 'I'm ob--liged to lie tumb-ling a-lone, a - - lone.' ___ 'I'm ob-liged to lie tumb-ling a-lone.'___

2 I said, 'My fair maid, where did you come from,
  Or are you some distance from home?
  'My home', replies she, 'is a burden to me,
  For I'm obliged', *etc.*

3 'When I was eleven, sweethearts I had seven,
  But then I was fitting for none;
  But now I am fit ne'er a one can I get,
  For I'm obliged', *etc.*

4 'My sister a girl was wed at sixteen,
  And she has fine babes of her own;
  And here I am now in my sweet twenty-one,
  I'm obliged', *etc.*

5 'I wish some brisk fellow would pity my case,
  And make me a bride of his own;
  For I vow and declare I shall die in despair
  If I lie one night longer alone, alone,
  If I lie one night longer alone'.

*The problem of the girl of 'sweet twenty-one' who is unable to find a suitable
'brisk fellow' seems less of a genuine feminine problem than masculine wishful
thinking, especially to some one living in the late twentieth century. There
are nevertheless some songs deeply concerned with the desire to avoid spinster-
hood, though others for one reason or another reject importunate suitors.*

63   **Green Bushes**

*A young man 'a-walking', as in so many English folk songs, 'one morning in
May', overhears a woman singing of her true love. He immediately offers her
rich clothing if she will marry him instead, but she rejects the offer. Almost
immediately, however, she changes her mind, on condition that he will be
'loyal and constant'. The erstwhile true love is naturally disappointed as he
sees the pair disappearing into the distance. The green bushes are both part of
the landscape and a symbol of virginity. The song dates from the 1760s,*

though it remained popular until the early years of this century. The fine, striding tune is often associated with 'The Cutty Wren'; Vaughan Williams collected it in Essex in 1904 with only a fragment of text, for which I have substituted words from a ballad sheet.

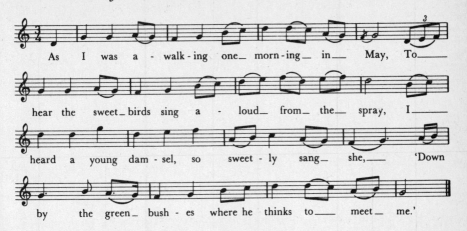

As I was a-walking one morning in May, To hear the sweet birds sing aloud from the spray, I heard a young damsel, so sweetly sang she, 'Down by the green bushes where he thinks to meet me.'

2 'I'll buy you fine beavers and a fine silken gown,
   I'll buy you fine petticoats flounced to the ground,
   If you'll but prove loyal and constant to me,
   And forsake your own true love and marry with me.'

3 'I want none of your beavers nor fine silken hose,
   For I never was so poor as to marry for clothes;
   But if you'll prove loyal and constant to me,
   I'll forsake my own true love and get married to thee.'

4 'Come let us be going, kind sir, if you please,
   Come let us be going from under these trees;
   For yonder he's coming, my true love I see,
   Down by the green bushes where he thinks to meet me.'

5 Oh, when he came there and found she was gone,
   He stood like some lambkin that was quite forlorn;
   'She is gone with another and forsaken me,
   So adieu the green bushes for ever', said he.

6 'Now I'll be like a schoolboy and spend my time in play,
   For I never was so foolishly deluded away;
   There is ne'er a false woman shall serve me so more,
   So adieu the green bushes, 'tis time to give o'er.'

119

64   Lovely Joan

Masculine strength against feminine guile: the contest must have been familiar for centuries. It has been the subject of many songs in which women by the exercise of superior wit out-manoeuvre men whose advances they find importunate. In some versions of 'Lovely Joan' it is a threatened rape which is averted; here, merely a seduction. The splendid melody was used by George Butterworth in his 'Folk Song Suite'; the text is as sprightly as the tune.

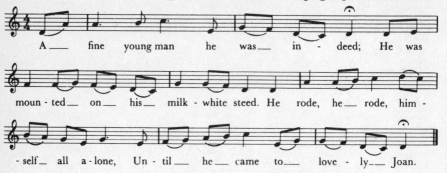

A — fine young man he was — in - deed; He was moun - ted — on — his — milk - white steed. He rode, he — rode, him - self — all a - lone, Un - til — he — came to — love - ly — Joan.

2 'Good morning to you, pretty maid';
   And 'Twice good morning, sir', she said.
   He gave her a wink, she rolled her eye;
   Says he to himself, 'I'll be there by and by.

3 'Oh, don't you think those pooks of hay
   A pretty place for us to play?
   So come with me like a sweet young thing,
   And I'll give you my golden ring.'

4 Then he pulled off his ring of gold;
   'My pretty little miss, do this behold.
   I'd freely give it for your maidenhead';
   And her cheeks they blushed like the roses red.

5 'Give me that ring into my hand,
   And I will neither stay nor stand,
   For this would do more good to me
   Than twenty maidenheads', said she.

6 And as he made for the pooks of hay
   She leaped on his horse and tore away.
   He called, he called, but it was all in vain;
   Young Joan she never looked back again.

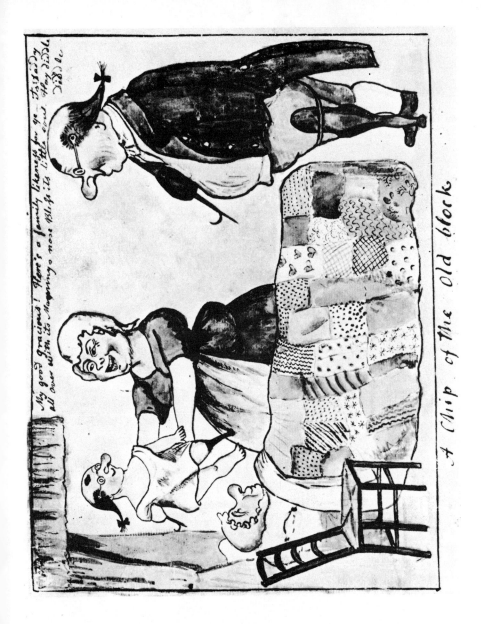

1. A drawing of about 1800. © National Maritime Museum.

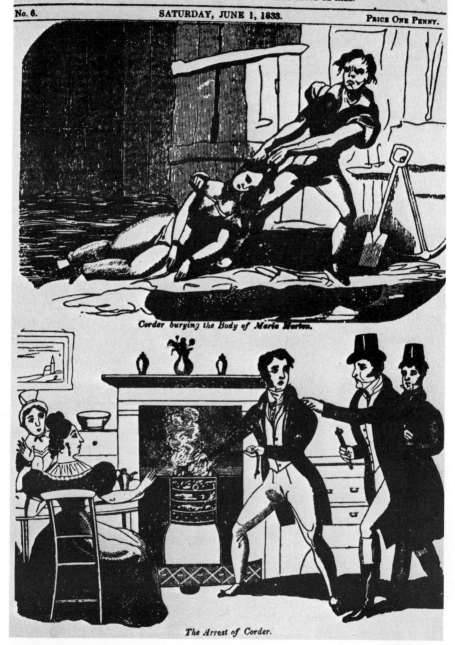

GOD'S
REVENGE AGAINST MURDER.

"WHOSO SHEDDETH MAN'S BLOOD, BY MAN SHALL HIS BLOOD BE SHED."

No. 6.   SATURDAY, JUNE 1, 1833.   PRICE ONE PENNY.

Corder burying the Body of Maria Marten.

The Arrest of Corder.

2. Drawings which appeared in a religious periodical on 1 June 1833. Louis James's *Print and the People 1819–1851*, Allen Lane, 1976.

3. A country fair.
W. H. Pyne's
Microcosm,
1808.

4. Ploughing with oxen. W. H. Pyne's *Microcosm*, 1808.

5. Haymaking at the turn of the century. © Radio Times Hulton Picture Library.

6. The thresher. William Hone's *Every-Day Book*, 1826.

7. In the hay field. W. H. Pyne's *Microcosm*, 1808.

8. Farmer visiting workers in the harvest field.
   W. H. Pyne's *Microcosm*, 1808.

9. Woodcut of a Scots chapbook and ballad seller of the late eighteenth century. © Bodleian Library.

10. Hunting the hare. From a seventeenth-century ballad in the Roxburghe Collection. © British Library.

11. Children in the Wood.
A ballad published
between 1819 and 1844.

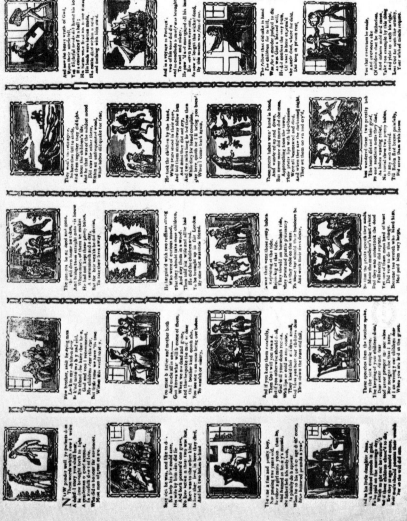

7 She didn't think herself quite safe,
No, not till she came to her true love's gate.
She's robbed him of his horse and ring,
And left him to rage in the meadows green.

65   Broomfield Hill

*A maid wagers a man that she can meet him in the countryside and depart again without losing her virginity. He, not surprisingly, is determined to win the double stake of maidenhead and money. She, in her turn, is full of confidence because a witch has given her a spell to keep him asleep. It consists of strewing broom at his head and feet, and in walking nine times round him. Broom, says Geoffrey Grigson, is 'one of the great landscape plants, and since it breaks into flower in May and June, one of the plants of love and romance in European poetry' (*The Englishman's Flora, Paladin, *1975, p. 138).*

*The story is at least seven hundred years old, and it has been appearing in ballad form in English since the eighteenth century. R. B. Johnson noted in 1894 that it 'is still popular in England, and is printed as 'The Merry Broomfield' by Mr Such, who told me, however, that he only sells it occasionally to country hawkers' (*Popular British Ballads, Ancient and Modern, *1894, vol. I, p. xxiii). It remains in oral tradition to this day. I collected this version from Walter Pardon, the Norfolk singer, in 1978.*

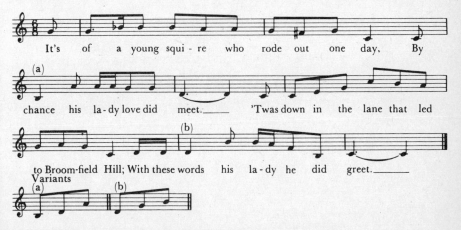

2 'A wager, a wager with you, pretty maid,
My one hundred pounds to your ten,
That a maid you shall go into yonder green broom
And a maid you shall never return.'

3 'A wager, a wager with you, kind sir,
  Your one hundred pounds to my ten,
  That a maid I shall go into yonder green broom,
  And a maid I shall boldly return.'

4 And when she arrived down in yonder green broom
  She found her love fast asleep,
  Dressed in fine silken hose, with a new suit of clothes,
  And a bunch of green broom at his feet.

5 Then nine times she did go to the soles of his feet,
  Nine times to the crown of his head;
  And nine times she kissed his cherry-red lips
  As he lay on his green mossy bed.

6 Then she took a gold ring from off of her hand
  And placed it on his right thumb,
  And that was to let her true love to know
  That his lady had been there and gone.

7 Then nine times she did go to the crown of his head,
  Nine times to the soles of his feet;
  And nine times she kissed his cherry-red lips
  As he lay on the ground fast asleep.

8 And when he awoke from out of his sleep
  'Twas then that he counted the cost,
  For he knew that his true love had been there and gone,
  And he thought of the wager he had lost.

9 He called three times for his horse and his man,
  The horse that he'd bought so dear;
  Saying, 'Why didn't you wake me out of my sleep
  When my lady, my true love, was here?'

10 'O master, I called unto you three times,
  And three times I blew on my horn;
  But I could not wake you from out of your sleep,
  Till your lady, your true love, had gone.'

11 'Farewell and adieu to our loved one in gloom,
   Farewell to the birds on Broomfield Hill;
   A maid she did go into yonder green broom,
   And a maid she remains for ever still.'

she took a gold ring . . . and placed it on his right thumb: thumb rings were common in
medieval times, which underlines the antiquity of the song's background.

66   The Crockery Ware

*'At twelve by the sun, or by signal from the possessor of one of the old
turnip-faced watches which descended from father to son, the teams would
knock off for the dinner-hour', wrote Flora Thompson in* Lark Rise *(1939,
ch. 3). 'Often the elders would sit out their hour of leisure discussing politics,
the latest murder story, or local affairs; but at other times . . . they would
while away the time in repeating what the women spoke of with shamed
voices as 'men's tales'. . . . Songs and snatches on the same lines were bawled
at the plough-tail and under hedges and never heard elsewhere.'*

*One such lively, home-made ditty is this song about what used to be a
perennial source of humour, the chamber pot: though that utensil is here only
the means by which a pert young lady causes her presumptuous wooer to retire
discomfited.*

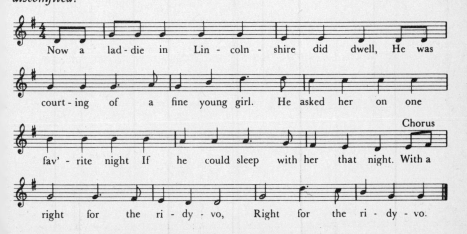

2 After gaining of her consent,
   Straightaway up to bed they went;
   She placed him in an old arm-chair
   And underneath was some crockery ware.

123

3 Then Johnny got groping in the dark,
   Thinking he was up to a lark;
   He blundered up against this bloody old chair,
   Then arse over head went the crockery ware.

4 Then the old girl woke up in a fright,
   Shouting out for a candle light:
   'Who goes there? I do declare,
   You're breaking all my crockery ware.'

5 Then the damsel in that bed she laid,
   Laughing at the game she'd played;
   Said: 'It's all right, John, I do declare,
   If you pay my mother for the crockery ware.'

6 So the very next morning the bill was made,
   And on the table it was laid;
   There was ten bob for the bloody old chair
   And two pound ten for the crockery ware.

7 Now all you laddies that are up to a lark,
   Never go courting in the dark;
   If you do, then I will declare,
   You'll pay bloody dear for the crockery ware.

the old girl: the young woman's mother.
ten bob: ten shillings (50 pence).

67   Three Maids A-milking

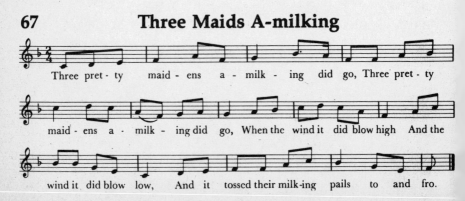

Three pret - ty maid - ens a - milk - ing did go, Three pret - ty
maid - ens a - milk - ing did go, When the wind it did blow high And the
wind it did blow low, And it tossed their milk-ing pails to and fro.

2 Then she met with a man that she did not know,
   O, she met with a man that she did not know,
   And she asked, 'Have you the skill?'
   And she asked, 'Have you the will
   To catch me a small bird or two?'

3 'Here's a health to the blackbird in the bush,
   Likewise to the merry ring-doo;
   If you'll go along with me,
   Then in yonder greenwood tree
   I will catch you a small bird or two.'

4 So I went till we stayed at a bush,
   We went till we stayed at two;
   And the pretty birds flew in,
   O, and you know what I mean,
   And I caught them by one and by two.

5 So, whilst, boys, that we have our fun,
   And we all drink down the sun,
   We will tarry till we drink down the moon.
   As birds of one feather
   We will all flock together,
   Let people say little or none.

The extra line in the last verse may be accommodated by repeating the first or second line of the tune.

After first appearing in print in the 1820s, this song continued to crop up from time to time, either on street ballads or in the oral tradition, until the end of the century. Its open sensuality caused problems for the Victorian collectors, who printed it infrequently, and then in either truncated or bowdlerized forms. In successive editions of Songs of the West *(1889–92 and 1905), Baring-Gould essayed both a complete re-write and a bowdlerization. Fortunately, he preserved in manuscript the original text, which is given here, from Roger Hannaford, of Lower Widdecombe, Devon.*

The first appearance in print of this song was in a garland (an eight-page booklet) of the second half of the eighteenth century. Its lazy sensuality, tinged with sentimentality, and couched in poetic diction ('flowery dell'), betrays its origin. Hardy's Tess heard her mother 'singing, in a vigorous gallopade, the favourite ditty of "The Spotted Cow"', while simultaneously wringing out the washing and rocking a child in its cradle (Tess of the d'Urbervilles, 1891, ch. 3). The song was widely known until recently; the version used here was recorded from the notable Yorkshire singer, Frank Hinchliffe, in 1976.

It was___ one mer - - ry morn - ing in May, As from ___ my cot ___ I strayed;___ Just at the dawn - ing of the day I met with a charm - ing maid.___

Verse 2

2 'Good morning', to this maid said I,
   'What makes you up so soon?'
   'Good morning, gentle sir', she cried,
   'I have lost my spotted cow.'

3 'No longer weep nor mourn for her,
   Your cow is not lost, my dear;
   I saw her down beneath yon grove,
   Come love, and I'll show thee where.'

4 Then hand in hand together we went,
   And crossed the flowery dell,
   Just at the dawning of the day,
   And love were all our tale.

5 All in the grove we spent the day,
   That semt to pass to' soon;
   We huddled and cuddled each other there,
   While brightly shone the moon.

6 Whenever in that grove I stray
   I go to view my flowers;
   She comes and cries, 'Kind gentle sir,
   I've lost my spotted cow.'

semt: seemed.   *While:* until.

69   The Mower

Not only in English, but also in French and Spanish folk song (and no doubt in other cultures, too), the mower with his scythe is often used as a symbol for sexual potency. Even the well known 'One Man Went to Mow' is thought to be a sexual metaphor. It is much less common for the lusty mower to have to confess himself unequal to his task, as he does here. It is one of the great strengths of folk song that it can deal with such matters, not merely with directness, but also with delicacy. Baring-Gould wrote somewhat ruefully, because he disapproved of the 'objectionable' words, that the song 'is a very favourite one throughout England'.

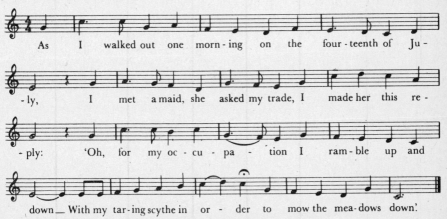

As I walked out one morn-ing on the four-teenth of Ju-ly, I met a maid, she asked my trade, I made her this re-ply: 'Oh, for my oc-cu-pa-tion I ram-ble up and down With my tar-ing scythe in or-der to mow the mea-dows down.'

2 She says, 'My handsome young man, if a mower that you be,
   Come, put your scythe in order and come along with me,
   For I have a little meadow long time been kept in store,
   And on the dew I can tell you true it never was cut before.'

3 He says, 'My canty dairymaid, what wages will you give?
  For mowing is hard labour unless the scythe be good.'
  'I'll give you a crown an acre, I solemnly declare,
  I'll give you a crown an acre and plenty of strong beer.'

4 He says, 'My canty dairymaid, I like your wages well,
  For my scythe it's in good order and we will have a spell;
  For on your lovely countenance I never saw a frown,
  My bonny lass I'll cut your grass that ne'er was trampled
     down.'

5 Like a lion, he being undaunted, he entered in her field,
  He said he'd mow her meadow down before that he would
     yield;
  He wrought from six till breakfast time till it went beyond his
     skill,
  He was forced to yield and quit the field for the grass was
     standing still.

6 He says, 'My canty dairymaid, oh do not on me frown,
  For although I mow all summer I cannot mow it down';
  Then she put her hand in her pocket and paid us down a
     crown:
  'Oh, when you come this way again, enquire for Betsy
     Brown.

7 'All in my little meadow there is neither hill nor rock,
  Oh, when you come this way again the cradle you may rock.'
  Come all you pretty fair maids wheresoever you may be,
  Oh, when you meet a plough boy, oh treat him kind and free;
  He ploughs the furrows deep and rambles up and down,
  With his taring scythe in order to mow the meadows down.

taring: large.   *canty:* lively.

The Ploughman's Glory

As I was a-walking one— morn-ing in spring, I—
heard a pret-ty plough-boy and so sweet-ly he did sing; And—
as he was a-sing-ing, O! these words I heard him say, 'There's no
life like the plough-boy's in the sweet— month of May.'

2 'There's the lark in the morning, she will rise up from her
    nest,
  And she'll mount the white air with the dew all on her
    breast;
  And with this pretty ploughboy, O! she'll whistle and she'll
    sing,
  And at night she'll return to her nest back again.

[3 If you walk in the fields any pleasure to find,
  You may see what the plowman enjoys in his mind;
  There he sees the corn grow, and the flow'rs for to spring,
  And the plowman's as happy as a prince or a king.

4 When his day's work is done that he has for to do,
  Perhaps to some country wake he will go;
  And there with his sweetheart he'll dance and he'll sing,
  And at midnight he'll return with his lass back again.

5 And as they return from the wake to the town,
  Where the meadows are mow'd and the grass is cast down;
  And if they chance to tumble among the green hay,
  'Come kiss me now or never', the damsel will say.

6 Next morning he rises to follow his team,
  Like a jolly, brisk plowman, so neat and so trim;
  If he kiss a pretty girl he will make her his wife,
  And she loves her young plowman as dear as her life.

7 Come, Molly and Sue, let's away to the wake,
There the plough lads will treat us with spice, ale and cake;
And if in coming home they should gain their ends,
Never fear but they will marry us and make us amends.

8 There is Molly and Dolly, there's Nelly and Sue,
There is Ralph, John and Will, and there's young Tommy,
　　too;
Each lad takes his lass to the wake or the fair,
Odzooks they look merry, I vow and declare.]

wake: fair.
from the wake to the town: 'from the wake *in* the town' makes more sense.

So far as farm workers went, the ploughman was at the top of the tree (or at least equal top with the shepherd). He took immense pride in his work, which he rightly saw as the foundation for the whole pyramid of society. Such a man was a highly desirable catch, and the girls had a touching faith that seduction by a ploughman would result in marriage. I doubt whether ploughmen had the same attitude. Frank Kidson published the song in his Traditional Tunes *(1891) after obtaining it (as we learn from a note in his manuscripts) from a Mr Thompson, himself a ploughman, of Flamborough`in North Yorkshire. Since the singer had only two verses, the remainder have been added from a broadside issued by Kendrew of York, under the title of 'The Plowman's Glory'. The song had the same title when it first appeared in print, in 1778. Mr Thompson's title was 'The Pretty Ploughboy' but the broadside has been followed in order to avoid confusion with no. 94.*

71　　　　The Barley Rakings

The young women in 'The Ploughman's Glory' (no. 70) trusted that seduction would swiftly lead to marriage. Pregnancy often did lead to a wedding, since the future wife had proved herself to be capable of bearing children. On the other hand, women were often left literally holding the baby, when their lovers decamped. The most frequent culprits were soldiers or sailors, travelling tinkers or tailors, and the itinerant harvesters.

In a broadside version of 'The Barley Rakings', published by Lund of York, the girl has a warrant drawn up for the arrest on a paternity charge of her man. He is brought back from Liverpool, which perhaps indicates that he was a sailor, or an Irish harvester on his way home. He successfully denies that he is the father of the child, and departs again 'to face all sorts of weather'. In this oral version, we are spared that episode; the song has a bitter-sweet quality, and is part lyric, part lament. The moral, if moral there be, is that young women should keep their wits about them.

'Twas in the prime of sum-mer-time when hay it was a-mak-ing, And har-vest time was com-ing on, and bar-ley was a-mak-ing. A lov-ing cou-ple met one day, they had a mind to style and play, And did not count it much as-tray, all in the bar-ley rak-ings.

2 When twenty weeks were gone and past the maiden lay
    a-crying;
When forty weeks were gone and past the maiden lay
    a-dying.
She sent a letter to her love, she bade him true and faithful
    prove,
Conjured him by the powers above, 'Remember the barley
    rakings'.

3 Oh, when this letter to him came he read it o'er and over,
He put it by – 'twas all the same, because he was a rover.
A message he sent back again to let her know 'twas all in vain,
And, 'Have no care and have no pain, and forget the barley
    rakings.

4 'I have so good a pair of shoes as e'er were made of leather,
I'll cock my beaver over my nose and face all wind and
    weather.
Oh, when that I have run my race, then if I find no better
    place,
Oh, then again I'll seek your face and remember the barley
    rakings.'

hay it was a-making . . . and barley was a-raking: it is not usual for the hay and corn harvests to be overlapping; the broadside text is more logical, since it has 'when hay it has been gotten'.

to style: to leap or dance.   *beaver:* hat.

The Nutting Girl

Come all you jo-vial fel-lows, come list-en to my song; It
is a lit-tle dit-ty and it won't con-tain you long; It's
[de-tain]
of a fair young dam-sel, she liv-ed down in Kent,
Rose one sum-mer's morn-ing, she a-nut-ting went.

Chorus

With my
fal lal lal, to me ral tal lal, Whack for the dear ol day, And
what few nuts that poor girl had She's threw them all a-way.

2 She then came to young Johnny as he sit on his plough,
She said, 'Young man I really feel I cannot tell you how.'
He took her to some shady broom and there he laid her
down;
Said she, 'Young man, I think I feel the world go round and
round.'

3 It's of this fair young damsel, she was nutting in a wood,
His voice was so melodious it charmed her as she stood.
[She had no longer power,] she could no longer stay,
And what few nuts she had, poor girl, she's threw them all
away.

4 Now come all you young women this warning by me take,
[take of mine]
If you should a-nutting go, please get home in time.
For if you should stay too late to hear that ploughboy sing,
You might have a young farmer to nurse up in the spring.

Here once more, the ploughman is seen as a figure of almost irresistible sexual attraction. Gathering nuts was – and is – a widespread country practice, though in September (which coincided with the beginning of autumn ploughing), rather than the summer, as the song has it. There was a saying that a good season for nuts meant a good season for babies, the following year. Cyril Poacher, who was born at Stone Common, near Blaxhall, Suffolk, learned his version of the song at the age of eight, in 1918, from his grandfather, Walter Ling.

73   The Thrashing Machine

The farm labourers' bitter opposition to the introduction of thrashing machines was one of the causes of the riots of 1830. It is odd to reflect that the machines have now largely disappeared, after being replaced by the combine harvester. However, they stayed long enough to be accepted as a familiar feature of the farming scene, and it was inevitable that singers well versed in the sexual symbolism of agricultural implements should see the possibilities of the thrashing machine, especially the variety powered by a horse. This home-made song is perhaps another from the disreputable repertoire mentioned by Flora Thompson (note, no. 66). It can still be heard in a few country pubs, usually to the tune of 'Villikins'. Cecil Sharp had a better one from William Nott of Meshaw, Devon.

It's of a young farm-er near Lon-don, 'tis said, He kept___ a ser-vant, a bloom-ing young maid; Her name it was Mol-ly, she was scar-cely six-teen, She would work ve-ry well at the thrash-ing mach-ine.

Chorus

Fal di dal did-dle di, fal de dal dee, Fal di dal did-dle, fal di dal dee.

2 'Oh, Molly', said master, 'the times are hard,
  Will you go with me into the farmyard?
  You harness young Dobbin, you know what I mean,
  I think we can manage the thrashing machine.'

3 'Oh, master', says Molly, 'what will missus say?'
  'Never mind', says master, 'she's making of hay,
  And while she is spreading the grass that is green,
  We can be working the thrashing machine.'

4 So the barn doors were open, young Dobbin stood inside,
  The farmer got on the machine for to ride;
  'Oh, master', says Molly, 'you think very clever, [fine?]
  I think we can manage the thrashing machine.'

5 So young Dobbin got tired of going round,
  He hangs to the traces he bows to the ground;
  Although once in good order he's now got a wen,
  Through working so hard at the thrashing machine.

6 'Oh', Molly says, smiling, 'we have had a loss,
  I think it requires a much stronger hoss;
  If Dobbin was strong as before he has been,
  I think, why! we would keep working the thrashing machine.'

7 Six months it passed over and, truth for to tell,
  Molly's front parlour began for to swell;
  And shortly after that she had got her wean,
  The fruits of her labour with the thrashing machine.

The Miller's Song

Although the miller was often harshly treated – and no doubt justifiably – in traditional lore (see note, no. 32), there were occasions when he was cast as hero. In this song, both the miller and his lass are happy with their bargain.

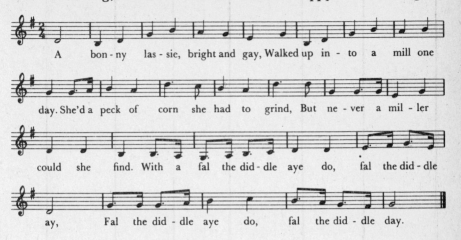

A bon-ny las-sie, bright and gay, Walked up in-to a mill one day. She'd a peck of corn she had to grind, But ne-ver a mil-ler could she find. With a fal the did-dle aye do, fal the did-dle ay, Fal the did-dle aye do, fal the did-dle day.

2 At length the miller 'e came in;
That pretty fair maid she did begin:
'A peck of corn I 'ave to grind,
But never a miller can I find,
With 'is fal the diddle', *etc.*

3 'My stones are up, my water's low,
My mill is not in tune to go';
But they talked of love, till love grew kind,
And then the mill begun to grind,
With 'is fal the diddle, *etc.*

4 'Now go you 'ome, my pretty dear,
For your corn's ground and my mill's clear;
But if it 'as been ground ten thousand times o'er,
I'm sure you never 'ad if ground so well before,
With my fal the diddle', *etc.*

5 Said this bonny lass, still blythe and gay,
'A bargain I will make this day;
I'll bring my corn here every year
To be ground at the same price as before,
With a fal the diddle aye do, fal the diddle ay,
That means I'll never, never have to pay.'

75   Oh, Once I Loved a Lass

A lover's night visit to his lass is one of the classic themes of folk song, and, indeed, of literature in general. Such visits were at times entirely unofficial, but there was a practice, known as bundling, which, though ostensibly clandestine, was sanctioned by tradition. In effect, this permitted pre-marital intimacy in order to ensure before marriage that a union would be fruitful. Putting it more simply, a Cambridgeshireman told a scandalized clergyman: 'But vicar, you wouldn't buy a horse before getting astride to see how it trotted'.

At the end of the visit, the inevitable parting is frequently lamented in western poetry in the form of an aube which regrets the shortness of the night and the coming of the dawn, heralded by the crowing of the cock. Finally in the song, there is the recollection in tranquillity of the night's 'sport and play', inspiring bitter-sweet emotion, especially when the lovers are separated for a time. In the reign of Henry VIII Englishmen were singing 'Westron wynde when wyll thou blow?/The smalle rain down doth rayne;/Oh, if my love were in my armys, /Or I in my bed agayne', which may be part of a version of 'Once I Loved', which was collected in Dorset in 1905. The melody has been printed in extenso so as to show the rhythmic and melodic variation which was once common in traditional singing.

1. Oh, once I loved a lass but she lo-vèd not me, Be-
4. Now my fa-ther keeps a cock and a wond-er-ful cock, And he

-cause I look-ed too poor; Now she all in good part has
crows in the morn-ing so soon. I thought it had been day when I

stole a-way my heart And will keep it for ev-er-more.
sent my love a-way But it proved to be the light of the moon.

2. O 'twas un-der my true love's win-dow one night, Yo!

there did I hol-loa so shil-lo, lit-tle shil-lo, lit-tle

shil-lo; My true love she a-rose and she

slipp-ed on her clothes And so soft-a-ly she let me in.

3. Yo! 'twas all the fore part of __ the __ night We did
both sport and play, play so pret-ty, play so pret-ty, __ play; And
all __ the __ last part of the __ night O she sleep-èd in my arms till day.

5. Now I'll be so true to my love as the sun __ that doth shine
O - ver the fal - low, the fal - low, __ fal - low __ ground, And if
she's not true to me as I am true to she __ I would
ra - ther she were lost than found.

76   **The Knife in the Window**

Now if maid-ens were sheep, love, and they fed on the
moun-tains, Now if maid-ens were sheep, love, and they fed on the
moun-tains, Then all the young men they would go and feed

Chorus

with them. Sing fal the ral i do, sing fal the ral day.

137

2 'Oh, Molly, my true love, may I come to bed to you?' (2)
'Oh, yes', she replied, 'you can come to bed with me.'

3 'Now the door it is bolted, I cannot undo it.' (2)
'Oh, now', she replied, 'you must put your knee to it.'

4 So I put my knee to it and the door flew asunder, (2)
And upstairs I went like lightning and thunder.

5 'Now your small things are tight, love, and I cannot undo
    them.' (2)
'Oh, now' she replied, 'there's a knife in the window.'

6 Now her small things fell off, her and I into bed tumbled, (2)
And I'll leave you to guess how we young couple fumbled.

*In the song usually called 'Hares on the Mountains' we hear that if young
women were variously and successively hares, blackbirds and thrushes, ducks,
fishes, then young men would hunt them with guns, go and bang the bushes,
turn drakes and follow, strip and swim after. This is not merely a series of
sexual metaphors, but an echo of the ancient songs and stories of metamor-
phosis, in which the pursued woman runs out of transformations and falls to
the man. In this version her resistance seems merely token, though metaphor is
by no means exhausted after the first verse.*

77   Seventeen Come Sunday

As I walked out one May morn-ing, One May morn-ing
ear-ly, 'Twas then I spied a pret-ty maid, So
hand-some and so clev-er. With my rue, rum, ray,
Fol the rid-dle ay, Whack fa loo-ra li - - do.

Chorus

2 Her shoes were black, her stockings white,
  And her buckles shone like silver;
  She had a dark and rolling eye,
  And her hair hung down her shoulders.

3 'How old are you, my pretty fair maid,
  How old are you, my honey?'
  She answered me quite cheerfully,
  'I am seventeen come Sunday.'

4 'Will you marry me, my pretty fair maid,
  Will you marry me, my honey?'
  She answered me quite cheerfully,
  'I dare not for my mammy.

5 'If you come down to my mammy's house
  When the moon is shining brightly,
  Then I'll come down and let you in
  And my mammy will not hear me.'

6 [I went to her mammy's house
  When the moon was brightly shining;
  She came down and let me in,
  And I lay in her arms till morning.]

7 'Oh, soldier, will you marry me?
  For now's your time or never.
  Oh, soldier, will you marry me?
  Or I'm undone for ever.'

8 And now she is a soldier's wife
  And sails across the brine, O.
  'The drum and fife is my delight
  And a merry man is mine, O.'

Mothers with nubile daughters were particularly wary of soldiers, who were proverbial for the girls they left behind. The man here is atypical, for he takes the girl with him to be at least a common-law wife. The song originated in the eighteenth century, and remained widely popular until the twentieth. Cecil Sharp alone collected 22 versions, but the one given here was recorded by Walter Pardon in 1978.

The Cuckoo

The deep grief of a woman deserted by her lover finds expression in this fine, melancholy lyric, which was known throughout Britain and America. It was one of the country songs which sailors took on their travels, which may be why in this version the sycamore tree usually found has been unaccountably changed into a 'sailor so free'.

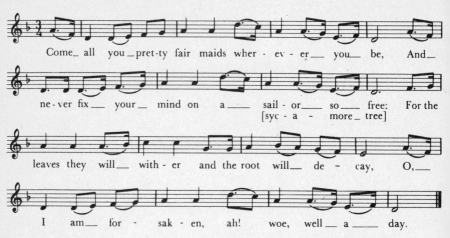

Come all you pretty fair maids wherever you be, And never fix your mind on a sailor so free: [sycamore tree] For the leaves they will wither and the root will decay, O, I am forsaken, ah! woe, well a day.

2 The cuckoo is a fine bird and she sings as she flies,
   She brings us good tidings, she tells us no lies;
   She sucks little birds' eggs to make her voice clear,
   And never sings cuckoo till the summer draws near.

3 O, meeting is a pleasure and parting is a grief,
   An inconstant lover is worse than a thief;
   A thief can but rob you and take all you have,
   An inconstant lover will bring you to the grave.

4 O the hours that I've passed in the arms of my dear
   Can never be thought of without shedding a tear;
   All hardships for him I would cheerfully bear,
   And at night on my pillow forget all my care.

The Banks of Sweet Primroses

A woman's grief at being deceived by a man causes her to reject his attempt to renew their relationship. The brief encounter is set in a verdant landscape, though the woman yearns towards a more desolate scene as a more fitting background for her sadness. However, her final warning to other 'fair maids' turns into an expression of hope. The song's title derives from what in most versions is the second couplet of the first verse: 'Down by the banks of the sweet primroses,/There I beheld a most lovely fair'.

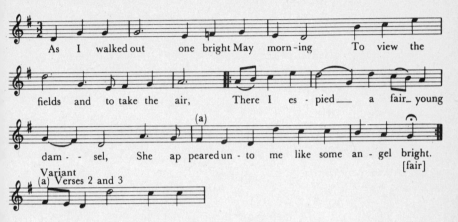

As I walked out one bright May morn-ing To view the fields and to take the air, There I es - pied_ a fair_ young dam - - sel, She ap peared un - to me like some an - gel bright. [fair]

Variant
(a) Verses 2 and 3

2 I said, 'My dear, where are you going?
  What is the cause of all your grief?
  I will make you as happy as any lady,
  If you will once more grant me relief.'

3 'Stand off, stand off, you are deceitful,
  You are a false and deceitful man;
  It was you that have caused my poor heart to wander,
  And to give me comfort it's all in vain.

4 'Then I'll go down to some lonely valley,
  Go down where no one there shall me find,
  Where the pretty little small birds do change their voices
  And every moment blows blustery wind.

5 'So all fair maids from me take a warning,
  Listen awhile to what I say:
  There's many a dark and a cloudy morning
  Brings forth a bright and sunshiny day.'

80   Fare Thee Well, Cold Winter

*A woman's infidelity has turned a man's love, first to hatred, then to indiffer-
ence. 'Farewell, She' is a frequent title for the song, though there are versions
from a feminine standpoint, called 'Farewell, He'. Under the title of 'Let him
go, let him tarry' the song enjoyed considerable popularity on the radio in the
late 1940s. The singer was Barbara Mullen.*

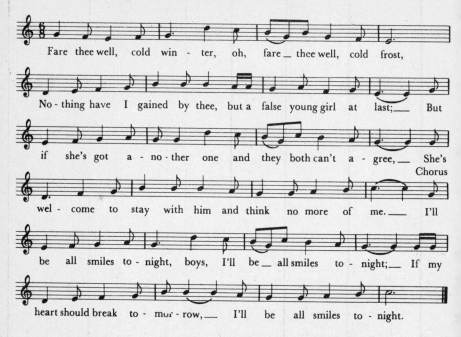

Fare thee well, cold win - ter, oh, fare _ thee well, cold frost,

No - thing have I gained by thee, but a false young girl at last;___ But

if she's got a - no - ther one and they both can't a - gree, ___ She's
Chorus

wel - come to stay with him and think no more of me.___ I'll

be all smiles to - night, boys, I'll be _ all smiles to - night;___ If my

heart should break to - mor - row, ___ I'll be all smiles to - night.

2 She wrote to me a letter to say that she was sad;
I quickly wrote the answer back to say that I were glad.
She may keep her paper and I will keep my time;
For what I'd have a true young girl I'd search the whole
    world round.

3 One day that I was walking all through the shady grove,
'Twas there I met my own true love; she handed me a rose,
Thinking I should take it, to never pass her by;
For what I'd have a true young girl I'd lay me down and die.

4 False, deceitful young girls are easy to be found;
For what I'd have a true young girl I'll search this world
    around.
And if she's got another one and they can't both agree,
She's welcome to stay with him, and think no more of me.

81　　The Water of Tyne

This exquisite lament was first published in 1793. The tune was taken down almost a century later from an old man at Hexham, Northumberland.

I can-not get to my love if I would dee, The_
wa-ter of Tyne runs be-tween him and me; And_
here I must stand with the tear in my e'e, Both_
sigh-ing and sick-ly my sweet-heart to see.

2　O where is the boatman, my bonny hinny?
　　O where is the boatman? Bring him to me,
　　To ferry me over the Tyne to my honey,
　　And I will remember the boatman and thee.

3　O bring me a boatman, I'll give any money,
　　And you for your trouble rewarded shall be,
　　To ferry me over the Tyne to my honey,
　　Or scull him across that rough river to me.

82　　The Brisk Young Sailor

A young woman loses her virginity, becomes pregnant, and is then deserted. Filled with sorrow and despair, she longs for death. This gloomy theme was popular among country singers, especially men, and it gave rise to a huge family of songs, usually with very fine tunes. Among the many titles are 'Apron Strings' ('Oh, when my apron strings were low,/My love followed me through frost and snow;/But now my apron strings are high,/My love passes by and never looks nigh'); 'I wish, I wish'; 'A bold (or Brisk) Young Farmer (or Sailor, or Lover, or Man)'; and, reflecting later adaptations, 'There is a Tavern (or Alehouse) in the Town'. The version printed here was sung by James Bayliff, a 70-year old carpenter of Barbon in Westmorland, and collected in 1909 by Anne Gilchrist.

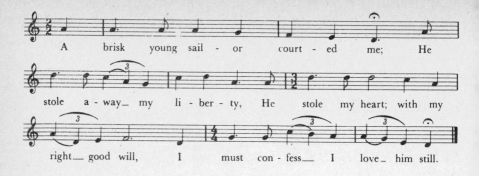

A brisk young sail - or court - ed me; He stole a - way_ my li - ber - ty, He stole my heart; with my right_ good will, I must con - fess_ I love_ him still.

2 There is an alehouse in the town,
   Where my love goes and sits him down,
   And pulls a strange girl on his knee –
   And isn't that a grief to me?

3 A grief to me, I'll tell you why,
   Because she has more gowld than I;
   But the gowld it'll waste and the beauty blast,
   And she'll come to a poor girl like me at last.

4 I wish my baby it was born,
   Set smiling on its nurse's knee;
   And I myself was in my grave,
   And the green grass growing over me.

5 I wish, I wish, but it's all in vain,
   I wish I was a maid again;
   But a maid again I never must be,
   Till an apple grows on an orange tree.

83 Sheepcrook and Black Dog

Laments by deserted lovers are by no means uncommon. In most cases the counter-attraction is another person, though sometimes the cause of parting is an occupation. The demands made by being a soldier or sailor are frequent reason (or excuse) for separation, but the departure and subsequent alienation of a servant are very unusual subject-matter for a song. In reality, however, the loss to villages of young women leaving to go into service was an everyday feature of rural life for two centuries or more. For a recent example, see Winifred Foley's autobiography, A Child in the Forest *(BBC Publications, 1974).*

Oh, spread the green bran-ches o-ver whilst I am young, So well did I like my love, so sweet-ly she sung. Was ev-er a man in such hap-py es-tate As me with my Flo-ra, fair Flo-ra so brave?

2 I will go to my Flora and this will I say:
  'Tomorrow we'll be married, it wants but one day.'
  'One day', said fair Flora, 'that day is to come,
  To be married so early my age is too young.

3 'We'll go for a service and a service we'll get,
  And perhaps in a few years after might substance and reap.'
  'Oh, don't go to service, leaving me here to cry.'
  'Oh, yes, lovely shepherd, I'll tell you for why.'

4 We got her to service and to service she went,
  To wait on a lady, which was her intent;
  To wait on a lady, and a rich lady gay,
  Who clothed fair Flora, fair Flora so brave.

5 A little time after a letter he sent
  With three or four lines in it, to know her intent.
  She wrote that she lived in such contented life
  That she never did intend to be a young shepherd's wife.

6 These words and expressions appeared like a dart:
  I'll pluck up my spirits and cheer up my heart;
  Oh, being that she'll never write to me so any more,
  Her answer convinced me quite over and o'er.

7 My ewes and my lambs, I'll bid them adieu,
  My bottle and budget I'll leave them here with you;
  My sheepcrook and my black dog I'll leave here behind,
  Since Flora, fair Flora, so changed her mind.

budget: sheepskin bag.

The Seeds of Love

The symbolism of plants and flowers is here used to retell the old story that the loss of virginity may bring sorrow in its wake. A woman rejects modesty, purity and courtesy (the violet, the lily and the pink), and chooses passion (the red rosebud), which leads to grief (the willow tree). In some cases the end is despair, with hope gone and only repentance left (thyme overcome by rue), but here, the conclusion is optimistic (with the trampled grass springing up again).

The earliest printed version I have seen is an eighteenth century slip song, 'The Red Rose Bud', though the song may date back to the previous century. There is a Lancashire tradition, almost certainly unfounded, that it was written by a Mrs Fleetwood Habergham, who, 'undone by the extravagance, and disgraced by the vices of her husband, soothed her sorrows by some stanzas' on her troubles. J. H. Dixon wrote in 1846 that 'This very curious old song is not only a favourite with our peasantry, but . . . has obtained popularity in more elevated circles'. The version given here was the first folk song ever collected by Cecil Sharp, who heard it by chance, sung by John England, a gardener, at Hambridge in Somerset, in 1903.

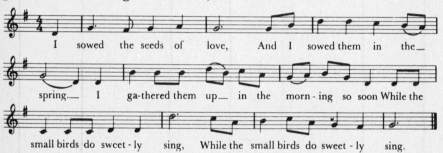

I sowed the seeds of love, And I sowed them in the spring. I gathered them up in the morning so soon While the small birds do sweetly sing, While the small birds do sweetly sing.

2 My garden was planted well
   With flowers everywhere,
   But I had not the liberty to choose
       for myself
   Of the flowers that I love so dear.

3 The gardener was standing by
   And I asked him to choose for me.
   He choosed for me the violet, the lily and
       the pink,
   But those I refused all three.

4 The violet I did not like
   Because it bloomed too soon.
   The lily and the pink I really overthink;
   So I vowed that I'd stay till June.

146

5 In June there was a red rosebud,
  And that's the flower for me;
  I oftentimes have plucked that red rosebud
  Till I gained the willow tree.

6 The willow tree will twist
  And the willow tree will twine.
  I oftentimes have wished I was in that
        young man's arms
  That once had the heart of mine.

7 Come all you false young men,
  Do not leave me here to complain,
  For the grass that have been oftentimes
        trampled under foot,
  Give it time, it will rise up again.

V

The Charming Bride: Marriage

85   The Ensilver Song

'Ensilver' was money distributed by the bridegroom immediately after a wedding in rural Yorkshire. With it the local men would adjourn to the village inn to sing the health of the bridal pair.

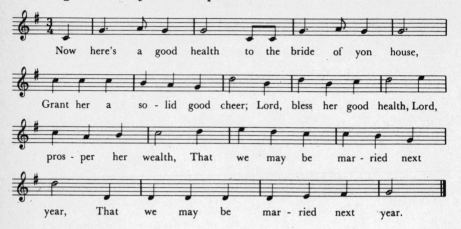

Now here's a good health to the bride of yon house,
Grant her a so-lid good cheer; Lord, bless her good health, Lord,
pros-per her wealth, That we may be mar-ried next
year, That we may be mar-ried next year.

2 Well, here's to the bride, good luck to the lass,
Grant her a solid good cheer;
And through her garter we'll pass each glass,
And may we be married, *etc.*

3 Our drink, O Lord, will better seem –
Grant her a solid good cheer –
When we remember where it has been,
And may we, *etc.*

4 Our glasses we'll lift now to the bridegroom,
Grant him a solid good cheer;
And the fellow that spills it he'll pay for t'next round,
And may we, *etc.*

5 It's fair to be seen, he's supped it off clean,
As any other man can;
And if that he please another at his ease,
And it shall be unto a good man. (2)

6 To the bridal pair we all will sing,
And grant them a solid good cheer;
In spite of Turk or Spanish king,
And may we be married next year. (2)

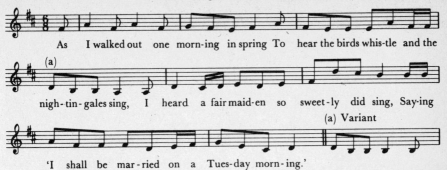

As I walked out one morn-ing in spring To hear the birds whis-tle and the

(a)

nigh-tin-gales sing, I heard a fair maid-en so sweet-ly did sing, Say-ing

(a) Variant

'I shall be mar-ried on a Tues-day morn-ing.'

2 I stepped up to her and thus I did say:
   'Pray, tell me your age and where you belong?'
   'I belong to the sign of the Bonny Blue Bell;
   My age is sixteen and you know very well.'

3 'Sixteen years old, love, is too young to marry;
   The other five years, love, I'll have you to tarry.'
   'You talk like a man without any skill;
   Five years have I tarried against my own will.

4 'On Monday night it is all my care
   To powder my locks and to curl my hair,
   And my two pretty maidens to wait on me there,
   To dance at my wedding next Tuesday morning.

5 'My husband will buy me a guinea gold ring,
   And at night he will give me a far better thing;
   With two precious jewels he'll be me adorning,
   When I am his bride, on Tuesday morning.

6 'My two pretty maids shall put me to bed,
   Then I'll bid adieu to my maidenhead;
   And over my true love my legs I will fling:
   "Good morning, fair maidens", on Wednesday morning.'

The fair maidens of folk song had a wit, a sprightliness and, at times, a lack of inhibition which would have horrified the conventional ladies of Victorian polite society. The girl here clearly had no intention of lying back and thinking of England on her wedding night. The song is perhaps better known as

'The Sign of the Bonny Blue Bell'. Vaughan Williams introduced a version of it into his opera, Hugh the Drover. *He also collected the set printed here, the rather fragmentary text of which has been filled out from a broadside. A tune called 'I mun be marry'd a Tuesday' appeared in print as early as 1708, which may indicate a seventeenth-century origin for the song.*

87   Bonny Blue Handkerchief

As I__ was a walk - ing one morn - ing in May, A beau - ti - ful young dam - sel came trip - pa - ling my way; With her cheeks red as ro - ses as beau - ti - ful she sung, With her bon - ny blue han - ker-chief tied un - der her chin.

2 'How so far are thou going?' as I took her round the waist.
 'I'm going to my work, sir, all in great haste,
 For to work in yon factory where the cotton they spin,
 With my bonny blue handkerchief tied under my chin.'

3 [When to kiss her sweet lips I was going to begin,
 'Stop, sir', she said, 'whilst I tell you one thing:
 He that kisses these lips must first show a gold ring,
 To this bonny blue handkerchief tied under my chin.'

4 With gold and with silver I tried all in vain,
 She smiled in my face and with scornful disdain
 Cried, 'It's not all your gold, sir, that one kiss will win
 From this bonny blue handkerchief tied under my chin.]

5 'This bonny blue handkerchief my love gave to me,
 He promised me the colour would never false be;
 And to him I'll prove true as the colour that's in,
 With my bonny blue handkerchief tied under my chin.'

6 [When he heard her so loyal he could not forbear,
He flew to her arms and called her his dear,
Saying, 'My dearest jewel, here's the gold ring
For that bonny blue handkerchief tied under thy chin.'

7 And to church they went and were married with speed,
And this loving couple live happy indeed;
When their day's work is over, so cheerily they sing,
With the bonny blue handkerchief tied under my chin.]

In spite of its rather priggish tone, this song was popular with countrymen until recent years. The tune and three verses come from a Sussex man who learned them from his father, a shepherd on the downs above Brighton. The rest of the words have been supplied from a broadside. Earlier versions (? eighteenth century) have the girl going not to the factory but 'to my mother to spin'.

88   When Shall We Get Married, John?

A woman looks forward with enthusiasm to her wedding but the husband-to-be is hopelessly unromantic and unimaginative. The song exploiting the humour of this contrast apparently dates back to the seventeenth century: the earliest text dates from 1776, but the tune is mentioned in 1683 (see Iona and Peter Opie, The Oxford Dictionary of Nursery Rhymes, *1977, p. 75). Versions circulated orally until well within living memory.*

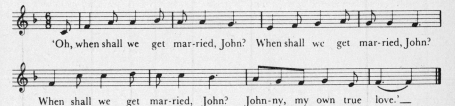

'Oh, when shall we get mar-ried, John? When shall we get mar-ried, John?
When shall we get mar-ried, John? John-ny, my own true love.'—

2 'We'll get married next Sunday morning, (3)
And doesn't thee think it'll do?'

3 'Can't we get married before, John, (3)
Johnny, my own true love?'

4 'Why, does't want to get married by moonlight, (3)
Surely the wench is mad.'

151

5 'Who shall we ask to the wedding, John, (3)
Johnny, my own true love?'

6 'Why, ask your father and mother, (3)
And doesn't thou think it'll do?'

7 'Can't we ask anyone else, John, (3)
Johnny, my own true love?'

8 'Why, does't want the king and queen, then? (3)
'Surely the wench is mad.'

9 'What shall we have for dinner, John, (3)
Johnny, my own true love?'

10 'We'll have some broad beans and fat bacon, (3)
And don't you think it'll do?'

11 'Can't we have anything else, John, (3)
Johnny, my own true love?'

12 'Why does't want duck and green peas? (3)
Surely the wench is mad.'

13 'What shall we do in bed, John, (3)
Johnny, my own true love?'

14 'Why, go to sleep to be sure. (3)
Surely the wench is mad.'

89   Three Weeks Before Easter

'The pangs of despisèd love' are amongst the keenest one can feel. This fine, lyrical song has been on men's lips for some three hundred years. As a street ballad, 'The forlorne lover', beginning with the words, 'A Week before Easter the day's long and clear', was entered in the Stationers' Register on 1st March, 1675. Vaughan Williams collected the version given here in Essex, in 1904. The words are a little garbled in places, but the power of the lament is undiminished.

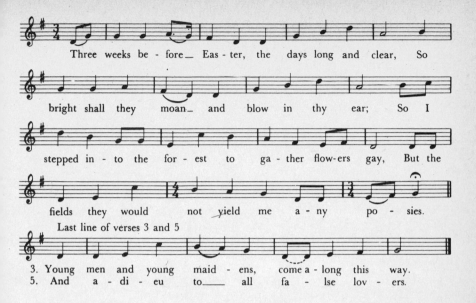

Three weeks be - fore_ Eas - ter, the days long and clear, So
bright shall they moan_ and blow in thy ear; So I
stepped in - to the for - est to ga - ther flow-ers gay, But the
fields they would not yield me a - ny po - sies.

Last line of verses 3 and 5

3. Young men and young maid - ens, come a - long this way.
5. And a - di - eu to__ all fa - lse lov - ers.

2 Young men and young maidens to church they do go,
   Young men and young maidens they do make a fine show;
   And I follow after with my heart full with woe,
   Was to how my false lover was guarded.

3 I saw my false lover all in the church stand,
   With a ring on her finger and a glove in her hand;
   And the parson he married her, and the words he did say,
   'Young men and young maidens, come along this way'.

4 Young men and young maidens to church they do go;
   I saw my false lover sat down to meat,
   And I sat myself by her but none could I eat,
   For the sight of my false lover was better than meat.

5 I saw my false lover take the candle to bed,
   With the tears in my eyes that dazzled my sight;
   I picked up my hat and I wished them goodnight,
   And adieu to all false lovers.

6 O dig me a grave both long, wide and deep,
   Trim it all over with flowers so sweet,
   So that I may lie down and take a long sleep,
   And that sleep will last me for ever.

So bright shall they moan . . . .: another version has, 'The sun it shone brightly and keen blew the air'.

The Charming Bride

As I walked out___ one sum - mer's morn, 'Twas
in the mer - ry month of June, In the search of a charm-ing
bride,_____ In the search of a charm - ing bride.___

2 I walkèd forty mile that day,
  I spied a cottage on my way,
  Which I never had seen before. (2)

3 I walkèd up to the garden gate,
  Although the night was very late,
  And I callèd to be let in. (2)

4 'O no, kind sir, that never can be,
  There's no one in this house but me;
  So I pray, young man, be gone.' (2)

5 Then she looked up to the glorious skies;
  It hailed, it rained, the winds blew high;
  And she callèd me back again. (2)

6 Then she came down and let me in,
  She kissed my cheeks, likewise my chin,
  And soon a game began. (2)

7. We spent that night in sweet content,
  Next mornin' to the church we went,
  And she made me a charming bride. (2)

A solitary woman is prudently disposed to turn the tramping stranger from her door, but relents because of the bad weather. At least this is her excuse, for it is she who takes the initiative in the 'game' which follows. In many songs, seduction is followed only by separation, but here the outcome is a wedding. The earliest English version of this delightful piece is a street ballad issued during the reign of James II (1685–88) under the title of 'John's Earnest

Request; Or, Betty's compassionate Love extended to him in a time of Distress'. The words and tune printed here were collected in Lincolnshire by the composer, Percy Grainger, in 1906.

91   The Cuckoo's Nest

As — I went a-walk-ing one day — in — May, I —
met a pret-ty maid, and — un-to her did say: 'To —
love I am in-clined, I will show — you my mind, For I'm
deep — ly en-gaged — with your cuck-oo's nest.' [Oh],
some like girls — that are fair of face, [And] —
some like a lass — with a nice trim waist; But —
give — me the girl — who'll — wrig-gle and twist At the
bot-tom of her bel-ly with the cuck-oo's nest.

2 'Oh, my darling', says she, 'I am innocent and young,
And I scarce can believe your false, deluding tongue;
Yet I see in your eyes and it fills me with surprise
That your inclination lies in the cuckoo's nest.'

3 'Oh, my darling', says I, 'if you see it in my eyes,
   Then think on it as fondness, and don't be surprised;
   For I'll marry you, I swear, and make you my dear,
   If you let me slip my hand in the cuckoo's nest.'

4 'Oh, my darling', says she, 'I can do no such thing,
   For my mother often told me it would be a great sin
   My maidenhead to lose, and then to be abused,
   And to have no more a-doing with the cuckoo's next.'

5 'Oh, my darling', says I, 'it wouldn't be a sin;
   Why, your common sense will tell you it's a pleasing thing.
   You were sent upon this earth to increase and do your best,
   And to help a man to heaven with your cuckoo's nest.'

6 'Oh, my darling', says she, 'now I cannot you deny,
   For you've fairly won my heart with the rolling of your eye;
   And I see it in your eyes, and your courage it doth rise,
   So gently slip your hand in the cuckoo's nest.'

7 This couple they were wed, and quickly went to bed,
   And now this pretty fair maid has lost her maidenhead;
   In their little country cottage they do each other bless,
   As they gaze upon the fruits of the cuckoo's nest.

The message of 'The Charming Bride' (no. 90) is quite clear, though almost entirely conveyed by implication rather than by statement. In contrast, 'The Cuckoo's Nest', while having a broadly similar theme (a sexual encounter which leads to marriage), implies very little and says a good deal, once the meaning of the central circumlocution is understood. The cuckoo's nest, says Eric Partridge, with uncharacteristic modesty, is the pudendum muliebre (Dictionary of Historical Slang, Penguin edition, 1972, p. 229). The metaphor, as intended, adds to the mood of strong and gleeful sexuality. No doubt for that reason the song has been extremely rare; indeed I have not seen it in print before, at least in the form given here. Versions of the tune, however, are widely known, sometimes with fragments of text, because of their use for Morris dancing. The melody I have used is from the notebooks of John Clare, a poet who was also an accomplished fiddler, in demand for village merrymakings.

Raking the Hay

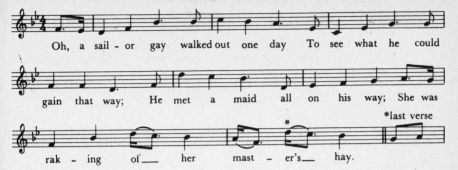

Oh, a sail - or gay walked out one day To see what he could
gain that way; He met a maid all on his way; She was
rak - ing of __ her mast - er's __ hay.

*
*last verse

2 'Good morning to you, maid so fair,
   How come you raking this hay so clear?
   Come, pull off your gown, throw away your rake,
   And gain with the sailor to yonder green gate.'

3 'What would my master say to me
   If I leave my work and gain with thee?
   He'd stop my wage, give me no pay,
   He'd stop my wages and turn me away.'

4 Now with kisses sweet and words so kind,
   Causèd this fair maid to change her mind;
   She pulled off her gown, threw away her rake,
   And gained with the sailor to yonder green gate.

5 Now six long months were gone and passed,
   And the ninth month brought a child at last;
   Then she cursed the hour, she cursed the day,
   She cursed the very hour she left her master's hay.

6 But 'leven months gone and twelve months passed,
   And the sailor he returned at last;
   He married her the very next day,
   So she blessed the very hour she left her master's hay.

'Joy after Sorrow' is the title of an eighteenth century slip-song, beginning: 'A
Sailor walking in the fields,/To see what pleasure Flora yields,/Where a
pretty maid stript in her smock,/Was busy a raking, busy a raking, all round
the haycock'. The sailor invites the girl to lay down her rake, put on her
gown, and go with him to 'yonder wake'. There, he 'gain'd this fair maid's

love', and, twenty weeks later, as soon as 'her rosy cheeks quite alter'd was', he married her.

The version given here is from the singing of Sam Larner (1887–1965), of Winterton, Norfolk. It contrasts in a number of ways with the earliest text. The girl is now wearing a gown, which the sailor asks her to remove: this is an updating, since, although women did strip to their smocks to make hay in the eighteenth century, they did not do so in the late nineteenth. Kilvert recorded some remarks on the subject in 1873 from an old lady, Sally Killing: 'She said when she was young, women never wore their gowns out hay-making. If a farmer saw one of his women working in her gown he would order her to take it off. She herself had been weeks without putting on her gown from Monday morning till Saturday night, in the hay harvest. The women had loose sleeves which they pinned on to their 'shift sleeves' and which covered their arms to the wrist from the sun' (Diary, single volume edition, 1964, p. 218). 'Yonder wake' has changed to 'yonder green gate': possibly a mishearing in oral transmission, but perhaps also a modernization, if wakes had lost their former importance in the area. Finally, Sam Larner's oral version has a much neater and more effective climax and dénouement than the printed text. The sailor disappears for a time, and returns only after the baby is born. The woman's joy after sorrow is thereby the more marked.

93   The Foggy Dew

When I was a ba-che-lor ear-ly and young I fol-lowed the weav-ing trade, And all the harm that ev-er I done was court-ing a ser-vant maid. I court-ed her in the sum-mer sea-son and part of the win-ter too, And ma-ny a night I walked with her all ov-er the fog-gy dew.

2 One night as I lay on my bed, as I laid fast asleep,
   There came a pretty, fair young maid and most bitterly she
      did weep.
   She wept, she mourned, she tore her hair, crying, 'Alas, what
      shall I do?
   This night I'm resolved to stay with you, for fear of the foggy
      dew.'

3 It was in the first part of the night we passed the time away,
   And in the latter part of the night she stayed with me till day;
   When broad daylight it did appear, she cried, 'I am undone.'
   'Hold your tongue, you foolish girl, the foggy dew is gone'.

4 'Suppose that we should have a child, would it cause us to
      smile?
   Suppose that we should have another, would it make us laugh
      awhile?
   Suppose that we should have another, another, and another
      one too.'
   'It would make you think of your foolish tricks, likewise the
      foggy dew.'

5 I love this young girl dearly, I love her as my life;
   I took this girl and I married her, and made her my lawful
      wife.
   I never told her of her fault, nor e'er intend to do,
   But every time she smiles on me I think on the foggy dew.

Something of a minor scandal was caused in the 1940s, when Benjamin Britten's arrangement of a student version of this song, sung on a gramophone record by Peter Pears, was banned by the BBC. Traditional versions have been widely known to collectors in Britain and America since the 1890s, but have seldom been published, at least until very recently. Of the eight variants found by Cecil Sharp, only one, with a skimpy text at that, was published prior to 1958, when James Reeves analysed the different versions in The Idiom of the People. *A great deal of time and ink has been expended in attempting to explain the meaning of the phrase, 'the foggy dew'. Perhaps it is best left as mysteriously evocative. One likely idea, however, seems to be that it is a corruption of 'bugaboo' or 'bogle bo', meaning ghost. Yet the earliest text which I have seen, an eighteenth-century street ballad entitled 'The Batchelor Brave', has 'foggy dew'.*

Two well-loved themes combine here. Parents, disapproving of a suitor whom they regard as their daughter's social inferior, arrange for his removal by the press gang. She, in turn, follows her lover 'to the wars' and secures his release, so that they can be married. The earliest form of the song seems to be a street ballad issued by Johnny Pitts, of Seven Dials, between 1802 and 1819, at a time when the press gang was either very active or a recent and vivid memory. 'The Pretty Ploughboy' remained on the lips of country singers for another 150 years; the version given here was recorded from Walter Pardon in 1977.

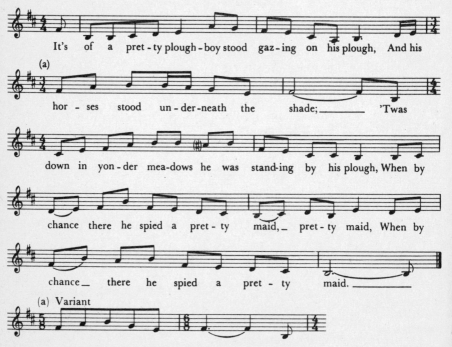

It's of a pret-ty plough-boy stood gaz-ing on his plough, And his

(a)

hor-ses stood un-der-neath the shade;_____ 'Twas

down in yon-der mea-dows he was stand-ing by his plough, When by

chance there he spied a pret-ty maid,_ pret-ty maid, When by

chance_ there he spied a pret-ty maid._____

(a) Variant

2 The song that he sung as he walkèd along:
'Pretty maid, you are of high degree.
If I should fall in love and your parents should know it,
The next thing they would send me to the sea, to the sea,
The next thing they would send me to the sea.'

3 And when the aged parents they came for to know
That her love was a-ploughing on the plain,
They sent for the press gang and pressed her love away,
And they sent him to the wars to be slain, to be slain,
And they sent him to the wars to be slain.

4 She went home and dressed herself all in her best,
  And her pockets she linèd with gold;
  With tears all in her eys she trudged along the streets,
  In search of her jolly sailor bold, sailor bold,
  In search of her jolly sailor bold.

5 The first man she met was a jolly sailor:
  'Have you seen my pretty ploughboy', she cried;
  'They've sent him on the deep, he's a-sailing with the fleet';
  And he said, 'My pretty maid, will you ride, will you ride?'
  And he said, 'My pretty maid, will you ride?'

6 She rode till she came to the ship her love was in,
  And unto the captain did complain;
  She said, 'I've come to seek for my pretty ploughboy,
  Who they've sent to the wars to be slain, to be slain,
  Who they've sent to the wars to be slain.'

7 One hundred bright guineas she did then lay down,
  So thrillèd her tale she told them o'er,
  Until she'd got her pretty ploughboy into her arms,
  And she hugged him till she'd got him safe on shore, safe on
      shore,
  And she hugged him till she'd got him safe on shore.

8 And when she had got her ploughboy into her arms,
  Where he had oft times been before,
  She set those bells to ring and so sweetly she did sing,
  Just because she met the lad that she adore, she adore,
  Just because she met the lad that she adore.

95   The Bonny Labouring Boy

*At least the eponymous pretty ploughboy (no. 94) was a stranger, but here
the daughter horrifies her parents by wishing to marry one of their own em-
ployees. Perhaps her father was one of the new fashioned farmers (no. 27) of
the late eighteenth and early nineteenth centuries, whom Cobbett and the
labourers detested. Certainly the song dates from that time. It was a firm
favourite with country people, and was quoted in* The Scouring of the

161

White Horse *(1858) by Thomas Hughes. The version given here (with two verses added from a broadside) was collected in 1907 from a man who learned his songs as a boy in Huntingdonshire, where 'he used to lead the horses when ploughing and the man who held the plough taught him them, while they were at work in the fields'. The tune is a variant of 'The Banks of Sweet Dundee'.*

As I rode out one morn-ing, being in the bloom of spring, I heard a love-ly maid com-plain, so griev-ous-ly — did sing, Say-ing, 'Cru-el were my par-ents, they did me so — an-noy, And they would not let me mar-ry my bon-ny lab-ouring boy.

2 Young Johnny was my true love's name, as you shall plainly see;
My parents they employed him their labouring boy to be,
To harrow, reap and sow the seed, and plough my father's land;
And soon I fell in love with him, as you may understand.

3 His cheeks were like the roses red, his eyes as black as sloes;
He's mild in his behaviour wherever that he goes,
He's manly, neat and handsome, his skin as white as snow;
In spite of my parents with my labouring boy I'll go.

4 My father thought to have me wed unto some lord or peer,
I being the only heiress of five thousand pounds a year.
I placed my heart on one true love and him I'll ne'er deny,
So this nation I will ramble with my bonny labouring boy.

5 My mother came one morning and took me by the hand,
And said she'd send young Johnny unto some foreign land.
She locked me in my bedroom, my comforts to annoy,
And kept me there to weep and mourn for my bonny
labouring boy.

162

[6 Nine hundred pounds and all my clothes I took that very
      night,
  And with the lad I did adore to Plymouth I took flight;
  His love it has entangled me, and that I can't deny,
  So to a foreign land I'll go with my bonny labouring boy.

7 This couple they got married and joined in unity,
  In peace and comfort for to live, in love and loyalty;
  Her parents' riches she disdains for her love and only joy,
  May prosperity attend her with her bonny labouring boy.]

8 So fill your glasses to the brim, let the toast go merrily round,
  Here's a health to every labouring boy that ploughs and tills
      the ground;
  And when his work is over his home he steers with joy,
  Saying, happy is the girl that weds a bonny labouring boy.

96   The Dumb Maid

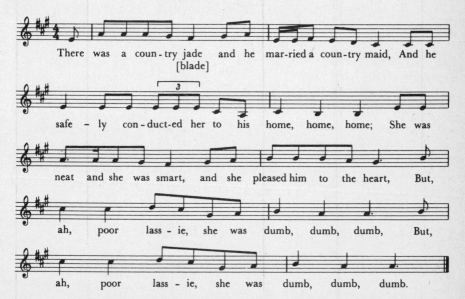

There was a coun-try jade [blade] and he mar-ried a coun-try maid, And he
safe - ly con-duct-ed her to his home, home, home; She was
neat and she was smart, and she pleased him to the heart, But,
ah, poor lass - ie, she was dumb, dumb, dumb, But,
ah, poor lass - ie, she was dumb, dumb, dumb.

2 She could brew and she could bake, and could sew and she
      could make,
  She could sweep round the house with her broom broom
      broom;

She could hang and she could wring and do any kind of thing,
But, ah, poor lassie, she was dumb, dumb, dumb. (2)

3 To the doctor then he went just to make himself content,
To get his missus cured of her mump, mump, mump;
Said the doctor, 'Of my heart, it is the easiest part
To make a woman speak that is dumb, dumb, dumb.' (2)

4 So the doctor in he brings and he cut her chattering strings,
And at liberty he set her tongue, tongue, tongue;
Then her tongue began to work and she began to talk,
Just as though she never had been dumb, dumb. (2)

5 Now these faculties she tried, and it filled the house with
    noise,
And rattled in his ears like a drum, drum, drum;
He bade her ill of strife, made the worry of his life:
'I wish this day and night she was dumb, dumb, dumb.' (2)

6 To the doctor then he goes and he just unfolds his woes:
'Oh, doctor, thou hast made me undone, done done;
For my wife she proves a scold and her tongue she will not
    hold:
I'd give any kind of thing if she was dumb, dumb, dumb.' (2)

7 'When I did undertake for to make thy wife spake,
'Twas a thing quite easily done, done, done;
But it's past the art of man, try the best that e'er he can,
To make a scolding woman hold her tongue, tongue, tongue.'

he cut her chattering strings: the remedy in
1526 was merely to place two aspen
leaves under her tongue.

He bade her ill of strife . . . .: in another version, this line reads: 'She bred a deal of
strife, made him weary of his life.'

*Songs and stories in dispraise of scolding wives are legion. The tale of the
dumb wife made to speak, much to the subsequent chagrin of her husband, was
probably already old when it was first printed, in 1526 (in* A Hundred
Merry Tales, *no. 62; see the edition by P. M. Zall, University of Nebraska
Press, Lincoln, USA, 1963). It was constantly reprinted in chapbooks for the
next three centuries. The earliest ballad version, 'The Dumb Maid; or the
Young Gallant Trappan'd', appeared in about 1678. The set given here is
from the singing of Mrs Freda Palmer, of Witney, Oxfordshire (1975).*

97 Come All You Young Ladies and Gentlemen

The scold, the slattern and the unfaithful: these are the three sorts of wife most frequently castigated in song. Here, the young man, having married in haste, repents, not at leisure but very quickly, on discovering that his wife is untidy and a spendthrift to boot.

Come all you young la-dies and gen-tle-men,— let me with your com-pa-ny min-gle:— Once I was young like you, and then I was hap-py and sin-gle. Till my mo-ther ad-vised me to wed un-til se-ven-teen I had tar-ried; I went off to the church in a trance one day, like a man to be mar-ried.

Chorus

O———— I wish I were sin-gle a-gain.————

2 My wife she came home in a pet and she burned my new boots to a cinder,
And the cat she kicked under the grate and the table threw out of the winder;
And the bed-clothes, kettle and broom, and the washing tub off she has carried,
And she sold both the poker and the tongs, so I wish I had never got married.

3 It's seldom we get a bit of meat – but once a month, or I'm generally mistaken;
Then it's old sheep's head and a pluck, and a small piece of liver and bacon.
She says bread and butter is dear, and business most shocking and horrid,
And I've often times wished I'd been dead before I ever got married.

4 Now I should be happy and jovial once more if I could once
    see all things right;
May Old Nick come and fetch her away some morning
    before it is daylight.
Come all you young men that are single of mind and pray
    don't you ever be hurried,
For if I were single again, I'd be cussed if I ever got married.

98   Willie Went to Westerdale

*The slatternly wife is an archetypal figure of fun, though in the days when
there was a very fine line between survival and starvation, inefficiency in
either marriage partner could be a very serious matter. There is a nineteenth-
century broadside version of the song with the ironic title of 'The Thrifty
Housewife', though I find its inclusion in Kidson and Moffat's* Children's
Songs of Long Ago *rather perplexing. This oral version is from Jack
Beeforth, who lived very near to Westerdale in North Yorkshire himself.*

2 He bowt her twenty good milk kies;
  Nineteen of them she let gan dry.

3 She never kerned but yance a year,
  And that's what made her butter so dear.

4 And when she kerned she kerned in her beeats,
  And for t' creamstick she put in her feeat.

5 She made her cheese and put it on t' shelf;
  She nivver turned t' cheese till t' cheese turned self.

6 And she roasted t' chicken both heead and feeat,
  Feathers and guts and all complete.

7 And she did a far worse trick than that,
  She let t' bairns shit in t' father's neetcap.

bowt: bought. *beeats:* boots.
kies: cows. *feeat:* feet.
kerned: churned (butter).

99   Oh, It Was My Cruel Parents

Oh, it was my cru-el pa-rents that did me first tre-pan;___ They mar-ried me to___ an' old man for the sake of mon-ey and land;___ If they'd mar-ried me to___ a young man___ with-out a pen-ny at all, He'd have took me in his arms and have loved me all the more.___

167

2 Oh, it's 'Hush, my dearest Nancy, oh, wait till we go to
        town,
  I'll buy you a lady's bonnet, likewise a mus-e-lin gown;
  There is no lady in the land your beauty can compare,
  And I'll buy you a little lapdog to follow you everywhere.'

3 'I want none of your little lapdogs nor none of your gentle
        care;
  It's a pity such an old man my beauty you should snare.
  I am but sixteen years of age and scarcely in my bloom;
  Oh, you are my cruel torment, both morning, night and
        noon.'

4 When he goes to bed at night he's as cold as any clay:
  His feet as cold at midnight as corpse, I've heard them say;
  His pipes are out of order and his old flute's never in tune.
  Oh, I wish that he was dead and a young man in the room.

5 [Now some they do persuade me to drown him in a well,
  And others do persuade me to grind him in a mill.
  I'd rather take my own advice and tie him to a stake,]
  And I'll get a big stick and wallop him until his bones I break.

trepan: entrap.
I've heard them say: 'that ever you did see' (reading from another version).

*Since the Renaissance young women in Western Europe have vigorously
claimed the right to choose husbands for themselves. When to the indignity of
a husband selected by parents is added disparity of age, bitterness and even
hatred result. The complaint of a young woman married to an old man is one
of the staple themes of folk song, though it is not often treated with the
strength of feeling expressed here. The song is rather uncommon, having
turned up in the oral tradition only a handful of times, and once on an
eighteenth-century broadside, entitled, 'Sally's Love For a Young Man'.*

100   Hey Down Derry

*The disastrous choice of husband here is apparently the girl's own. Her rejec-
tion of him is reasonably good-humoured, and couched in the form of a warning to others. I have a feeling that singers were more interested in the humour
than the warning.*

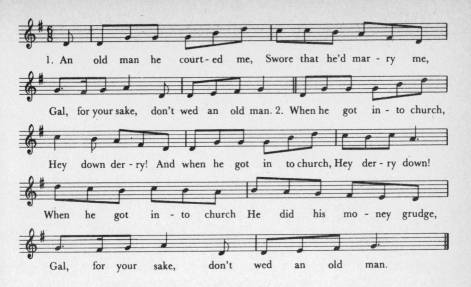

1. An old man he court-ed me, Swore that he'd mar-ry me,
Gal, for your sake, don't wed an old man. 2. When he got in-to church,
Hey down der-ry! And when he got in to church, Hey der-ry down!
When he got in-to church He did his mo-ney grudge,
Gal, for your sake, don't wed an old man.

3 When he got home to meat,
Hey down derry!
When he got home to meat,
Hey derry down!
When he got home to meat
He did grudge all I eat,
Gal, for your sake, don't wed an old man.

4 When he got home to bed . . .
He did not turn his head.
Gal, for your sake, don't wed an old man.

5 When he got fast asleep . . .
Out of bed I did creep,
Into the arms of a jolly young man.

101 The Parson With the Wooden Leg

*If a married couple is grossly mismatched in age, one of the results can be
infidelity; in songs, at least, young women married to old men quickly seek
the company of a 'jolly young man'. In other cases, differences not of age but*

of temperament lead one or both of a married pair to look elsewhere for sexual partners. In popular lore and literature, the feeling seems generally to be that the cuckolding of a husband is fair sport, and there are scores of songs on the subject. Few deal sympathetically with the plight of such a husband, or reflect that there is often a second victim in the cuckolder's wife. Among the professions which, it was thought, had particularly good opportunities for seducing other men's wives, was the clergy. The philandering cleric goes back at least to Chaucer's time, and no doubt beyond.

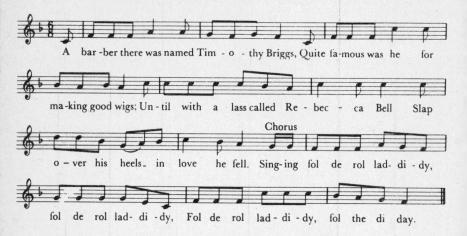

A barber there was named Timothy Briggs, Quite famous was he for making good wigs; Until with a lass called Rebecca Bell Slap over his heels in love he fell. Singing fol de rol lad-di-dy, fol de rol lad-di-dy, Fol de rol lad-di-dy, fol the di day.

2 They went to the church the knot for to tie
   To a wooden-legg'd parson named Jonathan Sly;
   And sure, if you'd seen him you'd laughed at him plump,
   As he mounted the pulpit with his old stump.

3 They'd only been married a week or two
   When Rebecca turned out a most terrible screw [shrew].
   'No comfort have I with this woman', he said;
   'I'll go back to the parson and I'll get unwed.'

4 He went to the parson; said he, 'Mr Sly,
   If I live with this woman I surely shall die.
   You said you would make us two into one;
   I've come to see now if I can't be undone.'

5 The parson he said, 'That's a thing rather new;
   I don't know that I've power my flock to undo.
   Here's hoping you lead a more happier life;
   I'll go round to your house and I'll lecture your wife.'

6 Now the barber, quite pleased, went taking his glass –
  The old parson stumped off to lecture the lass –
  But when he got home, Lor', what did he see,
  But the parson with Rebecca on top of his knee.

7 Now the barber bristled up every hair;
  Said he, 'Mr Parson, what are you doing there?'
  'You said you wanted undoing, my man,
  So you see I'm a-doing it as fast as I can.'

8 'I think I'm undone now if I never was before.'
  He kicked Mr Parson straight out through the door;
  He laid in the street and his wooden leg stood,
  Like a spade sticking up in a cartload of mud.

9 This couple from then they lived more reconciled,
  But nine months from that day she brought him a child.
  The barber hung himself up on a peg
  When he found his child born with a brand-new wooden leg.

102   It's of an Old Couple

In the nineteenth century the church was widely identified with the squire-archy, and inevitably was distrusted and disliked for it, at least by some. In later life Joseph Arch vividly remembered what he saw when he peeped into the communion service at Barford (Warwickshire) in 1833, at the age of seven: 'First, up walked the squire to the communion rails; the farmers went up next; then up went the tradesmen, the shopkeepers, the wheelwright, and the blacksmith: and then, the very last of all, went the poor agricultural labourers in their smock frocks. They walked up by themselves; nobody else knelt with them; it was as if they were unclean.' These same labourers seem to have enjoyed accusing the clergy of gluttony or lechery in their tales and songs. The story of 'The Man that Stole the Parson's Sheep' (S. O. Addy, Household Tales, 1895; reprinted in K. M. Briggs and R. Tongue, Folk-tales of England, Routledge, 1965, p. 117) is a case in point. The song, 'Parson and Bacon', accuses a Methodist parson (for the established church was not the only target) of stealing a man's bacon and also, by implication, his wife. In 'It's of an Old Couple' the intention seems to be that we should be amused both at the parson's morals (in some versions the clerk of the parish, rather than the parson) and the husband's gullibility.

171

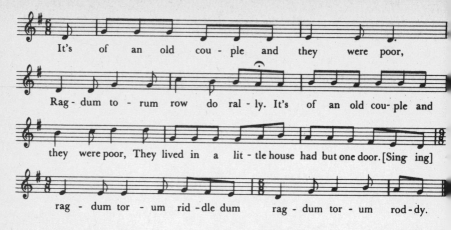

It's of an old cou - ple and they were poor,

Rag - dum to - rum row do ral - ly. It's of an old cou- ple and

they were poor, They lived in a lit - tle house had but one door.[Sing ing]

rag - dum tor - um rid -dle dum rag - dum tor - um rod - dy.

2 The old man he was often gone from home; (2)
The old wife got tired of sleeping alone.

3 The parson of the parish who lived close by, (2)
And often with the old woman did lie.

4 The old man he came home about twelve o'clock, (2)
And at the little door he did knock.

5 She said, 'My dear husband, will you be so kind (2)
To fetch me an apple to please my mind?'

6 The old man he went out and got up a tree; (2)
Up jumped the parson and away got he.

7 He brought her an apple, put it on the shelf. (2)
'If you want another, go fetch it yourself.'

103   Coming Home Late

The extravagance of tongue-in-cheek lies and fanciful tall stories is one of the perennial sources of pleasure and humour in folk tales, anecdotes and songs. Here, it is allied with another staple, the foolish cuckold. The song, first printed in the eighteenth century as 'Our Goodman', is widely known in Britain and America. The Dubliners' recording, under the title of 'Seven Nights Drunk', was very popular in the early 1970s. The version given here was collected in Sussex in 1977.

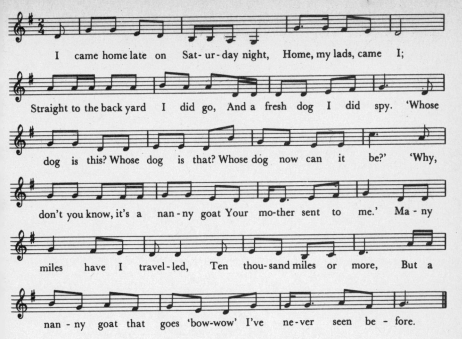

I came home late on Sat-ur-day night, Home, my lads, came I;

Straight to the back yard I did go, And a fresh dog I did spy. 'Whose

dog is this? Whose dog is that? Whose dog now can it be?' 'Why,

don't you know, it's a nan-ny goat Your mo-ther sent to me.' Ma-ny

miles have I travel-led, Ten thou-sand miles or more, But a

nan-ny goat that goes 'bow-wow' I've ne-ver seen be-fore.

2 I came home late one Sunday night,
Home, my lads, came I;
Straight to the back door I did go,
And a fresh coat I did spy.
'Whose coat is this? Whose coat is that?
Whose coat now can it be?'
'Why, don't you know, it's a rolling pin
Your mother sent to me.'
Many miles have I travelled,
Ten thousand miles or more,
But a rolling pin with armholes in
I've never seen before.

3 I came home late one Monday night,
Home, my lads came I;
Straight to the bedroom I did go,
And a fresh hat I did spy.
'Whose hat is this? Whose hat is that?
Whose hat now can it be?'
'Why, don't you know, it's a chamber pot
Your mother sent to me.'
. . . But a chamber pot with a lining in
I've never seen before.

173

4 I came home late one Tuesday night,
Home, my lads, came I;
Straight to the bedroom I did go,
And a fresh face I did spy.
'Whose face is this? Whose face is that?
Whose face now can it be?'
'Why, don't you know, it's a new-born babe
Your mother sent to me.'
. . . But a baby's face with whiskers on
I've never seen before.

a rolling pin: in most versions this is reserved until a final verse, sung only in the right company. The coat is normally explained as a blanket, which brings the retort: 'But a blanket with bright buttons on I've never seen before.'

104   The Mole Catcher

Adultery must be as old as marriage. What the Victorians and Edwardians felt to be profoundly shocking about this song was not the subject matter, however, but the ribald glee with which it was treated. According to Baring-Gould, who took down a version in Devon in 1888, 'The original words were very gross and I did not note them'. He adds: 'In the British Museum is an early Garland, and in the list of contents on the cover is 'The Mole Catcher', but the song has been torn out, probably for the same reason that prevented me from taking it down.' It was not until 1960 that a full text of the song appeared, when James Reeves printed a manuscript version which had been taken down some fifty years earlier (The Everlasting Circle, p. 191). *Orally, the song was widely known in country districts, though why it usually refers to Manchester or Warrington is not clear. The version printed here comes from East Anglia.*

In War - ring - ton town at the sign of the plough There lived a mole catch - er and I'll tell you how. [Sing - ing tu - re li day, fol lad - dy li day.]

174

2 And he had a wife, both gallant and gay;
   She with an old farmer so oft times would play.

3 The mole catcher being a man well skilled in his trade,
   He oft times walked out with his trap and his spade.

4 He go out in the morning and stay out till night
   Whilst the old farmer was a-kissing his wife.

5 Mole Catcher being jealous of the very same thing,
   He stepped into the house to see him come in.

6 He saw the old farmer hop over the stile,
   Which caused the mole catcher behind for to smile.

7 He pulled his good woman down on to his lap;
   'Now,' says the mole catcher, 'I have you in my trap.'

8 And upstairs they go and fulfil their design;
   Mole catcher he followed them softly behind.

9 And when that they got in the midst of the sport,
   He catches the old farmer by the tail of his coat.

10 He catched the old farmer all by his coat flap,
    Saying, 'Now I've caught you in my mole trap.'

11 'I'll make you pay dear for tilling my ground:
    The sum of the money is full ten pound.'

12 'Ten pound', said the farmer, 'I never shall mind;
    That scarcely will cost me one penny a time.'

13 So now to conclude and finish his loss,
    The old farmer go home to the sign of the cross.

14 He go no more to the sign of the plough,
    For spending his money he could not tell how.

sign of the cross: the reference may be to paying for the support of an illegitimate (cross-bred) child.

An amusing situation frequently found in folk narratives is that of the wife's lover taking refuge in a chimney, chest or cupboard when her husband returns unexpectedly. Interest and humour then lie in the dénouement: the lover's escape or his discomfiture at the hands of the husband. Cuckolds are seldom accorded much sympathy in folk songs, but the case alters when the wife's lover belongs to the despised trade of tailor.

In fair London town a young damsel did dwell, With her wit and her beauty none could her excel; With her wit and her beauty none could her excel, And her husband he was a bold drover.

Chorus

Fal - da - ral lur - i - li - day.

2 A groggy old tailor he livèd close by,
And all on this here damsel he cast a sly eye;
'Ten guineas I'll give if I can with you lie,
For your husband he is a bold drover.'

3 The bargain was made and upstairs they did run,
And they jumped into bed; soon the music begun.
They huddled, they cuddled, they both fell asleep,
And they never once thought of the drover.

4 In the middle of the night when the drover came home
He knocked at the door with the palm of his hand.
'O, hide me, O, hide me', the tailor he cried,
'For I hear the loud knock of the drover.'

5 'There's a dusty old cupboard hangs over the door,
Where you can get in so snug and secure.

I will go down and I'll undo the door,
And I'll let in my husband, the drover.'

6 So she undone the door and her husband walked in,
With her kiss and her compliments she welcomed him in.
'For your kiss and your compliments I don't care a pin,
For you don't care a damn for the drover.'

7 'O, husband, O husband, there's no firestuff,
And if you're in bed you'll be quite warm enough.'
'There's a dusty old cupboard hangs over the door,
Which this night I shall burn', said the drover.

8 'Dear husband, now will you grant me my desire,
For that cupboard's too good to be burnt on the fire.
In it I've a gamecock I much do admire' –
'Then I'll fight your gamecock', said the drover.

9 He knocked this old cupboard right down on the floor,
He knocked the old tailor all over and o'er.
He kicked him, he hit him, knocked him heels over lugs.
'I've cooked your gamecock', said the drover.

106   The Grey Hawk

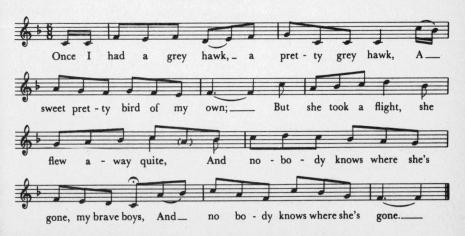

Once I had a grey hawk, – a pret-ty grey hawk, A sweet pret-ty bird of my own; — But she took a flight, she flew a-way quite, And no-bo-dy knows where she's gone, my brave boys, And — no bo-dy knows where she's gone. —

2 So through the green forest I rambled away
And across the green fields I did stray;
I hollered, I whooped, I played on my flute,
Not my sweet pretty bird could I find, my brave boys,
Not my sweet pretty bird could I find.

3 So over the green hills I rambled away
And along the green paths I did stray.
Lo, there I did spy my sweet pretty bird,
And close by the side of a man she did lay,
She was close by the side of a man.

4 Now he that has got her is welcome to her
To do the best with her he can;
But whiles he have got and I have her not,
I will hawk with her once now and then, my brave boys,
I will hawk with her once now and then.

5 So happy the man who hath a good wife,
Far happier is he that hath none;
But cursèd is he who courteth his friend's,
When he hath a good wife of his own, my brave boys,
When he hath a good wife of his own.

*A husband uses the metaphor of a lost hawk to lament his wife's leaving him
for another man. His sorrow (albeit mitigated by the sly resolution to 'hawk
with her once now and then') is expressed in words which first appeared in a
street ballad of about 1667, 'Cupid's Trappan; or, Up the Green Forest'.
The version given here was recorded in 1977 from Bob Roberts, who was
born in Dorset in 1909, spent most of his life in Suffolk, and has just retired
from skippering a coaster sailing out of the Isle of Wight.*

107   The Trees They Do Grow High

*There is a theory that the child husband of this song was a young Scots laird
called Urquhart of Craigston, who died in 1634. However, in Fletcher's
Two Noble Kinsmen, published in the same year, one of the characters
sings a snatch of the 'old ballad'. It seems likely, therefore, that Craigston was
woven into an existing ballad. Nevertheless, the piece has a fine antic reso-
nance, even though the first full text to appear was a rifacimento by Robert
Burns (in 1792). The sad story retained its place in the affections of country
singers until very recently; the version given here was recorded from Walter
Pardon of Norfolk in 1975.*

The trees they do grow high, the leaves they do grow green, The
time is long past, love, you and I have seen. It's a
cold win-ter's night when you and I must bide a-lone, Though my
bon-ny lad is young he's a-grow-ing,— grow-ing,— Though my
bon-ny lad is young he's a-grow-ing.

(a) Last verse

2

etc.

2 'O, father, dear father, you've done me much wrong:
You've married me to a boy who I fear is too young.'
'O, daughter, dear daughter, if you stay at home with me,
A lady you shall be while he's growing, growing,
A lady you shall be while he's growing.

3 'We'll send him to college for one year or two.'
'Perhaps then my love to a man he will grow.'
'I'll buy you white ribbons to tie around his bonny waist,
So the ladies shall know that he's married, married,
So the ladies shall know that he's married.'

4 At the age of sixteen he was a married man,
At seventeen the father of a son;
At the age of eighteen, love, his grave was a-growing green,
So she saw the end of his growing, growing,
So she saw the end of his growing.

5 I made my love a shroud of the holland, oh, so fine,
And every stitch I put in it the tears came tricking down;

179

And I'll mourn his fate until the day I die,
But I'll watch o'er his child while it's growing, growing,
But I'll watch o'er his child while it's growing.

6 Now my love is dead, in his grave doth lie;
The grass that's all o'er him it groweth so high.
Once I had a sweetheart but now I've got never a one;
Fare you well, my own true love, for growing, growing,
Fare you well, my own true love, for growing.

108   **The Dark-eyed Sailor**

'Twas of a come-ly young la-dy fair, Who was walk-ing out for to take the air; She met a sai-lor whilst on her way, So I paid at-ten-tion,— So I paid at-ten-tion to hear what they did say. So I paid at-ten-tion,— So I paid at-ten-tion to hear what they did say.

2 He said, 'Pray, lady, why roam alone?
The day's far spent and the night's coming on.'
She cried whilst tears from her eyes did fall,
' 'Twas the dark-eyed sailor,
'Twas the dark-eyed sailor that provèd my downfall.

3 ' 'Tis two long years since he left the land,
A golden ring he took off my hand;
We broke that token, here's half with me,
Whilst the other lay rolling,
Whilst the other lay rolling at the bottom of the sea.'

180

4 Said William, 'Lady, drive him from your mind,
    There's other sailors as good you'll find.
    Love turns aside and soon cold doth grow
    Like a winter's morning,
    Like a winter's morning with the ground all covered with
        snow.'

5 These words did Phoebe's young heart inflame;
    She said, 'Upon me you shall play no game.'
    She drew a dagger and loud did cry:
    'For my dark-eyed sailor,
    For my dark-eyed sailor a maid I'll live and die.'

6 [Then half the ring did young William show;
    She seemed distracted 'midst joy and woe,
    Saying, 'Welcome, William, I've lands and gold,
    For my dark-eyed sailor,
    For my dark-eyed sailor, so handsome, true and bold.']

7 Now in a cottage down by the sea
    They're joined in wedlock and well agree.
    O maids, be true whilst your love's away,
    For a cloudy morning,
    For a cloudy morning brings forth a sunshine day.

two long years: in most versions, seven.

The broken token is well known in folk narrative: two lovers on parting break a token such as a ring, and retain half each; when their separation is over the joining again of the token will symbolically cement their reunion. There was also a practical consideration: people changed so much after long periods apart that they might well need some conclusive form of identification on meeting again. A dearly-loved theme was that of a man returning to his sweetheart without being recognized, and testing her love by asking her to marry him. She steadfastly refuses until he suddenly produces the token to reveal his true identity.

Like so many songs, this seems to have originated in the late eighteenth century, been printed on street ballads in the early nineteenth, and survived in oral tradition until the twentieth. Indeed, it was so common that one has the feeling that many collectors did not bother to note it. The song was widely popular in country areas: the self-styled King of the Norfolk Poachers, who was born in about 1860, remembers hearing it at harvest homes (I Walked by Night ed. L. R. Haggard, 1935); almost every country singer of note had a version of it. The one given here comes from a man identified only as Jack, whom E. J. Moeran recorded in East Anglia in 1947.

VI
Up to the Rigs:
Sport and Diversion

109   **Up to the Rigs**

In Lon-don ci-ty I made my way, A-long Cheap-side I

chanced to stray; A fair la-dy I there did meet, I

                                                Chorus

greet-ed her with kiss-es sweet. I was up to the rigs,

down to the jigs, Up to the rigs of Lon-don town.

2 She took me to some house of fame;
  Boldly there she did step in.
  Loudly for supper she did call;
  She said to me, 'You'll pay for all.'

3 The supper over, the table clear,
  She called me a jewel and a dear.
  She called for wine, both white and red;
  The chambermaid prepared the bed.

4 Between the hours of one and two
  She asked me if to bed I'd go.
  Immediately I gave consent,
  Up to the bedroom we both went.

5 Her lips they were so sweet and red,
  I cuddled and kissed her there in bed;
  And while she lay there fast asleep
  Out of the bed then I did creep.

6 I stole her watch, her silken gown
  Her silver snuff-box and five pound;
  Away I crept into the night,
  Taking the lot for my delight.

7 Now all young men, just list to me,
  With pretty girls you may make free.
  In case misfortune should betide,
  Keep right away from old Cheapside.

Rigs: goings on.
house of fame: house of ill fame is presumably intended.

The sailor and the countryman, alike unused to the wiles and ways of the city, were regarded as fair game by swindlers, sharpers and prostitutes. In many a song the innocents return sadder and wiser than when they came, but here the guile of the countryman proves to be superior. No doubt for this reason, the song was held in particular affection by country singers. This version comes from Walter Pardon of Norfolk.

110   I'm a Young Man from the Country

The eponymous young man is alive to the dangers presented successively by the pickpocket, the pawn-ticket swindler and (although the third verse is rather confused) the pimp. The song seems to be a fragment from a longer original, but I have not been able to trace any other version.

It was down in North-amp-ton-shire where I heard of var-ious news, All the shows and fan-cies of migh-ty Lon-don town; So I took it in-to my head one day I'd tramp that place to see: I'm a young man from the coun-te-ry and I'm far too wide a-wake, I'm a

2 As I was stand staring in a shop window at a handsome chain
  and a golden locket,
A London chap behind me stopped, shoved his hand into my
  pocket.
Says I, 'Young man, your hand is on the wrong place, you're
  making it rather free:
I'm a young man from the countery but you can't pickpocket
  me.'

3 Then another chap stepped up to me and swore that he would
  nick it;
He said, 'Young man, I've pawned my watch and I want to
  sell the ticket.'
So I kep' a sharp watch on his game and soon I showed to he:
'I'm a young man from the countery but you cannot ticket
  me.'

4 Now up stepped a dashing lady and by my side did keep;
  Her cheeks were all rubbed up with paint just like we mark
    our sheep.
  Saying, 'Here's a shilling for thee, lad,' and she offered one to
    me.
  I'm a young man from the countery but I'm far too wide
    awake.

111   Rotherham Statutes

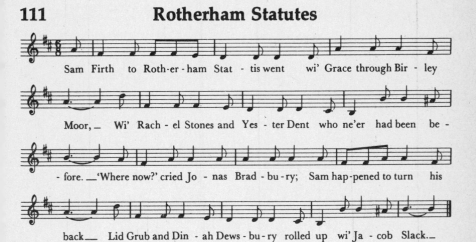

Sam Firth to Rother-ham Stat - tis went   wi' Grace through Bir - ley Moor,— Wi' Rach-el Stones and Yes-ter Dent who ne'er had been be-fore.— 'Where now?' cried Jo - nas Brad-bu-ry; Sam hap-pened to turn his back— Lid Grub and Din - ah Dews-bu-ry rolled up wi' Ja - cob Slack.—

2 They merrily jogged it on apace until they came to th' town.
  'Some puts up at t' *Cranes*', says Grace, 'but I'll put up at t'
    Crown.'
  Grace's cheeks were red, her eyes were black, so tight was
    every rag.
  Sam's soles were just two inches thick, wi' here and there a
    brag.

3 Sam Firth and Grace had ta'en their place wi' Tet through t'
    Nether Green;
  Jim Walsh and Fan stood next to Grace, Goff Thomson stood
    between.
  Jonathan Crookes were t' first to bid, he stared 'em fair i' th'
    face;
  He looked at Tet and then at Lid but fixed his mind on Grace.

4 Now Grace to go seemed very loth, and leave Sam Firth
    behind;
  Says Jonathan Crookes, 'I'll have you both, but not again
    your mind.
  Seth Merrill knows what beast I keep; I've forty acres of land,
  Three mares, a horse, and twenty sheep, and I live at Woober
    Stand.'

5 Then Goff and Sam and Grace and Lid took right away to th'
    Crown.
  Jim Walsh and Deborah Frost were there, Kit Lidget and
    Zanker Brown.
  The fiddler played so sweet and clear, he far excelled the lark;
  He played 'em 'Farewell, Manchester', and warbled until dark.

6 When night came on the game began, they drank hot ale and
    gin;
  Grace's face was like the rising sun and Sam felt warm within;
  So when they'd paid and ta'en their place the fiddler soon
    struck off,
  Sam crossed o'er a couple wi' Grace and Mat led through wi'
    Goff.

7 Sam set to Dinah Dewsbury, then reeled about wi' Sall;
  He singled wi' Jonas Bradbury, then danced again wi' Nell;
  Then he flew up the middle and reeled about wi' Kit;
  His pumps just touched the fiddle and brake it bit through bit.

8 Sam stared, his hair stood quite erect, and Grace's sun went
    down;
  Goff Thompson says, 'We must collect', and so says Zanker
    Brown.
  Sam tipped Goff two shillings i' hand; he'll mind better for t'
    time to come,
  So they all set off to Woober Stand to dance where there's
    more room.

brag: hobnail.   *Woober Stand:* Hoober Stand, a monu-
again your mind: against your inclination.   ment near the village of Hoober, three
                                         miles north-west of Rotherham.

*'At the Fairs and Statutes it (an open space near the College Inn in Jesus
Gate, now called College Street) was the great centre of attraction, and it was
especially so at the Hiring Statutes (commonly called the 'Stattis'), the rustic*

carnival of the year. Then brawny men, stout lads, and buxom country lasses mustered from the whole surrounding country, in high and unsophisticated glee, to renew with rough heartiness many an old acquaintance, and perhaps many a rustic vow. It was a time when village fathers and mothers met, with great delight, their sons and daughters who were living in different and distant services, and with them seemed again to renew their youth, and share with all the glee of the youngster the manifold amusements which crowded around them on every hand, and in every new and noisy form. . . . Those days of simple, hearty, honest enjoyment have passed away. Where are now the robust farming men with their smart and curiously braided smock frocks, and the long waggon whips, the emulative cracking of which in the church yard was one of the sights (and sounds) of the day? — and where, in their serviceable dresses, and simple but becoming finery, are the blooming country lasses, "when least adorned, adorned the most"? The statute hiring fair, as such, has lost its use; and as a cheerful holiday for the re-union of country friends . . . and is now mainly a rendezvous for the disorderly and dishonest, for triflers and tricksters, and ought long since to have been abolished.' So wrote John Guest, in his Historic Notices of Rotherham (1879, p. 356), though the Rotherham directories continued to describe the 'stattis' (held on the eve, day and morrow of the feast of St Edmund (20 November) and the five days following) as a hiring fair until at least 1922.

The song, one of a huge number on such subjects, shows both the 'rustic carnival' and the business of hiring.

112   Sedgefield Fair

Owd Dick-ie Thomp-son 'e 'ad a grey mare, 'E took 'er a-way to Sedge-field Fair. 'E browt 'er back, oh, yis, 'e did, Be-cause 'e 'adn't a far-thin' bid. Sing-ing ti-ti fa ler-ie, fi-re up Ma-ry, Up-to the jigs of Sedge-field Fair.

187

2 Now he turned her away into Wragby Wood,
   He thowt his owd mare might deea some good;
   But she ran her awd heead right intiv a tree:
   'Gor, dang', said Dick, 't'owd mare'll dee.'

3 Now he browt some hay all in a scuttle;
   Her poor owd belly began to ruttle.
   He browt her some corn all in a sieve:
   'Gor, dang', says Dick, 't'owd mare'll live.'

4 Now he took her away into t' field to ploo,
   To see what good his owd mare could do;
   But at ivvery end she let a great fart:
   'Gor, dang', says Dick, 'we'll ploo till dark.'

5 Now all his sheep got intiv his fog
   And he sent away home for t' black and white dog;
   And at ivvery end he gave a great shout,
   Was: 'Get away by 'em and fetch 'em out.'

6 Then all his hens got intiv his corn
   And he swore he would shoot 'em as sure as he's born;
   So he got his owd gun and he squinted and squared,
   But he missed t'owd hens and shot his grey mare.

Sedgefield: in County Durham.   Jack Beeforth, was born at Wragby on
Wragby Wood: the singer of this song,   Fylingdales Moor in North Yorkshire.

Perhaps the best known of all fair songs is 'Widdecombe Fair', which can be dated from its reference to Uncle Tom Cobleigh, who died in 1794. However, the song is neither confined to Devon, nor did it necessarily orginate there. Indeed, its essential feature is neither the fair, nor Tom Cobleigh and all, but the death of a mare. I believe that this death has a deeper significance as a sort of fertility sacrifice. (Compare 'The Derby Tup' or 'The Old Horse', nos. 145 and 140.) Such meaning has long since been lost at the conscious level, and almost all that remains is boisterous broad humour.

113   Strawberry Fair

Moralistic writers in the eighteenth and nineteenth centuries loved to castigate the sexual licence which, they claimed, attended all fairs. Population statistics show that they had a point. For example, 'at Bromley, Kent, there was a bulge of bastard births each year in December-January, about nine months after the spring fair' (R. W. Malcolmson, Popular Recreations in English Society, *Cambridge, 1973, p. 78).*

When Baring-Gould took down 'Strawberry Fair' from a Devon singer in 1891, he was horrified by the 'very indelicate' words, which he accordingly re-wrote. Ironically, his doctored version became widely known as a result of being taught in schools, but the original text is given here.

As I was a-going to Straw-b'ry Fair, Ri tol ri tol, rid-dle tol de li-do, I saw a fair maid-en of beau-ty rare, Tol de dee. I saw a fair maid-en go sell-ing her ware As she went on to Straw-b'ry Fair, Ri tol ri tol, rid-dle tol de li do, Ri tol ri tol, rid-dle tol de dee.

2 'O, pretty fair maiden, I prithee, tell;
My pretty fair maid, what do you sell?
O, come tell me truly, my sweet damsel,
As you go on to Strawberry Fair.'

3 'O, I have a lock that doth lack a key,
O, I have a lock, sir', she did say.
'If you have a key then come this way,
As we go on to Strawberry Fair.'

4 Between us I reckon that when we met
The key to the lock it was well set;
The key to the lock it well did fit,
As we went on to Strawberry Fair.

5 'O, would that my lock had been a gun,
I'd shoot the locksmith for I'm undone;
And wares to carry I now have none,
That I should go to Strawberry Fair.'

114   **Home from the Fair**

Come Nan - ny, come Pol - ly, come Dan - ny, come Bob - by, Keep

house like good bairns while I go to the fair. Be

stea - dy and qui - et, don't ramp and don't ri - ot, And

may - be I'll bring you an ap - ple or pear. And

may - be I'll bring you an ap - ple or pear.

*At this point, the third verse continues as follows:

(Faster)

A whis - tle to blow and a dol - ly to show, A

whip for a race and a fan for the face, A

top that 'll spin and a bell that 'll ring, And a

Tempo primo

trum - pet and drum to make you all mum. For

gran - ny, dear gran - ny's come home from the fair. For

gran - ny, dear gran - ny's come home from the fair.

2 Now Polly and Nanny had tea for old granny
  Too soon by an hour and a half, I declare,
  The kettle boiled over and scalded poor Rover,
  And left him a patch on his back wi'out hair. (2)

3 Come, dears, I forgive you, 'twas foolish to leave you
  All by yourselves while I went to the fair,
  So take from my wallet the toys you'll find in it,
  A whistle to blow and a dolly to show,
  A whip for a race and a fan for the face,
  A top that'll spin and a bell that'll ring,
  And a trumpet and drum to make you all mum,
  For granny, dear granny's come home from the fair.
  For granny, dear granny's come home from the fair.

*I have not seen this charming little song elsewhere. It has a strong flavour of
the eighteenth century, paralleled in the simplicity and directness of the children's prints of that age. The use of 'to ramp' (verse 1) with the meaning of
'to rampage' was also widespread in the eighteenth century, though it lingered
into the nineteenth: John Clare was quite fond of it.*

115   I Went to Market

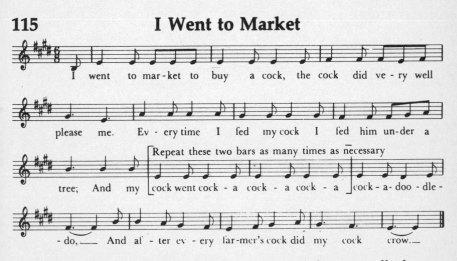

2 I went to market to buy a hen, the hen did very well please
    me.
  Every time I fed my hen I fed her under a tree;
  And the hen went caddle-ca,
  Cock went cock-a, cock-a doodle do,
  And after every farmer's cock did my cock crow.

3 . . . duck . . . quack
4 . . . goose . . . cackle
5 . . . pig . . . (snorting noise)
6 . . . sheep . . . baa
7 . . . cow . . .moo

8 I went to market to buy a wife, the wife did very well please
    me.
  Every time I fed my wife I fed her under a tree;
  And my wife said 'dammit' and cow went moo,
  And sheep went baa and pig went (snort),
  And goose went cackle and duck went quack,
  And hen went caddle-ca,
  Cock went cock-a, cock-a doodle do,
  And after every farmer's cock did my cock crow.

Farmyard noises have perennial appeal, and this jolly song has many parallels and many versions, the first having been printed in 1849 under the title of 'My Cock Lily-Cock'. However, the fun has a few serious overtones, one of which is the reference to buying a wife. The sale and purchase of wives really did take place, though not as the completely degrading ceremony shown by Hardy in The Mayor of Casterbridge, *but as a form of poor man's divorce by consent (for which see, for example, my* Rigs of the Fair *(with Jon Raven), Cambridge, 1976, pp. 25–8).*

116   John Barleycorn

*Sir James Frazer suggested that the story of John Barleycorn parallels the ancient belief in a vegetation spirit killed for the sake of the fertility of the crops (*Adonis, Attis, Osiris, *1906, p. 189). A more straightforward explanation is that he merely personifies the life-cycle of the barley grain which is used for brewing beer. 'A pleasant new ballad about the murther of John Barleycorn' is first mentioned in Murray's* New English Dictionary *of 1620, though the oldest extant copy dates from 1624. It has been sung to a variety of tunes, and given rise to a number of sequels, such as 'Hey, John Barleycorn' and 'The Little Barleycorn'. Robert Burns rewrote it some time between 1774 and 1784 (*Songs, *pp. 22–4); some two hundred years later, Ted Hughes appears to have been inspired by it to write his poem, 'The Golden Boy' (*Season Songs, *Faber 1976, pp. 39–40). Meanwhile, both John Barleycorn and his song have kept their popularity with countrymen.*

There were three men came out of the west their
fortunes for to try, And these three men made a
solemn vow, John Barleycorn should die. They
ploughed, they sowed, they harrowed him in, throwed clods upon his
head, And these three men made a solemn vow, John
Barleycorn was dead.

Last verse

Here's John Barleycorn in the
nut brown bowl and cider in a can, But
John Barleycorn in the nut brown bowl will prove the strongest man.

2 And there he lay for some little time till the rains from heaven
   did fall,
   When little Sir John sprung up his head, made liars of them
   all.
   They let him stand till midsummer, when he grew both pale
   and wan,
   And little Sir John he growed a long beard, much like unto a
   man.

3 They hired men with scythes so sharp who cut him off at the
   knee;
   They rolled him and tied him by the waist and served him
   most barbarously.
   They hired men with sharp pitchforks who pricked him to the
   heart,
   But the loader he served him worse than that for he tied him
   to the cart.

4 They carried him away unto a barn, a prisoner to endure,
   But soon they fetched him out again and laid him on the
        floor.
   They hired men with crabtree sticks, who cut him skin from
        bones,
   But the miller he served him worse than that, for he ground
        him between two stones.

5 They flung him into a cistern deep, and drowned him in
        water clear,
   And the brewer he served him worse than that, for he brewed
        him into beer.
   Now barleycorn is the best of grain that ever was sown on
        land:
   It will do more than any other grain by the turning of your
        hand.

6 It will turn a boy into a man and a man into an ass,
   It will turn your gold into silver and your silver into brass.
   It will make the huntsman hunt the fox who never wound a
        horn,
   It will bring the tinker to the stocks, the people for to scorn.

7 Here's John Barleycorn in the nut-brown bowl and cider in a
        can,
   But John Barleycorn in the nut-brown bowl will prove the
        strongest man.

crabtree sticks: flails.

117   When Jones's Ale Was New

*A combination of good humour with a modicum of social comment seems to
have been a successful formula for this ancient convivial song, which can still
be occasionally heard from country singers. It was first published, as 'Jones ale
is newe', in 1594, though copies are extant only from the reprint of 1656.
There was a further publication, with a tune similar to those still current, in
d'Urfey's famous* Pills to Purge Melancholy *(vol. V, 1719, p. 61), when
the tradesmen mentioned were cobbler, broom-man, ragman, pedlar, hatter,
tailor, porter, shoemaker and weaver, with the addition of a Dutchman and a
Welshman. With considerable variation in its protagonists, the song remained
popular throughout the nineteenth century. Richard Jefferies in an early story
has a village mason who (appropriately) knows his own verse ('The Midsummer Hum', 1876).*

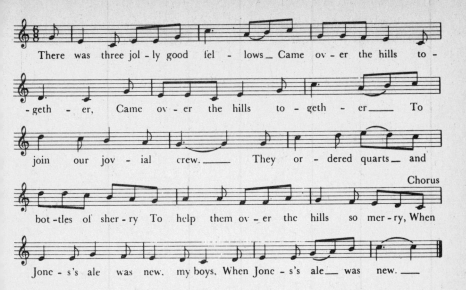

There was three jol-ly good fel-lows— Came ov-er the hills to-geth-er, Came ov-er the hills to-geth-er___ To join our jov-ial crew.___ They or-dered quarts— and bot-tles of sher-ry To help them ov-er the hills so mer-ry, When

Chorus

Jone-s's ale was new, my boys, When Jone-s's ale— was new. ___

2 The next to come in was a tinker
  And he was no small beer drinker, (2)
  To join our jovial crew.
  'Have you got any old pots and pans or kettles to fettle?
  My rivets are made of the very best metal
  And all your holes I very soon settle.'

3 The next to come in was a mason,
  His hammer it did want facing, (2)
  To join our jovial crew.
  He flung his mallet against the wall,
  He wished all the churches and chapels would fall;
  Then there would be work for us all.

4 The next to come in was a thatcher,
  No man couldn't be much fatter, (2)
  To join our jovial crew.
  He flung his old hat upon the ground
  And swore he'd spend just half a crown
  To drink the health of all around.

5 The next to come in was a dyer,
  He sat himself by the fire, (2)
  To join our jovial crew.
  The landlady told him to his face
  The chimney corner was his place,
  And there he could sit and dye his face.

195

6 The next to come in was a soldier
With a firelock on his shoulder, (2)
To join our jovial crew.
The landlady's daughter she came in,
He kissed her between the nose and the chin;
My word, the quarts of ale rolled in.

facing: '(?) fashioning' (note in MS).

118   The Barley Mow

*Dixon wrote in 1846 that 'This song is sung at country meetings in Devon
and Cornwall, particularly on completing the carrying of the barley, when the
rick, or mow of barley, is finished.' Some ten years later Chappell added that
it was still well known in many counties and in Hertfordshire 'frequently sung
by the countrymen in ale-houses after their daily labour.' A number of versions have been noted from oral tradition in recent years, and the song has
enjoyed a new lease of life as a favourite in folk song clubs.*

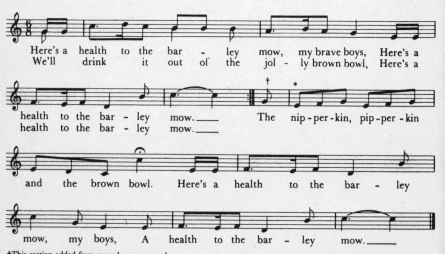

†This section added from second verse onwards.
*Repeat this bar as necessary.

2 We'll drink it out of the nipperkin, boys,
Here's a health to the barley mow.
The nipperkin, pipperkin and the brown bowl,
Here's a health to the barley mow, my boys,
A health to the barley mow.

196

3 We'll drink it out of the quarter-pint, boys . . .
The quarter-pint, nipperkin, *etc.*

4 We'll drink it out of the half a pint, boys . . .
The half a pint, quarter-pint, nipperkin, *etc.*

5 We'll drink it out of the pint, my brave boys . . .
The pint and the half a pint, quarter-pint, nipperkin, *etc.*

6 We'll drink it out of the quart, my brave boys . . .
The quart and the pint and the half a pint, quarter-pint,
nipperkin, *etc.*

7 We'll drink it out of the pottle, my boys . . .
The pottle, the quart and the pint and the half a pint,
quarter-pint, nipperkin, *etc.*

8 We'll drink it out of the gallon, my boys . . .
The gallon, the pottle, the quart and the pint and the half a
pint, quarter-pint, nipperkin, *etc.*

9 We'll drink it out of the half-anker, boys . . .
The half-anker, gallon, the pottle, the quart and the pint and
the half a pint, quarter-pint, nipperkin, *etc.*

10 We'll drink it out of the anker, my boys . . .
The anker, half anker, the gallon, the pottle, the quart and
the pint and the half a pint, quarter-pint, nipperkin, *etc.*

11 We'll drink it out of the half-hogshead, boys . . .
The half-hogshead, the anker, half-anker, the gallon, the
pottle, the quart and the pint and the half a pint,
quarter-pint, nipperkin, *etc.*

12 We'll drink it out of the hogshead, my boys . . .
The hogshead, half-hogshead, the anker, half-anker, the
gallon, the pottle, the quart and the pint and the half a
pint, quarter-pint, nipperkin, *etc.*

13 We'll drink it out of the pipe, my brave boys . . .
The pipe and the hogshead, half-hogshead, the anker,
half-anker, the gallon, the pottle, the quart and the pint
and the half a pint, quarter-pint, nipperkin, *etc.*

14 We'll drink it out of the well, my brave boys . . .
   The well and the pipe and the hogshead, half-hogshead, the
      anker, half-anker, the gallon, the pottle, the quart and
      the pint and the half a pint, quarter-pint, nipperkin, *etc.*

15 We'll drink it out of the river, my boys . . .
   The river, the well and the pipe and the hogshead,
      half-hogshead, the anker, half-anker, the gallon, the
      pottle, the quart and the pint and the half a pint,
      quarter-pint, nipperkin, *etc.*

16 We'll drink it out of the ocean, my boys,
   Here's a health to the barley mow.
   The ocean, the river, the well and the pipe and the hogshead,
      half-hogshead, the anker, half-anker, the gallon, the
      pottle, the quart and the pint and the half a pint,
      quarter-pint, nipperkin, pipperkin and the brown bowl,
   Here's a health to the barley mow, my boys,
   A health to the barley mow.

pottle: half-gallon.
anker: eight-gallon cask.

hogshead: 50-gallon cask.
pipe: cask holding two hogsheads.

119   The Punch Ladle

'Punch' comes from the Hindi word, panch *(five), because of its five ingredients, spirit, water, lemon-juice, sugar and spices. The word was first recorded in English in 1669, but I would estimate the song to date from about a century later. I cannot help feeling that it has overtones of smuggling, for customs duties were very high at that time, and ordinary people would seldom have been able to enjoy punch made from spirits acquired through legitimate channels. The mysterious last verse may well refer to a dead smuggler. This is speculation. What is sure, is that the song was popular in country districts long after the passing of the old smugglers. Alfred Williams, for example, found it 'fairly well known from Malmesbury to Oxford' in 1914–16 (Folk Songs of the Upper Thames, 1923, p. 88). He quotes this toast, which he heard recited at the end of the song: 'Here's to the large bee that flies so high./The small bee gathers the honey;/The poor man he does all the work/And the rich man pockets the money.'*

Come all you bold heroes, give an ear to my song, I'll
sing in the praise of good brandy and rum; There's a
clear, crystal fountain near England shall roll, Give
me the punch ladle, I'll fathom the bowl. I'll

Chorus

fathom the bowl, I'll fathom the bowl, Give
me the punch ladle, I'll fathom the bowl.

2 From France we get brandy, from Jamaica comes rum,
 Sweet oranges and lemons from Portugal come;
 Strong beer and good cider are England's control,
 Give me the punch ladle, I'll fathom the bowl.

3 My wife she comes in when I sit at my ease,
 She scolds and she grumbles and does all she please;
 She may scold and may grumble till she's black as a coal,
 Give me the punch ladle, I'll fathom the bowl.

4 My father he lies in the depths of the sea,
 With no stone at his feet – what matters for he;
 There's a clear, crystal fountain, near him it doth roll,
 Give me the punch ladle, I'll fathom the bowl.

stone: tomb-stone.

120 Good English Ale

In recent years campaigns for beer traditionally brewed and served have been very widely supported. One hopes that songs like this will help the good cause.

When I was a lit-tle 'un my fa-ther did say, 'When

ev-er the sun shines that's time to make hay: And

when hay is cart-ed, don't nev-er you fail To

rall. Chorus **slower**

drink farm-er's health in a pot of good ale.' Ale, ale,

good Eng-lish ale,— Filled up in pew-ter it tells its— own tale.

Some folks like rad-ish-es and some cur-ly kale, But

give I boiled pars-nips and a good dish of 'ta-ters, And a

lump of fat ba-con and a quart of good ale.

2 I pities tee-totallers, they drinks water neat;
It must rot their stomachs and give 'em damp feet.
I allus did say, a man couldn't get stale
On broad beans and bacon and pots of good ale.

3 When men goes to parliament their pledge for to keep,
They does nothing else but just sit there and sleep.
The next that I vote for will be a female,
If she'll keep awake with a pot of good ale.

121 Mowing Match Song

In the nineteenth century the men of the moorland area round Saddleworth, a wedge of Yorkshire projecting westwards into Lancashire, were renowned as mowers. 'Every lad', wrote the local poet, Ammon Wrigley (Songs of a

Moorland Parish, *Saddleworth, 1912)*, '*who had the wind and limb prided himself on his scythe-work. The hand-loom weaver on the hillside had generally a little farm attached to his loom, and his lads were taught to mow as soon as they had the strength to swing a scythe. . . . The best men . . . formed themselves into teams or "fleets". On Friarmere there was the "Black Fleet of Denshaw", and the "Light Fleet of Denshaw". The "fleet" system was simply the banding together of the crack mowers of the two valleys, which meant that where there was mowing to let they were almost certain to secure it.*'

In 1842 a contest was arranged between two crack scythemen for a prize of £10 – a very large sum at the time, to be won by the man able to mow the greater area in two hours. John Lawton ('Curly') was from the Friarmere (the old name for the Denshaw Valley), otherwise known as the Top End. His opponent was Thomas Winterbottom (Tom o' th' Fearnlee) of Greenfield, the champion of the Lower End. Wearing, as was the custom, only 'shirt and shoon', the mowers met at Brimmy Croft, 'in the long meadow which runs towards the Moorcock road at Marshbottom.' Unfortunately, however, the contest was badly organized. The ground was not staked out, so that the mowers worked rather haphazardly, avoiding heavy grass, and cutting into each other's path. After two hours, each had mowed over 3,000 square yards, but it was found impossible exactly to measure their respective amounts, and the match was declared void. Curly and the Top Enders appealed against the decision, claiming a win, but the result was not changed. The dispute was never settled, and there was quarrelling and bitterness between the two factions for many years afterwards. Perhaps Curly was the moral victor at least, since Tom o' th' Fearnlee had overtaxed his powers in the contest, and was never the same man again.

The 'man's song' about the match, so called because it was sung at barn dances after the women and children had gone home was written by Jack o' Racker's, a slubber working at the time at Slackcote Mills. Becket Whitehead of Delph still knew part of the song in 1952, and his text has been filled out here with some verses noted by Ammon Wrigley. Even so, the full epic has yet to be recovered.

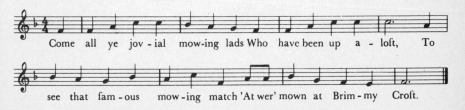

Come all ye jov-ial mow-ing lads Who have been up a-loft, To see that fam-ous mow-ing match 'At wer' mown at Brim-my Croft.

2 It wer' Curly up o' th' Freermere
   An' one fro' th' Lower End,
   An' what those lads did mow that day
   Ther's ne'er no two con mend.

3 Neaw Curly wer' a teamer mon
  For Millses, up i' th' wood;
  Among the Top End mowers
  Ther' wer' not one as good.

4 An' of o' the lads i' Frieslond
  'At shapped at mowing weel,
  Ther' one, coad Tom o' th' Fearnlee
  Could mak 'em lie at th' heel.

5 Fro' th' Gronge an' th' Castleshay they come,
  Sich likely lads, and strung,
  Wi' necks as red as feightin' cocks,
  An' backs as brod as lung.

6 Then Curly poo'ed his breeches off
  An' thrut 'em up o' th' wo'.
  Says one, 'Young Tom'll mak thee fain
  To doff thi shirt an' o'.'

7 Then Curly's wife come up i' th' thrung,
  'Neaw, Jack, my lad', said she,
  'If theaw gets licked wi' th' Lower End
  Theaw'll lie no more wi' me.'

8 They marched up to Denshaw
  Wi' their scythe-pows shoulder height;
  Says one, 'Ther's nowt i' th' Lower End
  Con oather mow or feight.'

9 Mony an owd trail hunter
  An' mony a rare owd hound,
  An' the finest lads at wrastlin'
  For fifty miles around.

10 An' o' those Shoredge tossers
   An' gambelers an' o',
   An' o' those Brewery weighvers
   Wer' sittin' in a row.

11 Ther' weren't a pheasun among 'em,
   They'd every one been tried;
   An' gam' wer' those fro' th' Castleshay
   An' th' same deawn Denshaw side.

12 Said Bill o' Breb's, 'Howd off a bit,
    Aw'd like yo' foak to know
    We'n browt a lad fro' th' Lower End
    To larn yo' heaw to mow.'

13 Says one, 'Theaw'll see when th' match is o'er,
    Theaw'll ha' no reawm to crow,
    For nowt 'at comes fro' th' Lower End
    Con oather feight or mow.'

14 Then Curly stepped into his grass
    An' cut just nine feet wide,
    An' made his scythe blade whistle wol –
    It wer' his country's pride.

15 Says one when Tom had cut a swathe,
    'That puts yo' i' th' shade;
    He maks the grass fair dance again
    To th' music of his blade.'

16 Neaw Curly wer' not satisfied
    Abeawt his measurement;
    He sent for Harry o' th' Turney Bonk
    But Yollow-breeches went.

Freermere: Friarmere.
no two con mend: no two can improve on.
teamer mon: waggoner.
Frieslond: Friesland.
shapped at: shaped at.
coad: called.
Gronge: Grange.
feightin': fighting.
poo'ed: pulled.
thrut 'em up o' th' wo': threw them up on
    the wall.
scythe-pows: scythe handles.
trail hunter: trail hunting, still carried on
    in some areas such as the Lake District,
    is cross country racing for hounds, fol-
lowing a scent made by rags, saturated
with oil of aniseed, dragged along the
ground.
tossers: players of pitch and toss.
gambelers: gamblers; mowing contests
    attracted heavy betting.
weighvers: weavers.
pheasun: faint-hearted one.
gam': game.
Harry o' th' Turney Bonk: Harry Buckley
    of Turney Bank, a great expert on
    'kesting' (estimating) the area mowed.
yollow-breeches: yellow-breeches, the
    nickname of another expert, called
    Shaw.

Becket Whitehead's tune is the first part of 'The Nutting Girl' (no. 72). If this is found
to be a little monotonous, the even-numbered verses can be sung to the second part of
the tune, with the original chorus added: 'An' what those lads did mow that
day./Ther's ne'er no two con mend.'

Wa'ney Cockfeightin' Sang

Long after it was outlawed in 1835 cock fighting retained a hold on the popular affection. Indeed, dark hints are dropped from time to time that it has continued in clandestine fashion until today. Eighteenth-century cockpits have been preserved at Welshpool (behind the National Westminster Bank) and in the Welsh National Folk Museum at St Fagan's, Cardiff.

At the Westmorland Musical Festival in 1905, John Collinson, the forty-three year-old village blacksmith from Casterton, won the prize with a local version of a cocking song once well-known throughout northern England, and dating probably from the early 1830s. Anne Gilchrist, who met Collinson in 1909, found out how he obtained the song from his father-in-law, a noted cockfighter in his time: 'Thinking this old song would have a good chance of obtaining a prize, he set off on foot from Casterton to Hutton Roof – a place of which they say "Out of the world, and then come Hutton Roofers". Alas, when he arrived, the old cocker . . . had forgotten the song. It was three days before his son-in-law's patience was rewarded by the return of the old man's memory. Then, secure with it in his own, the blacksmith brought the song home. But, as he remarked, it cost him more than the value of the prize in loss of work through absence.' ('Some Old Westmorland Folk-Singers', in Journal of the Lakeland Dialect Society, *no. 4, November, 1942, p. 8). She goes on to say that the chorus (which incidentally differs from the text given here) was 'sung with great energy and emphasis, being: 'With a hip and a hey, and a loud huzzay!/But the Black was t' strang for the Bonny Grey!' – with a curious kick-off like a hiccup from the second syllable of "bonny" which made it "bonny-y grey".'*

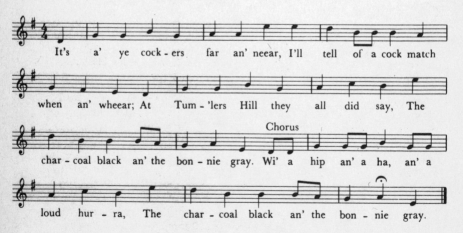

It's a' ye cock-ers far an' neear, I'll tell of a cock match when an' wheear; At Tum-'lers Hill they all did say, The char-coal black an' the bon-nie gray. Wi' a hip an' a ha, an' a loud hur-ra, The char-coal black an' the bon-nie gray.

2 When these two cocks com to be shewn
  The North Sceeal lads shouts 'We'll fight none;
  Reason's why', they all did say,
  'The charcoal black's t' big for the gray.

3 It's to the house t' tak a cup;
   This cock match it was soon made up.
   Ten guineas a side these cocks will play,
   The charcoal black an' the bonnie gray.

4 These cocks hedn't struck past two or three blows
   When Biggar lads cries, 'Now we lose',
   Which med 'em all both wan an' pale:
   They wished they'd fought for a gallon o' ale.

5 Miley Heslom com sweerin' down,
   He'd bet a guinea to a crown;
   If our black cock he gits fair play
   He'll drive off the sod the bonnie gray.

6 Now this black cock he hes lost,
   Which med Biggar lads to sweear and corss:
   They wished they'd nivver com that day
   T' Tum'lers Hill t' see the play.

Final chorus
Wi' a cooal black breast an' a silver wing
Six brothers of his fought befoor the king.
Wi' a hip an' a ha an' a loud hurra,
An' away they went wi' the bonnie gray.

Wa'ney: Walney Island, just off Barrow-
    in-Furness.
Tum'lers Hill: Tumbrel Hill.
North Sceeal: North Scale.

Biggar: village on the island.
Miley Heslom: Miles Haslam, a Barrow
    worthy.
sweerin': swaggering.

123 The Bell Ringing

The church bells are still part of the fibre of many English villages, with their tale of life and death, rejoicing and sorrow. The bell ringers, too, are still adding pages to the record books by their feats of skill and endurance. The tune of this song is based on the sound of bells, perhaps those of the village of Ashwater, on the west side of Dartmoor.

One day in Oc - to - ber, nei - ther drunk - en nor—
so - ber, O'er Broad - bu - ry Down I was wend - ing my
way; When I heard of some ring - ing, some danc - ing and
sing - ing, I ought to re - mem - ber that Ju - bi - lee
Day. *Chorus* 'Twas in Ash - wa - ter Town the bells they did
soun', They rang for a belt and a hat laced with
gold; But the men of North Lew rang so stea - dy and
true That there nev - er were bet - ter in Dev - on I'm told.

2 'Twas misunderstood, for the men of Broadwood
Gave a blow on the tenor should never have been;
But the men of North Lew rang so faultlessly true,
A difficult matter to beat them I ween.

3 They of Broadwood being naughty then said to our party,
'We'll ring you a challenge again in a round;
We'll give you the chance at St Stephen's or Launceston –
The prize to the winner's a note of five pound.'

Chorus
'Twas in Callington Town the bells next did soun',
They rang, *etc.*

4 When the match it came on at good Callington
The bells they rang out o'er the valleys below.
Then old and young people, the hale and the feeble,
They came out to hear the sweet bell music flow.

Chorus
'Twas at Callington Town the bells then did soun',
They rang, *etc.*

5 Those of Broadwood once more were obliged to give o'er,
They were beaten completely and done in a round.
For the men of North Lew pull so steady and true
That no better than they in the west can be found.

Chorus
'Twas at Ashwater Town, then at Callington Town,
They rang, *etc.*

Ashwater, North Lew, Broadwood (Widger): all villages near Broadbury Down, west of Dartmoor.
St Stephen's, Launceston, Callington: all in Cornwall.

124   I'Anson's Racehorse

The I'Ansons are a Yorkshire family, still in existence, and famous for an eighteenth century member, Frances, the lass of Richmond Hill, and for a whole series of racehorse trainers. The song may refer to William (1810–1881), despite calling him Charles since he was the most famous in the nineteenth century, with two Derby and two St Leger winners to his credit in the 1860s.

On the four - teenth day of Ju – ly last, A horse fair at__ New - mar - ket was, And ma – ny fine gen - tle -men [race] then did re - sort All for__ to see__ such live - ly sport. To my lad - dy O, pad - dy O, fal - de - dal, la - ra - di, do.__

2 There was a gentleman of great fame,
Charles I'Anson, Esquire, and that was his name;
And he had a kinsman who had got a mare
Called 'Little Dunee', with her cropped ears.

3 [He went to his kinsman and thus he did say,
  'I have matched your mare to run this day;
  I have matched your mare to run this day
  Against Mr Oliver's lively bay.'

4 'For fifty, for fifty', the little boy cries,
  I am afraid the mare will lose the prize.'
  'O no', says the uncle, 'I'm sure she will beat,
  For there is a guinea to a shilling against the first heat.'

5 The trumpet did sound and the drums did beat.
  Says the boy to his uncle, 'I'll lose the first heat.'
  'You know very well the good trim of your mare,
  You may lose the first heat if you think you dare.'

6 The gentlemen rode round the course,
  Betting their money on every post,
  Saying, 'I will lay you eight to five
  That the little dun mare will lose the prize.']

7 The jockeys were weighed, likewise the whips,
  And then the bold riders began for to strip;
  The little dun mare as I've heard say
  Carried twelve pounds more than the lively bay.

8 The gentlemen rode around the course,
  Saying one to another, 'Our money is lost.'
  Which made the bold gentlemen stamp and swear:
  'The devil take you and your little dun mare.'

9 [Now since my mare has won the race
  She shall not stop very long in this place;
  For she has won as much money this very day
  As my man can count and carry away.]

125   Hare Hunting Song

A hunter worth his salt usually feels considerable respect, sympathy and affection for his quarry. Such feelings are a little lacking here, though there is a certain admiration for the hare. In their fascinating book, The Leaping Hare *(Faber, 1972, p. 65), George Ewart Evans and David Thomson quote a*

Norfolk countryman on the respective merits of hare-coursing and hare hunting: 'I don't see coursing hounds so cruel as the hunting hounds. Because a coursing hound only runs a hare about two minutes at the most, and it's killed. They catch it nearly in the same field. Well, a hare hunt, that will last twenty minutes or half an hour; until that hare is racing about so it can't run any more. That's a terrible run! I once shot a hare running from the hounds. . . . Well, when I opened that hare I was never so much surprised. There wasn't a mite of blood in it! That blood was all gone to pink bubbles. She'd been chased for over a quarter of an hour and her blood was all gone to pink bubbles.'

The song first appeared in the Vocal Enchantress (1783), but this version was taken down by Frank Kidson from a Mr Cropper at the Westmorland Musical Festival in 1902. A still different text appears in a publication currently available, Songs of the Fell Packs (without date, place or imprint). There is a little note inside the cover: 'Traditional tunes are handed down vocally, while many other popular tunes can be adapted at will.'

The morn-ing looks charm-ing, all na-ture looks gay, Then a-
-way, my brave boys, to your hor-ses a-way; For that
pride of all plea-sures, in-quest-ing the hare, You___
have not so much as a mo-ment to spare.___ Lar-ri-li-day, li-
-day, li-day, li-lar-ri, li-lar-ri-li-day.___

2 Hark the lively tuned horn, how melodious it sounds,
   To the musical notes of the merry-mouthed hounds.
   In yon stubble field you will find her below;
   'See now', cries the huntsman, 'Hark to him, see now.'

3 See, see where she goes, and the hounds are in full view,
   Such harmony Handel himself never knew –
   Over the hedges and ditches, to us are no bounds,
   For the world is our own while we follow the hounds.

4 Over highlands and lowlands, through woodlands we fly,
  Our horses at full speed and our hounds at full cry;
  So matched in their speed and so equal they run,
  Like the turn of a spear or the rays of the sun.

5 When the old hands press forward 'tis a very sure sign
  That the hare, though a stout one, begins to decline;
  For a chase of two hours and more she has led:
  'She is down.' – 'Look about you.' – 'They have her.' – 'Ware
      dead.'

6 Then how glorious a death, to be honoured with sounds
  Of a horn and a shout and the chorus of hounds.
  Here's a health to all hunters and long be their lives;
  May they never be crossed by their sweethearts and wives.

126 The Huntsman

According to Barrett, this is 'a Northamptonshire song, often printed as a broadside or sheet song, and found in collections of sporting ditties dated from the first decade of the present century' (English Folk-Songs, 1891, p. 43). I obtained this version from Walter Pardon of Norfolk in 1978.

The sun had just peeped his head o'er the hills, The
plough boy is whist-ling a-cross the fields; The
birds are a-sing-ing so sweet on each spray; Said the
hunts-man to his hounds, 'Tal-ly ho, hark a-way.
Chorus Tal-ly
ho, hark a-way, tal-ly ho, hark a-way, Tal-ly
ho, tal-ly ho, tal-ly ho, hark a-way.'

2 'Come, my brave sportsmen, come, make no delay,
   Quick, saddle your horses and let's brush away;
   For the fox is in view and he's kindled with scorn,
   Come, my brave sportsmen, come, join the shrill horn.'

3 He led us a chase for sixteen long miles
   Over the hedges, over ditches, over gates, and over stiles.
   The huntsman came up with his musical horn:
   'We shall soon overtake him, for his brush drags along.'

4 He led us a chase six hours in full cry:
   Tally ho, hark away, now soon he must die.
   We will cut off his brush with a hallooing noise,
   And we'll drink a good success to all fox hunting boys.

127   We'll All Go A-hunting Today

What a fine hunt-ing day, it's as balm-y as May, When the
hounds to our vil-lage did come. Ev-ery friend will be there and all
trou-ble and care Will be left far be-hind them at home. See
ser-vants on steeds on their way___ And sports men in scar-let dis-
-play.___ Let us join the glad throng that goes laugh-ing a-long, And we'll

Chorus

all go a-hunt-ing to-day. So we'll all go a-hunt-ing to-
-day,___ All na-ture looks smil-ing and gay.___ Let us join the glad
throng that goes laugh-ing a-long, And we'll all go a-hunt-ing to-day.

211

2 Farmer Hodge to his dame says, 'I'm sixty and lame,
   Times are hard, yet my rent I must pay;
   But I don't care a jot if I raise it or not,
   For I must go a-hunting today.
   There's a fox in the spinny they say,
   We'll find him and have him away;
   I'll be first in the rush and I'll ride for his brush,
   For I must go a-hunting today.'

3 As the judge sits in court he gets wind of the sport
   And he calls the court to adjourn,
   As no witness had come and there's none left at home –
   They have gone with the hounds and the horn.
   Says he, 'Heavy fines you must pay
   If you will not your summons obey;
   But it's very fine sport so we'll wind up the court,
   And we'll all go a-hunting today.'

4 And the village bells chime, there's a wedding at nine,
   When the parson unites the fond pair.
   When he heard the sweet sound of the horn and the hound,
   And he knew it was time to be there.
   Says he, 'For your welfare I pray,
   I regret I no longer can stay:
   You've been safely made one, we must quickly be gone,
   For we must go a-hunting today.'

5 None were left in the lurch for all friends were at church
   With beadle and clerk, aye and all;
   All determined to go and to shout 'tally ho',
   And the ringers all joined in the rear.
   With bride and bridegroom in array
   They one to the other did say,
   'Let us join the glad throng that goes laughing along,
   And we'll all go a-hunting today.'

6 There's the doctor in boots to a breakfast that suits
   Of home-brewed ale and good beef.
   To his patients in pain says, 'I've come once again
   To consult you in hope of relief.'
   To the poor his advice he gave way,
   And the rich he prescribed them to pay,

But to each one he said 'You will quickly be dead
If you don't go a-hunting today.

7 'And there's only one cure for a malady, sure,
Which reaches the heart to adjure.
It's the sound of the horn on a fine hunting morn,
And where is the heart wishing more?
For it turneth the grave into gay,
Makes pain into pleasure give way,
Makes the old become young and the weak become strong,
If they'll all go a-hunting today.'

*This splendid celebration of the pleasures of fox-hunting will not please those
who oppose the sport. It was a firm favourite, from Cornwall to Cumberland,
in the early years of this century, having been written just about in between,
for the North Warwickshire Hunt. The composer was one W. Wilson, but I
have been unable to find any more details of him.*

VII

The Life of a Man:
Seasons and Ceremonies

'To him who acts with reason the beauty of all things doth appear': such a sentiment might have been penned by Rousseau himself. Although W. A. Barrett obtained the song (at Shoreham, Sussex) in the late nineteenth century, the picture of rural life which it gives seems to be one of pre-industrial, pre-enclosure innocence.

Come all you lads and las - ses, I'd have you give at - ten - tion To these few__ lines that I'm a - bout to write here. 'Tis of the four__ sea - sons of the year that I shall men - tion, The beau - ty of all things__ doth ap - pear. And now__ you are young__ and all in__ your pros-per - it - y, Come cheer up your hearts and re - vive like the spring. Join__ off in pairs like the birds in Feb- ru- ar - y That St. Val - en - tine's Day it__ forth do bring.

2 Then cometh Spring, which all the land doth nourish;
The fields are beginning to be decked with green.
The trees put forth their buds and the blossoms they do
flourish,
And the tender blades of corn on the earth are to be seen.
Don't you see the little lambs by the dams a-playing?
The cuckoo is singing in the shady grove.
The flowers they are springing, the maids they go a-Maying,
And in love all hearts seem now to move.

3 Then cometh Summer, and then to each beholder
  The fields are bedecked with hay and corn.
  The mower he goes forth with a scythe upon his shoulder
  And his bottle of beer so early in the morn.
  Then harvest days, when everyone must labour and must
      swelter,
  The reaper, the mower, the farmer comes along
  To cut down the corn and to lay it in the shelter,
  And at night drink a health with a merry song.

4 Next cometh Autumn with the sun so hot and piercing;
  The sportsman goes forth with his dog and his gun
  To fetch down the woodcock, the partridge and the pheasant,
  For health and for profit as well as for fun.
  Behold, with loaded apple-trees the farmer is befriended,
  They will fill up his casks that have long laid dry.
  All nature seems to weary now, her task is nearly ended,
  And more of the seasons will come by and by.

5 Next cometh Winter when outdoor work's suspended;
  The thatcher and the thresher go to work in the barn,
  Their coats new and thick, or with flannel neatly mended,
  Each follows his task to keep himself warm.
  'Tis very cold and pinching, the air is fresh and chilly,
  All streams they are bound up by ice and by frost.
  All nature seems decayed instead of reviving,
  The beauty of all things appears to be lost.

6 When night comes on with song and tale we pass the wintry
      hours;
  By keeping up a cheerful heart we hope for better days.
  We tend the cattle, sow the seed, give work unto the
      ploughers,
  And with patience wait till winter yields before the sun's fair
      rays.
  And so the world goes round and round, and every time and
      season
  With pleasure and with profit crowns the passage of the year.
  And so through every time of life, to him who acts with
      reason
  The beauty of all things doth appear.

St Valentine's Day: it was believed that the birds chose their mates on this day.

215

129   What's the Life of a Man?

Memento mori: the feeling here is poignant, and reminiscent of the expression of the transitory nature of human life found in a number of seasonal songs, and in some epitaphs. The song appeared on broadsides in the nineteenth century under the title of 'The Fall of the Leaf', though it was considerably improved by the refining and polishing action of oral circulation. Oral versions remain popular with country singers, the most recent recording having been made by Harry Holman of Copthorne, Sussex, who completes his performance with this toast: 'Time like an ever-flowing streams rolls on,/And could we judge the time aright/We would split an arrow in its flight,/And we should be as one' (When Sheepshearing's Done, Topic 12TS254, 1975). The version given here was collected by Vaughan Williams in Wiltshire in 1904.

As —— I was a-walk-ing one morn— at my ease, A-
Chorus What's the life of a man an-y more— than a leaf, For

view - ing the leaves as they fell from the trees, Their——
man— has a sea - son and why should he grieve? Be - -

rol - ling, full mo - tion ap - peared— fine and gay, Like the
- low in the wide world he ap - pears— fine and gay, Like the

leaf they must with - er and soon fade a - way.
leaf he shall with - er and soon fade a - way.

2 If you seen the green leaves a short time ago,
  A rolling full motion appearing to grow;
  But the frost came upon them and withered them all.
  Like the leaf he must wither and down he must fall.

3 If you look in yonder churchyard many names there you'll
    see,
  They went from this world like a leaf from a tree.
  Afflicted and wounded at least they must fall:
  Like the green leaf it did wither and down it did fall.

Apple Tree Wassail

'On Twelfth Eve, in Devonshire, it is customary for the farmer to leave his warm fireside, accompanied by a band of rustics, with guns, blunderbusses, etc., presenting an appearance which at other times would be somewhat alarming. Thus armed, the band proceed to an adjoining orchard, where is selected one of the most fruitful and aged of the apple trees, grouping round which they stand and offer up their invocations in the following doggerel rhyme: "Here's to thee,/Old apple tree!/Whence thou mayst bud,/And whence thou mayst blow,/And whence thou mayst bear/Apples enow:/Hats full,/Caps full,/Bushels,/bushels, sacks full,/And my pockets full, too!/Huzza! huzza!" The cider-jug is then passed around, and, with many a hearty shout, the party fire off their guns, charged with powder only, amidst the branches' (Illustrated London News, 11 January, 1851). Similar ceremonies were carried out in at least eleven English counties (Cornwall, Devon, Gloucestershire, Herefordshire, Kent, Shropshire, Somerset, Surrey, Sussex and Worcestershire), and still are carried out at Trusham (Devon) and Roadwater and Carhampton (Somerset), the last two on Old Twelfth Night (17 January).

Down in___ the lane __ there sits an old fox, A-
-mouch-ing and lick-ing his dir-ty old chops.
[munch-ing?]

2 Shall we go catch him, my boys if we can?
   Ten thousand to one if we catch him or none.

3 Catch him or none, catch him or none,
   Ten thousand to one if we catch him or none.

4 Wassail, wassail all over the town,
   Our cup it is white and our ale it is brown.

5 The great dog of Langport has burnt off his tail,
   And this is the night we go singing wassail.

6 I will go home to old mother Joan
   And tell her to put on a big marrow bone.

7 Boil it and boil it and skim off the scum,
   And we will have porridge when we do go home.

8 Wassail, wassail all over the town,
Our cup it is white and our ale it is brown.

(Spoken)
Bud, blossom, bloom and bear,
Ready to tear,
So that we shall have apples and cider next year.

Hat fulls, cap fulls, three bushel bag fulls,
Little heap under the stair,
Cider running out gutter holes.
Hip, hip, hurrah.

Our cup it is white: wassail bowls were sometimes made of ash or beech.
The great dog of Langport: this may be a reference to the defeat of the Danes at Langport in 993.

131   Shrove Tuesday Song

On Shrove Tuesday or the day before, children used to go round 'shroving' or 'Lent-crocking'; in other words, collecting anything towards a feast of pancakes which villagers cared to give. They announced themselves with a little song. This one, to a variation on 'Pop Goes the Weasel', was sung at Baldon, Oxfordshire.

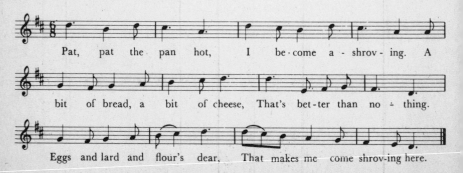

Pat, pat the pan hot, I be-come a-shrov-ing. A
bit of bread, a bit of cheese, That's bet-ter than no - thing.
Eggs and lard and flour's dear, That makes me come shrov-ing here.

132   Pace Egging Song

'Pace' is from the Latin word for Easter, and pace egging was the practice of collecting eggs and other eatables by touring the houses and farms in one's locality. Little groups of men would either perform a pace egg play (like other seasonal plays, a semi-ritual enactment of death and rebirth), or would dress as some of the characters and present themselves simply with a song. St George, Admiral Nelson, Lord Collingwood, Mrs Pankhurst: these are just a few of the wide range of possibilities. These practices were largely confined to the north-western counties of Cheshire, Lancashire, Westmorland, Cumberland, and parts of Yorkshire, where some remains of pace egging can still be found. This song comes from Marple in Cheshire, where Mr Arthur Hulme remembered it being sung by children between 1895 and 1900.

Here comes three or four jov-ie lads, all in a row. We've [of one mind] come a pace eg-gin', we hope you'll prove kind. Prove kind, prove kind, with your eggs and small beer, We hope you'll re-mem-ber it's pace eg-gin' time. For the *Chorus* did-dle dol, for the day, for the did-dle dol de day.

2 The next that comes in is Lord Nelson, you see,
With a bunch of blue ribbon tied under the knee;
With a star on his breast, like a diamond do shine,
I hope, *etc.*

3 The next that comes in is the miner, you see,
With his round hat and candle he works underground;
He works underground to get neighbour's coal,
At six in the morning he pops down yond hole.

With his round hat and candle: this reference must take the verse back to at least 150 years ago, and probably indicates that the song is even older.

Swinton May Song

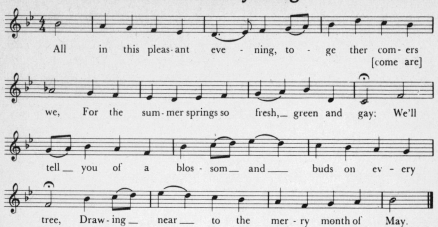

All in this pleas-ant eve - ning, to - ge ther com- ers
[come are]
we, For the sum- mer springs so fresh,_ green and gay: We'll
tell _ you of a blos - som _ and _ buds on ev - ery
tree, Draw-ing _ near _ to the mer - ry month of May.

2 Rise up, the master of this house, put on your chain of gold,
  We hope you're not offended [with] your house we make so
      bold.

3 Rise up, the mistress of this house, with gold along your
      breast,
  And if your body be asleep we hope your soul's at rest.

4 Rise up, the children of this house, all in your rich attire,
  For every hair upon your head shines like the silver wire.

5 God bless this house and harbour, your riches and your store;
  We hope the Lord will prosper you, both now and evermore.

6 So now we're going to leave you in peace and plenty here,
  For the summer springs so fresh, green and gay;
  We shall not sing you May again until another year,
  For to draw you these cold winters away.

Swinton: in South Lancashire; then a hamlet.
harbour: arbour (?).

'While reading one evening towards the close of April, 1861', wrote a correspondent (John Harland) in Chambers' Book of Days, *'I was on a sudden
aware of a party of waits or carollers who had taken their stand on the lawn in
my garden, and were serenading the family with a song. There were four
singers, accompanied by a flute and clarinet; and together they discoursed most
simple and rustic music. . . . Inquiry resulted in my obtaining from an old*

'Mayer' the words of two songs, called by the singers themselves 'May Songs', though the rule and custom are that they must be sung before the first day of May. . . . He says that the Mayers usually commence their singing rounds about the middle of April, though some parties start as early as the beginning of the month. The singing invariably ceases on the evening of the 30th April' (vol. I, 1862, p. 546).

134   Peterborough May Song

One of the classic descriptions of the May revels of old is from the horrified pen of Philip Stubbes: 'Against May, Whitsonday, or other time, all the young men and maids, old men and wives, run gadding over night to the woods, groves, hills and mountains, where they spend all the night in pleasant pastimes; and in the morning they return, bringing with them birch and the branches of trees, to deck their assemblies withal. . . . I have heard it credibly reported (and that viva voce) by men of great gravity, that of forty, or a hundred maids going to the wood overnight, there have scarcely the third part of them returned home undefiled. These be the fruits which these cursed pastimes bring forth' (Anatomie of Abuses, written in 1583). It is a far cry from such full-blooded sport to the children's garlands of recent times, though something of the antic passion remains in the May Day ceremonies at Padstow in Cornwall.

'The May Day Garlands are of various forms,' wrote Charles Dack, 'those in Peterborough are formed of two hoops fastened together to form a globe and a stick or stave through the centre. The hoops are decorated with flowers and ribbons, and when the children possess one, the best doll is fixed on the stick inside the garland. Two girls carry the garland which is carefully covered with a white cloth. This is lifted at the houses and the wondrous garland is exposed while the children sing the following song, which is the favourite May Day song in the city' (Weather and Folk Lore of Peterborough and District, 1911).

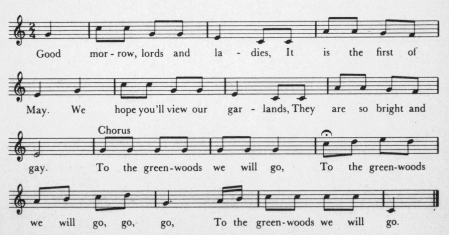

Good mor-row, lords and la-dies, It is the first of May. We hope you'll view our gar-lands, They are so bright and gay. *Chorus* To the green-woods we will go, To the green-woods we will go, go, go, To the green-woods we will go.

2 This bunch of May it looks so gay,
  Before your door it stands;
  It is but a sprout but it's well spread out
  By the work of our Lord's hands.

3 The cuckoo sings in April,
  The cuckoo sings in May;
  The cuckoo sings in June,
  In July she flies away.

4 I'm very glad the spring has come,
  The sun shines out so bright;
  The little birds upon the trees
  Are singing for delight.

5 The roads are very dusty,
  Our shoes are very thin;
  We have a little money box to put our money in.

135 Helston Furry Dance

The people of Helston still celebrate the coming of spring, and by one of those curious quirks of fortune, their melody achieved 'top of the pops' status nationwide, in 1978. Under the title of 'Cornish May Song', it was first published in 1802 in Edward Jones's Bardic Museum, *with these comments: 'The inhabitants of Cornwall, being a remnant of the Ancient Britons, still retain some of their ancient customs, as the Welsh do. This old traditional ballad is the source of conviviality to the inhabitants of the town and neighbourhood of Helston, in Cornwall, where it is always sung, and universally danced by them, on the eighth of May, when they hail the summer with peculiar rejoicings, rural revelry, festivity, and mirth. . . . The custom now is this: at break of day, the commonalty of Helston go into the fields and woods, to gather all kinds of flowers, to decorate their hats and bosoms, to enjoy the flowery meads, and the cheruping (sic) of the birds; and during their excursions, if they find any person at work, they make him ride on a pole, carried on men's shoulders, to the river, over which he is to leap in a wide place, if he can; if he cannot, he must leap in, for leap he must, or pay money. After this rustic sport is over, they then return to the town, and bring their flowery garlands or summer home (hawthorn boughs, sycamore, &c.). They then form themselves into various dancing groups with the lasses, and they jig it, hand in hand, all over the town; claiming a right of dancing through any person's house, in at one door, and out at the other, and so through the garden: thus they continue . . . until it is dark.'*

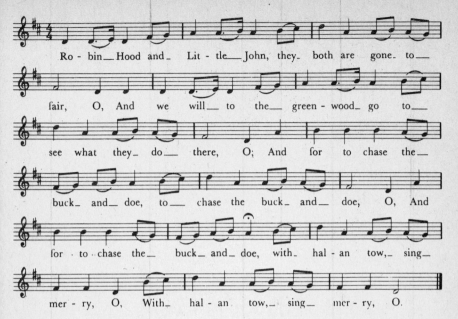

Ro - bin — Hood and — Lit - tle — John, they — both are gone — to —
fair, O, And we will — to the — green - wood — go to —
see what they — do — there, O; And for to chase the —
buck — and — doe, to — chase the buck — and — doe, O, And
for · to · chase the — buck — and — doe, with — hal - an tow, — sing —
mer - ry, O, With — hal - an tow, — sing — mer - ry, O.

2 We were up as soon as day for to fetch the summer home, O,
The summer and the May, O, for summer is a-come, O;
And winter is a-gone, O, and summer is a-come, O,
And winter is a-gone, O, with halan, *etc.*

3 Those Frenchmen they make such a boast, they shall eat the
grey goose feather, O,
And we will eat up all the roast in very land where'er we go;
And we will eat up all the roast: sing halan, *etc.*

4 Saint George next shall be our song, Saint George he was a
knight, O;
Of all the kings in Christendom King Georgie is the right, O.
In every land that e'er we go, sing halan tow and George, O,
Sing halan tow and Georgie, O.

5 Bless Aunt Mary with power and might; God send us peace
in merry England;
Pray send us peace both day and night, for ever more in
merry England.
Pray send us peace both day and night: with halan tow, sing
merry, O,
With halan two, sing merry, O.

Furry: the word is derived either from the Middle English word, *ferrie,* implying a church festival, or from the Celtic, *feur,* meaning a holiday or fair.
halan: calends (first of month).
tow: garland.

223

136   Bell Tune

Beltane (of which word the title of this song may be a corruption) was the Celtic festival which began on May Eve (30 April, or, in the case of the old-style calendar, 11 May). Fairies, evil spirits and witches were thought to be particularly active at that time, and to ward off their influence, greenery was strewn on the thresholds of houses and mountain ash crosses were placed over the doors. For the same purpose, fires were lit on the hills and in the fields, the smoke from which had the additional benefit of purifying the cattle and crops. On May Day itself there was a mock battle between the forces of winter and those of summer, with the latter invariably winning.

The meaning of the song seems to be that a girl is tempted to join in a witches' orgy, but is saved by the young man who agrees to marry her. It was sung at Stockenbrig, St Michael's-on-Wyre, in the Fylde, a remote part of Lancashire, between 1849 and 1853, both on May Days and at Lammas (1 August, three months later). It was first published in 1936, and caused some eyebrows to be raised by its exoticism. The collector M. W. Myres, added this information two years later, partly in response to the suggestion that his tune was surprisingly similar to that of 'Buffalo Girls', an American song popular in the mid-nineteenth century (which, incidentally, enjoyed a new vogue in the late 1940s): 'I 'collected' it in this way. I have a friend with, fortunately, a particularly retentive memory. She had often heard her father sing this song, and was told by him how he and several others used to sing it at St Michael's-on-Wyre in the Fylde. I have the names of several of them. I knew that the tune is said not to be the original one . . . Some of the singers belonged to families that had come from Sutherlandshire, for horse breeding or to bring sheep and cattle for the fells. This may push the origin back into Scotland, but the song was sung at St Michael's. Old John Crampton, the singer that I knew well, was descended on his mother's side from the Raes. . . . As regards date of singing, I gather that May-day and Lammas were regular times . . . , but it was also sung when the young fellows got together at other times.'

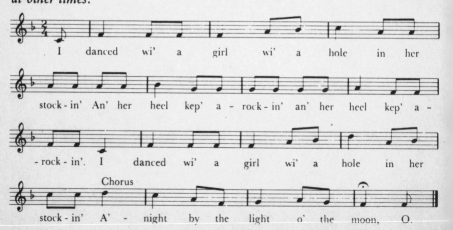

2 We'd a mind to tak the wood, but she dang it were accursed,
   An' she dang it were awakken, an' she dang it were awakken.
   We'd a mind to take the wood, but she dang it were accursed.

3 We dangled on a stane an' it lifted an' it thwacken,
   An' it lifted an' it moaned, an' it lifted an' it moaned.
   We dangled on a stane an' it lifted an' it thwacken.

4 She shivered on my shooder an' she clung my necken closer,
   An' she clung my soul to freeten, an' she clung my soul to
      freeten.
   She shivered on my shooder an' she clung my necken closer.

5 She ran me 'hint the clearin' an' we watched the folk
      a-dancin',
   An' her mither were a-prancin', an' her mither were
      a-prancin'.
   She ran me 'hint the clearin' an' we watched the folk
      a-dancin'.

6 Their heids were clad as beasties an' she cried her fayther
      nozzlin',
   An' she speired her brither ruttin', an' she speired her brither
      ruttin'.
   Their heids were clad as beasties an' she cried her fayther
      nozzlin'.

7 She had soul as white as Mary an' nae sinner yet had touched
      her,
   An' she clung 'til me to wed her, an' she clung 'til me to wed
      her.
   She had soul as white as Mary an' nae sinner yet had touched
      her.

8 'Fore the light wi' dark had striven I had dang her for my
      wife,
   An' I took her soul for life, an' I took her soul for life.
   'Fore the light wi' dark had striven I had dang her for my
      wife,
   God ha' benison upon the moon, O.

tak the wood: go to the woods?   *'hint:* behind.
she dang: she swore.   *speired:* saw.

225

137   The Mallard

At a harvest home, when men relaxed in triumph after the safe gathering of the crops, songs might well have been sung to celebrate bountiful creatures like the little mallard, which provided good eating and perhaps stood as a symbol for the fruitfulness of nature. This is a Berkshire version of the song, taken down in 1907 by W. G. Arkwright, who had it from his 'wife's uncle, the Rev. Maunsell Bacon, vicar of Swallowfield, who knew it from a boy at Lambourn Woodlands near Hungerford, and afterwards wrote it down from the dictation of the original singer.'

O I have a-yut. O what have I yut? I've a-
-yut the toe o' my mal-lard.   'Tis a toe-toe,
nip-pens and all, O I have a-yut o' my mal-lard-y O, So
good a mit woo my mal-lard.   A voot-voot, a toe-toe.

*Second and subsequent verses continue with this section as shown, repeating it as often as necessary.

2   O I have a-yut. O what have I yut?
     I've a-yut the voot o' my mallard.
     A voot-voot, a toe-toe, nippens and all,
     O I have a-yut o' my mallardy O,
     So good a mit was my mallard.

3 Leg   4 Thigh   5 Hip   6 Rump   7 Side   8 Wing
     9 Back   10 Neck   11 Head   12 Eye   13 Bill

14   O I have a-yut. O what have I yut?
     I've a-yut the tongue o' my mallard.
     A tongue-tongue, a bill-bill, an eye-eye, a head-head, a
         neck-neck, a back-back, a wing-wing, a side-side, a
         rump-rump, a hip-hip, a thigh-thigh, a leg-leg, a
         voot-voot, a toe-toe,
     Nippens and all,
     O I have a-yut o' my mallardy O,
     So good a mit was my mallard.

yut: ate.   *So good a mit:* so good as it was.

Far back in history, songs such as this were presumably connected with animal sacrifice and fertility ritual. (Not that they can be traced back very far: the earliest version of this song, better known as 'The Red Herring' or 'The Jolly Herring', is in a manuscript of 1831). Little trace of solemnity now remains, and we are left with a convivial song of tongue-twisting virtuosity. Oddly enough, there must have been a more literal meaning at one time, since the red herring was once a staple of the diet of the poor. A further irony is that the 'king of the fish' is now becoming a rare and expensive delicacy. The singer was Johnny Doughty, a Brighton fisherman, born in 1903. The words italicised were spoken.

*Repeat these bars as necessary

3 Herrings' *backs* – fishing smacks.
4 Herrings' *fins* – needles and pins.
5 Herrings' *bellies* – jam and jellies.
6 Herrings' *tails* – buckets and pails.

7 But what shall we do with the herrings' *guts*?
Turn them into comic cuts.
Herrings' guts – comic cuts,
Herrings' tails – buckets and pails,
Herrings' bellies – jam and jellies,
Herrings' fins – needles and pins,
Herrings' backs – fishing smacks,
Herrings' eyes – puddings and pies,
Herrings' heads – loaves of bread and all such things.

139   Souling Song

All Souls' Day (2 November) was instituted in A.D. 993 as an occasion when the faithful might alleviate the sufferings of souls in purgatory by prayer and almsgiving. On this day and its eve people used to go about asking for alms (often in the form of specially baked soul cakes), reinforcing their requests with chants, songs, and plays. As with many traditional observances, souling is now a children's activity (and confined to parts of Shropshire and Cheshire), but adult performances of the soulers' play still go on in due season, especially at Antrobus in Cheshire. This song comes from Middlewich in the same county.

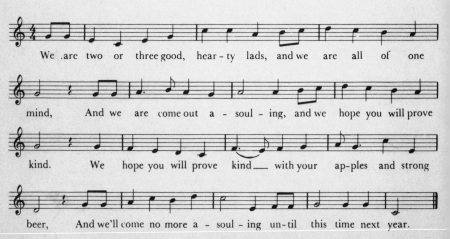

We are two or three good, hear-ty lads, and we are all of one mind, And we are come out a-soul-ing, and we hope you will prove kind. We hope you will prove kind— with your ap-ples and strong beer, And we'll come no more a-soul-ing un-til this time next year.

2 Step down into your cellar and see what you can find;
  If your barrels be empty we hope you'll prove kind.
  We hope you'll prove kind with your apples and strong beer,
  And we'll come no more a-souling until this time next year.

3 God bless the master of this house, the mistress also;
  God bless his sons and daughters that round his table go.
  We hope you will prove kind with your apples and strong
      beer,
  And we'll come no more a-souling until this time next year.

4 God bless his men and maidens, his cattle and his store,
  And all that lie within your gates, we wish you ten times
      more.
  We wish you ten times more with your apples and strong
      beer,
  And we'll come no more a-souling until this time next year.

140   The Old Horse

Prologue

By leave, you gen-tle-men all, Your par-don I do crave, For mak-ing bold to come To see what sport you'll have.

Song

This is my poor old horse that has car-ried me ma-ny a mile, O-ver hed-ges, o-ver dit-ches, o-ver high barred gate and stile; But now he has grown old—and his na-ture does de-cay,— He's forced to snap at the short-est grass that grows a-long— the way.

Chorus

Poor old horse! Poor old horse!

Prologue

2 There's more in company,
  They're following close behind;
  They've sent us on before,
  Admittance for to find.

3 These blades they are but young,
  Never acted here before;
  They'll do the best they can,
  And the best can do no more.

Song

2 His coat it was once of the linsey-woolsey fine,
  His mane it grew at length and his body it did shine;
  His pretty little shoulders that were so plump and round,
  They're both worn out and aged, I'm afraid he is not sound.

3 His keep it was once of the best of corn and hay
  That ever grew in cornfields or in the meadows gay,
  But now into the open fields he is obliged to go,
  To stand all sorts of weather, either rain or frost or snow.

4 His hide unto the tanner I will so freely give,
  His body to the dogs; I would rather him die than live.
  So we'll hang him, whip him, strip him, and a-hunting let
      him go,
  He's neither fit to ride upon or in the team to draw.

Last chorus
Poor old horse! Let him die!

At Christmas a play called 'The Old Horse' was performed in several counties by mummers going from door to door. In Nottinghamshire and Derbyshire the players had 'the skull of a horse, painted black and red, and supported on a wooden fore-leg. A man in a stooping posture, and covered with a cloth, represents the body of the horse, and, from the inside, snaps its formidable jaws at the company' (M. H. Mason, Nursery Rhymes and Country Songs, 1878, p. 49). In Yorkshire there was 'great noise and histrionic display' and 'Young women pretend to be frightened at the way in which the horse opens his wide jaws, and the awful manner in which he clashes them together' (S. O. Addy, A Glossary of Words used in the Neighbourhood of Sheffield, 1888, p. 164). The essential feature of the play was the death and resurrection of the horse. There was little solemnity, indeed, there was a great deal of knockabout fun, but for all that the ritual and the song have profound reverberations.

Six Jolly Miners

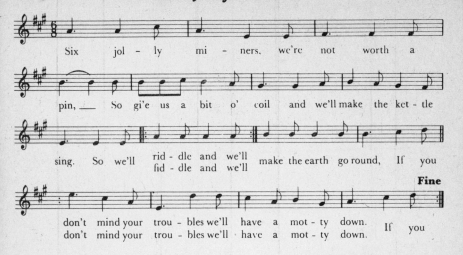

Six jol - ly mi - ners, we're not worth a pin, __ So gie us a bit o' coil and we'll make the ket - tle sing. So we'll rid - dle and we'll / fid - dle and we'll make the earth go round, If you

don't mind your trou - bles we'll have a mot - ty down.
don't mind your trou - bles we'll have a mot - ty down.   If you

Fine

2 Two came from Derby and two from Derby town;
  The others came from Oughtibridge, and they all came
      rolling down.
  So we'll riddle, *etc.*

3 Come on you jolly colliers and put your jackets on,
  We work for Newton Chambers and he's a gentleman.
  Chambers in his chariot, Newton's in his gig,
  Hairs on a donkey's back and bristles on a pig. (2)

Not worth a pin: have no money.
coil: coal.
motty: metal tally which a miner attached to a tub of coal which he had hewn so that his earnings could be credited accordingly.
Oughtibridge: village north-west of Sheffield, on the Penistone road.
Newton Chambers: former mine owners.

In some of the villages north of Sheffield, 'Jolly Minering' was a house-visiting custom, carried on between Christmas Eve and New Year's Day. Small groups of children would go round, their faces blackened with coal dust, wearing an old jacket and cap, and carrying shovels, picks and a riddle. One would carry a lantern (generally a candle in a jam jar) and a tin in which to collect money. They would knock on the door, and then sing, while doing the actions of picking, shovelling and riddling. They sang a somewhat corrupt fragment of a longer ballad in praise of miners which is still found in some parts of the country in a full, but non-ritual form. (See for example, Bob Copper, Songs and Southern Breezes, Heinemann, 1973, p. 286). *By a curious reversal of the common hand-me-down process, while the children's traditional observance has declined, the song has been taken up by adults and* sung in carol sessions at public houses in the locality mentioned. This version was recorded at Ecclesfield in 1973, and may be heard, together with the carols of the area, on the record, A People's Carol (*Leader LEE 4065, 1974*).

142   The Fleecy Care

Many villages have carols which they claim as their own. In some cases, these are local variants of standard items; in others, survivors from now-forgotten hymns; and occasionally, genuinely unique. This one, which comes, I believe, into the last category, is from the village of Napton in Warwickshire.

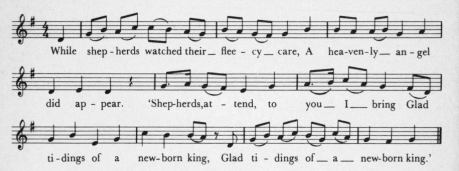

While shep-herds watched their— flee-cy— care, A hea-ven-ly— an-gel did ap-pear. 'Shep-herds, at-tend, to you— I— bring Glad ti-dings of a new-born king, Glad ti-dings of— a— new-born king.'

2 'In Bethlehem's town this blessed morn
   A Saviour of mankind is born;
   Born of a spotless virgin pure,
   Free from all sin and guile secure. (2)

3 'In swaddling clothes this babe behold,
   No costly garb his limbs enfold.
   Laid in a manger, there you will find
   The great redeemer of mankind. (2)

4 'Arise, your tender care forsake;
   With hasty steps your journey take
   To David's city – there you will see
   The pattern of humanity. (2)

5 'To save us from eternal death
   The great Messiah came to earth.
   Then let us with united voice
   Sing, Alleluia, all rejoice.' (2)

'By many European peoples', wrote Sir James Frazer, '— the ancient Greeks and Romans, the modern Italians, Spaniards, French, Germans, Dutch, Danes, Swedes, English, and Welsh — the wren has been designated the king, the little king, the king of birds, the hedge king, and so forth, and has been reckoned among those birds which it is extremely unlucky to kill. . . . Notwithstanding such beliefs, the custom of annually killing the wren has prevailed widely both in this country and in France. . . . Down to the present time the 'hunting of the wren' still takes place in parts of Leinster and Connaught (in Ireland). On Christmas Day or St Stephen's Day the boys hunt and kill the wren, fasten it to the middle of a mass of holly and ivy on the top of a broomstick, and on St Stephen's Day (26 December) go about with it from house to house, singing: "The wren, the wren, the king of all birds,/St Stephen's Day was caught in the furze;/Although he is little, his family's great,/I pray you, good landlady, give us a treat." Money or food (bread, butter, eggs, etc.) were given them, upon which they feasted in the evening' (Golden Bough, 1 vol. ed. Macmillan, 1963 (originally 1922), pp. 536–7).

In England such rituals died out in the nineteenth century, but the song survived. This version is from Edmund Hawkins, a singer and morris dancer, of Adderbury, Oxfordshire. When he sang 'every one' 'he stamped violently, so much so that his wife asked him to be quiet, but he said that was the right way and it reminded him of old times.'

2 'What shall us shoot?' says Richard to Robin.
'What shall us shoot?' says Robin to Bobbin.
'What shall us shoot?' says Jonathan Young.
'What shall us shoot?' boys every one.

3 'I see a wren.'

4 'We'll all shoot together.'

5 'She's down, she's down.'

6 'How shall us get her home?'

7 'We'll borrow feyther's cart.'
Or, 'We must hire a waggon.'

8 'How shall us get her in?'

9 'We must hire some ropes.'

10 'We'll all heave together.'

11 'How shall us cook her?'

12 'We'll buy a furnace.'

13 'We must hire a cook.'

14 'What shall us give her?'

15 'We must give her the feathers.'

16 'That won't be enough.'

17 'We must give her the bones.'

18 'The feathers will choke her.'

19 'The feathers have choked her.'

20 'So the poor cook is dead.'

21 'What shall us do wi' the braath?' [broth]

22 'Gi'e 't the poor o' the parish.'

Presumably, the appropriate question is missing before verses 10, 11 and 13.

144　　The Grampound Wassail

'Wassail' derives from the Anglo-Saxon wes hal, *meaning 'be whole' (cf. 'hale and hearty' in modern English) or 'be of good health'. The wassailers with their drinking bowl and their joyful songs toured the households and farms at Christmastide, bringing good luck for the coming year. They still linger in a few places, especially in the West Country. This song comes from the village of Grampound, in Cornwall, where it is still sung, as can be seen from Paul Jennings,* The Living Village, Hodder, 1968, p. 80.

Was-sail, was-sail, was-sail, __ was-sail! And joy __ come to __ our jol-ly was-sail. Now __ here at this house we first will be seen. To drink the king's health such a cus-tom has been; Now un-to the mas-ter we'll drink his good health, We hope he may pros-per in vir-tue and wealth. With our __ was-sail, was-sail, was-sail, was-

Dal Segno

-sail __ and joy. Was-sail __ and joy __ to our jol-ly was-sail.

2 In a friendly manner this house we salute,
　For it is an old custom, you need not dispute;
　Ask not the reason from where it did spring,
　For you know very well it's an old ancient thing.

3 Now here at your door we orderly stand
　With our jolly wassail and our hats in our hand.
　We do wish you good health unto master and dame,
　To children and servants we do wish the same.

4 It has been the custom, as I've been told
　By ancient housekeepers in days of old,
　When young men and maidens together draw near
　They fill up our bowls with cider or beer.

5 Come fill up our wassail bowl full to the brim,
　See, harnessed and garnished so neat and so trim,
　Sometimes with laurel and sometimes with bays
　According to custom to keep the old ways.

Pause for drink

6 Methinks I do smile to see the bowl full,
 Which just now was empty and now filled do grow
 By the hands of good people, long may they remain
 And love to continue the same to maintain.

7 Now neighbours and strangers we always do find
 And hope we shall be courteous, obliging and kind;
 And hope your civility to us will be proved
 As a piece of small silver in token of love.

Pause for collection

8 We wish you great plenty and long time to live
 Because you were so willing and freely to give
 To our jolly wassail most cheerful and bold,
 Long may you be happy, long may you live bold.

9 We hope your new apple trees prosper and bear,
 That we shall have cider again next year;
 For where you've a hogshead we hope you'll have ten,
 That you will have cider when we come again.

10 We hope all your barley will prosper and grow,
 That you may have barley and beer to bestow;
 For where you've a bushel we hope you'll have ten,
 That you will have beer when we come again.

11 Now for this good liquor to us you do bring,
 We'll lift up our voices and merrily sing,
 That all good householders may continue still
 And provide some good liquor our bowl for to fill.

12 Now for this good liquor, your cider or beer,
 Now for the great kindness that we have had here,
 We'll return our thanks, and shall still bear in mind
 How you have been bountiful, loving and kind.

13 Now for the great kindness that we have received
 We return you our thanks and shall take our leave;
 From this present time we shall bid you adieu
 Until the next year when the time do ensue.

14 Now jolly old Christmas is passing away;
   According to custom this is the last day
   That we shall enjoy along with you to bide,
   So farewell old Christmas, this merry old tide.

145   The Derby Tup

*'The Derby Ram', as it is better known, was already comonplace by 1739,
when the vicar of St Alkmund's Church, Derby, wrote at the end of a letter
to his son: 'And thus I conclude this long story; almost as long a tale as that of
the Derby Ram' (quoted in Opie,* The Oxford Dictionary of Nursery
Rhymes, *1977, p. 146). The version given here was learned in the late
1930s by three singers at present living in Leicester, who have recently performed it, together with the vestigial play which goes with it. There is a
short, spoken prologue ('Here comes me and our owd lass,/Short o' money
and short o' brass;/Pay for a pint and let us sup,/Then we'll do the Derby
Tup'), and a passage of dialogue after the first verse: 'First speaker: Well,
owd lass, we ought to kill this tup, I think. Have we a butcher in this house?
Second speaker: Our Bob's a blacksmith. First: I never asked for a blacksmith; I want a butcher. Second: Well, our Bill's a butcher. First: Well, will
you fetch 'im, then? Second: Bill, come here. Third speaker: Right, yes,
what d'y' want? First; We want this tup killin'. Third: Well, that's easy
done. Where d'y' want it stickin', 'eads or tails? First: 'Eads, to be sure.
Third: Right.' Mr Robert Moon, one of the performers, writes: 'This is sung
on New Year's Eve going round as a group in the public houses of the Derbyshire village where I lived as a boy. The village was Brimington, near Chesterfield. It was sung in other villages when I was a boy, but the tradition, I
am afraid, is dying out. . . . We do have another member to the team (in
addition to the three speakers), he taking the part of the Ram, for which we
made a Ram's head, complete with eyes, teeth, and horns, as you will note we
sing about, also he is dressed in a fur coat to represent the wool on his back'
(private communication, 1973).*

2 The wool upon his back, sir, reached up into the sky;
  The eagles built their nests there, for I heard the young ones
    cry.

3 The wool upon his belly, it dragged upon the ground;
  It was sold at Derby town, sir, for forty thousand pound.

4 The space between the horns, sir, was far as man could
    reach,
  And there they built a pulpit but no one in it preached.

5 The teeth that were in his mouth, sir, were like a regiment of
    men,
  And the tongue that hung between, sir, would have dined
    'em twice and again.

6 This ram jumped o'er a wall, sir, his tail caught on a briar;
  It reached from Derby town, sir, all into Leicestershire.

7 And of this tail so long, sir, the length you know full well,
  They made a goodly rope, sir, to toll the market bell.

8 All the maids in Derby came begging for his horns
  To take them to the coopers to make them milking gawns.

9 The little boys of Derby, they came to beg his eyes,
  To roll about the streets, sir, they being of football size.

10 The butcher that killed this ram, sir, was drowned in the
    blood,
  And all the people of Derby were carried away in the flood.

  Indeed, sir, it's the truth, sir, for I was never taught to lie,
  And if you go to Derby, sir, you may eat a bit of the pie.

146   One, O

*Under the title of 'Green Grow the Rushes, O', this is perhaps the best
known English folk song. It was sung in Cornwall both by chapel congrega-
tions and by carol singers at Christmas. In Norfolk it was a favourite at
harvest home celebrations. Eton schoolboys enjoyed it, and Sir Arthur Sulli-*

van introduced it into The Yeomen of the Guard. *The song still delights boy scouts round their campfires and rugby players (albeit with widely divergent words) in their baths. Versions have been reported in Breton, Flemish, Hebrew, German, Greek and medieval Latin ('Unus est Deus'). Part of its appeal lies in the mysterious quality of the allusions and in the poetic quality of the words. 'They sang exquisitely', wrote John Moore in* Portrait of Elmbury *(1945, p. 81), 'and with a sort of reverential air, as if they knew it was strong magic, which indeed it is.'*

Enormous ingenuity and energy have been expended in attempting to explain the song. The most recent and most convincing theory has been advanced by Bob Stewart in his Where is Saint George? Imagery in English Folk Song *(Moonraker Press, Bradford-on-Avon, 1977). He suggests that this was originally a mnemonic for the kabbalistic doctrine of the ten stages between heaven and earth, pictures in the tree of life. The twelve verses of many versions represent a Christian overlay. Whatever the truth may be, the song continues to fascinate.*

1 O, I'll sing you one, O.
   What is your one, O?
   One is one and all alone and never more shall be, so.

2 O, I'll sing you two, O.
   What are your two, O?
   Two are the lily-white boys, clothed with green, O;
   One is one and all alone and never more shall be, so.

3 Three, the drivers . .

239

4 Four, the gospel makers, and . . .
5 Five, the thimbles in your bosom . . .
6 Six, the six great walkers, and . . .
7 Seven, the seven stars in the sky, and . . .
8 Eight, the able rangers, and . . .
9 Nine, the nine great shiners, and . . .
10 Ten, the ten commandments . . .
11 Eleven, the evangelists, and . . .
12 O, I'll sing you twelve, O.
   What are your twelve, O?
   Twelve, the twelve apostles, and
   Eleven the evangelists, and
   Ten, the ten commandments,
   Nine, the nine great shiners, and
   Eight the able rangers, and
   Seven, the seven stars in the sky, and
   Six, the six great walkers, and
   Five, the thimbles in your bosom,
   Four, the gospel makers, and
   Three, the drivers,
   Two are the lily-white boys clothed with green, O;
   One is one and all alone and never more shall be, so.

One: God.
  Two: the astrological sign of the Gemini.
Three: understanding, eternity, and the great mother. Other suggestions are: the Three Fates, the Three Wise Men.
Four: the evangelists.
Five: the pentagram, or five-pointed star. 'It is the shape of a man standing upright with arms outstretched. The Qabalah uses this symbol to suggest that a fifth element of divinity, present in man, may control or discipline the Elements' (Stewart).

Six: the six proud walkers may have been accidentally imported from another song. The sixth stage in the tree of life is linked with the sun or the principle of harmony and beauty.
Seven: The Pleiades.
Eight: the archangel Raphael, the Keeper of the Gates of Dawn.
Nine: the angels of the ninth sphere were the 'brightly shining ones', who looked after the business of transporting souls into and out of bodies at birth and death.
Eleven: the twelve apostles, less Judas.

147 The Tree in the Wood

It is clear from some versions that this song refers to the cycle of life. One, appropriately called 'The Everlasting Circle' (collected by Baring-Gould and published for the first time in full in the book of the same name), follows the

feathers to a bed, and thence: 'All on this bed a lad did lie . . . with this lad a
maiden she did sleep . . . in this maiden a baby was made . . . out of this
baby a boy he did grow . . . the boy did lay on the ground an acorn . . . out
of this acorn did grow a great tree' (1960, p. 101). The song has enjoyed
extraordinary popularity; in addition to a score of times in England, it has
been reported from Ireland, Scotland, Wales, Canada, America, France, Brit-
tany, Switzerland and Denmark. The earliest printing seems to have been in
1878, which is surprising, considering the primitive feeling of the cycle.

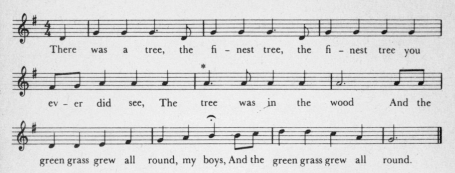

There was a tree, the fi - nest tree, the fi - nest tree you
ev - er did see, The tree was in the wood And the
green grass grew all round, my boys, And the green grass grew all round.

*Repeat this bar as necessary for succeeding verses.

2 There was a bough, the finest bough, the finest bough you
      ever did see;
   The bough was on the tree, the tree was in the wood,
   And the green grass grew all round, my boys,
   And the green grass grew all round.

   *And so on, successively introducing: branch, twig, a nest, some eggs,
      some birds, some feathers, some fleas, some bones, some
      marrow.*

   Last verse
   There was some marrow, the finest marrow, the finest
      marrow you ever did see;
   The marrow was on the bones, the bones were in the fleas,
      the fleas were on the feathers, the feathers were on the
      birds, the birds were in the eggs, the eggs were in the
      nest, the nest was on the twig, the twig was on the
      branch, the branch was on the bough, the bough was on
      the tree, the tree was in the wood,
   And the green grass grew all round, my boys,
   And the green grass grew all round.

SOURCES AND NOTES

Songs are unpublished unless otherwise stated

I FELLOWS THAT FOLLOW THE PLOUGH: WORK

1 The Green Grass
C. Carey, *Ten English Folk Songs,*
1915, p. 10.
2 The Oxen Ploughing
S. Baring-Gould, *English Minstrelsie:
a National Monument of English Song,*
8 vols, Edinburgh, 1895–7; vol. II,
p. 97.
**3 All Jolly Fellows that Follow
the Plough**
Sung by Arthur Lane (1884–1975),
farm worker, Corvedale, Shropshire;
collected by Philip Donnellan, 1974.
The tune given is as sung for the
second verse. A meeting with Arthur
Lane is described in John Seymour's
The Countryside Explained (Faber,
1977, pp. 12–17).
4 The Ploughboy
J. Broadwood, *Old English Songs,*
1843, no. 6.
5 Twankydillo
Sung by Samuel Willett (b. *c.* 1830),
baker, Cuckfield, Sussex; collected
by Lucy Broadwood, 1891 (L. E.
Broadwood and J. A. Fuller Maitland, *English County Songs,* 1893,
p. 138).
6 The Blacksmith
Sung by Mr Carter, fisherman,
King's Lynn, Norfolk; collected by
Ralph Vaughan Williams, 10.1.1905
(British Library Add. MSS 54187,
vol. III, p. 226).
7 A Lincolnshire Shepherd
Text: written by Jesse Baggaley
(1906–1976), of Lincoln. Tune: by
Maurice Ogg, Coleby, Lincs.
**8 Come All You Valiant
Shepherds**
Sung by Mr Burrage, Capel, Surrey;
collected by Ralph Vaughan Williams, 4.8.1908 (MS I 256).
9 Pleasant Month of May
Bob Copper, *A Song for Every Season,* Heinemann, 1971, p. 228. The
song can be heard, sung by the Copper family, on the record, *A Song for
Every Season* (Leader LED 2067).

10 Turnit Hoeing
Sung by Charles Parsons, Knole
Farm, Long Sutton, Somerset; col-
lected by Cecil Sharp (1859–1924),
September, 1903 (MS in the library
of Clare College, Cambridge).
11 The Rosebuds in June
M. H. Mason, *Nursery Rhymes and
Country Songs,* 1877, p. 55.
12 Tarry Woo'
Sung by Mr John Mason, Dent,
North Yorkshire; collected by Ralph
Vaughan Williams, 10.8.1904 (JFS II
215; also in my *Room for Company,*
Cambridge, 1971, p. 16).
13 The Rambling Comber
Sung by Henry Burstow
(1826–1916), bootmaker, Horsham,
Sussex; collected (tune) by Lucy
Broadwood, 2.5.1893; words sent on
later by Burstow (Broadwood Papers, Cecil Sharp House).
14 The Reaphook and the Sickle
H. Sumner, *The Besom Maker,* 1888,
p. 13.
15 All of a Row
Baring-Gould, *Minstrelsie,* vol. II,
p. 34.
16 The Jolly Waggoner
Sung by Mr Rose, landlord of the
Bridge Inn, Acle, Norfolk; collected
by Ralph Vaughan Williams,
14.4.1908 (MS I 34 (2).) In verse 1,
line 1, 'when' has been substituted
for 'oh'; and in the last line of the
same verse, 'none' for 'more'.
17 The Country Lass
Sent to Lucy Broadwood by Samuel
Willett (for whom, see no. 5) in
1890, with this comment: 'I write
everything from memory, both
words and music' (Broadwod Papers).
18 The Farmer's Boy
As no. 3
19 Joe the Carrier's Lad
Sung by Frank Hinchliffe, Holme
Valley, Yorkshire, on the record, *A
Fine Hunting Day: Songs of the Holme

Valley Beagles (Leader LEE 4056, 1975); recorded by David Bland. This may have been learned from a sheet music copy.

20 The Old Cock Crows
Sung by Derek and Dorothy Elliott

on the record, *Yorkshire Relish* (Traditional Sound Recordings TSR 025, 1976). This version derives from the singing of Kit Jones of Redmire, Yorkshire.

II A HEALTH TO THE MASTER: DEFERENCE AND PROTEST

21 Harvest Home Song
W. A. Barrett, *English Folk-Songs*, 1891, no. 7, p. 12.
22 God Speed the Plough
Sumner, p. 5.
23 The Jolly Thresherman
Sung by Mr Earle, Leith Hill Place, Surrey; collected by Ralph Vaughan Williams, October or November, 1904 (MS II 284).
24 The Old Farmer
Barrett, no. 17, p. 30. 'This song is popular in Sussex, in Cambridgeshire, and in Essex' (Barrett's note).
25 The Rigs of the Time
Sung by John ('Charger') Salmond, retired ferryman, Stalham, Norfolk; recorded at the Eel's Foot Inn, Eastbridge, Leiston, Suffolk by E. J. Moeran, 7.11.1947, and subsequently broadcast in a BBC programme. Previously published in my *Painful Plough*, Cambridge, 1972, p. 40.
26 The Labouring Man
Sung by Mr Sparks, Dunsfold, Surrey; collected by Lucy Broadwood, 1898 (*Journal of the Folk Song Society* (JFS), Vol I, 1899–1904, p. 198).
27 The New-fashioned Farmer
Sung by Mr John Denny (b. 1839), Nevinton, Essex; collected by Ralph Vaughan Williams, 25.4.1904 (MS II 124, under the title of 'The Old-fashioned Farmer'). The singer knew only the chorus and first four lines, so I have supplied the remainder of the text from a broadside without imprint in Cecil Sharp's Collection of Street Ballads (at Cecil Sharp House).
28 The Tythe Pig
Sung by J. Helmore (miller), South Brent, Devon; collected by F. W. Bussell (Baring-Gould MSS, no. XXIX, Plymouth Central Library).

Only the tune and two verses are in the manuscript, and the third verse reads: 'O then out spake &c. See Songs of the West'. In *Songs of the West* (1905 edition) there is the identical tune and seven verses with this note: 'There are ten verses in the original. I have cut them down to seven. . . . Words and air taken from Robert Hard. Sung also by J. Helmore.' Faced with these difficulties, I have given the material in the manuscript and added the remainder of the text from a broadside with the title of 'The Sucking Pig', printed by J. Catnach of London (Cecil Sharp Broadside Collection).
29 The Parson and the Clerk
Sung by Phil Tanner (1862–1950), Llangennith, Gower; collected by Maud Karpeles, 22.4.1949. © Folktracks and Soundpost Publications. Together with other songs sung by Phil Tanner, this was issued on a record by the English Folk Dance and Song Society in 1968 (LP 1005).
30 The Mare and the Foal
Sung by Mr George Hill, East Stonham, Suffolk; collected by E. J. Moeran, 1921 (JFS VIII, 1927–31, pp. 270–1).
31 Good King Arthur
Sent to Lucy Broadwood by a Worcestershire correspondent (Broadwood Papers).
32 The Miller and His Three Sons
Sung by Mr Greenwood, schoolmaster, at the Duncombe Arms, Westerdale, Yorkshire; collected by Ralph Vaughan Williams, 13.7.1904 (MS III 8).
33 We Poor Labouring Men
Sung by an unnamed singer at East Meon, Hampshire; collected by

Francis Jekyll, probably in 1909 (M. Dawney (ed.), *The Ploughboy's Glory*, EFDSS, 1977, p. 46).

34 Mutton Pie
Communicated by Mr Maurice Ogg, Coleby, Lincs., who learnt it in 1974 from one of his wife's relatives, and subsequently added verses 'picked up from here and there'. Mr Ogg says that 'many versions of the same song' are sung in his locality.

35 O the Roast Beef of Old England: New Version
Text: Howard Evans (ed.), *Songs for Singing at Agricultural Labourers' Meetings*, London and Leamington, n.d., p. 15. Tune: W. Chappell, *Popular Music of the Olden Time*, 1859, p. 636.

36 An Old Man's Advice
Sung by Walter Pardon (b. 1915), carpenter, Knapton, Norfolk; collected by Roy Palmer, 29.3.1978.

37 I've Livèd in Service
Sung by Mrs Verrall, Monks Gate, Horsham, Sussex; collected by Ralph Vaughan Williams, 24.5.1904 (MS II 142).

38 The Brisk Young Butcher
Sung by Jack Beeforth (b. 1891), hill farmer, Wragby, N. Yorks.; collected by David Hillery, 22.6.1974.

39 Rap-a-tap
Sung by Bob Hart (1892–1978), Snape, Suffolk, on the record, *Flash Company* (Topic 12TS243, 1974); recorded by Tony Engle, September, 1973.

40 The Rest of the Day's Your Own
Written by J. P. Long and W. David, published in *Old Time Comic Songs*, No. 1, 1915. Bob Arnold can be heard singing it on the record, *Mornin' All* (Argo ZFB 83, 1972).

III   THE HIGH GALLOWS TREE: CRIME

41 Robin Wood and the Pedlar
Sung by George Trainer, Haywards Heath, Sussex; collected by Mike Yates, 14.2.1964.

42 Spare Me the Life of Georgie
Sung by Mary Haynes, Hartlebury, Worcs.; collected by W. R. Clay, 30.11.1908 (W. R. Clay *Four Folk Songs from Hartlebury*, Kidderminster, n.d., no. 1). The singer learned the song from a dairy maid in Upton Warren parish in 1851.

43 Gilderoy
Sung by Henry Burstow (for whom, see no. 13). The tune was noted by Lucy Broadwood in 1893 and the words sent on by Burstow in 1894 (Broadwood Papers). The song was published in part in JFS II, 1907, p. 240.

44 The Three Butchers
Sung by Mr James Punt, East Hornden, Essex; collected by Ralph Vaughan Williams, 21.4.1904 (MS II 60). Only one verse was noted. The remainder of the text has been supplied from a broadside printed by J. Catnach (in Vaughan Williams'

Scrapbook of Broadsides, no. 6016–7 at Cecil Sharp House).

45 Bold Turpin
As for no. 44 (MS II 58). The half line which has been added in square brackets is wanting in the MS.

46 The Box Upon Her Head
Text: 'from Mrs Coomber, August, 1906; taken down by W. G.' (Gilchrist Papers at Cecil Sharp House). Mrs Coomber was from Kent. The text is marked 'sung to the tune of "The Banks of Sweet Dundee"', but I have preferred 'The Box Upon Her Head', as sung by Mrs Bowker, Sunderland Point, Lancashire, with a chorus and fragment of text, collected by Anne Gilchrist (Broadwood Papers). In the original of verse 8, line 3, the last word is in the plural, but I have changed it to the singular to avoid the hilarity of modern audiences.

47 Salisbury Plain
Sung by Mr and Mrs Verrall, Horsham, Sussex; collected by Ralph Vaughan Williams, 8.10.1904 (MS II 260). The text appears to be in the handwriting of Henry Burstow. The

song has previously been published (JFS II, 1906, p. 196 and R. Vaughan Williams and A. L. Lloyd, *The Penguin Book of English Folk Songs*, 1959, p. 95), though on neither occasion was the text of the MS given in full. It now appears in print for the first time, though the spelling has been regularized.

48 Australia
Details as for no. 39.

49 The Lincolnshire Poacher
Sung by Joe Saunders, traveller, at Biggin Hill, Kent; collected by Stephen Sedley, 1967. The singer has only a few lines of text, and the remainder has been supplied from R. Bell, *Ballads and Songs*, 1857, pp. 216–7, with verse 4 added from Chappell, p. 732.

50 The Nottingham Poacher
Sung by George Dunn (1887–1975), chainmaker, Quarry Bank, Staffordshire; collected by Charles Parker, April, 1971 (Roy Palmer, Katharine Thomson and Pamela Bishop, *Songs of the Midlands*, E. P. Publishing, 1972, pp. 71–2). The first verse is a combination of the words printed in the book, and those sung by George Dunn on his record (Leader LEE 4042).

51 Lads of High Renown
Sung by Walter Pardon (for whom, see no. 36) on the record, *A Proper Sort* (Leader LED 2063, 1975); recorded by Bill Leader. The title, 'The Poacher's Fate', is used on the record, but Walter Pardon has always known the song by the one given here.

52 Van Dieman's Land
Sung by Mr Broomfield, East Hornden, Essex; collected by Ralph Vaughan Williams, 22.4.1904 (MS II 69).

53 Hares in the Old Plantation
Sung by Noah Fisher at the Horseshoes, Tibbenham, Diss, Norfolk; collected by Ralph Vaughan Williams, 20.12.1911 (MS 8vo C 27). The last two and a half verses have been supplied from an unnamed singer at the Bell, Willingale Doe, Essex; collected by Ralph Vaughan Williams, 14.4.1904 (MS II 35).

54 Row Dow Dow
Sung by Joe Saunders (for whom, see no. 49); collected by Stephen Sedley, 1967. Pop Maynard can be heard singing this song on the record, *Ye Subjects of England* (Topic 12T 286, 1976).

55 Henry, My Son
Sung by George Dunn (for whom, see no. 50); collected by Roy Palmer, 3.12.1971 (*Songs of the Midlands*, p. 65). George Dunn can be heard singing this song on the record, LEE 4042.

56 The Babes in the Wood
Sung by Mrs Jenner (probably b. 1837), a native of Penshurst, Kent; collected by Anne Gilchrist, probably in 1907 (Gilchrist Papers). Since the singer had only the first verse and chorus the remainder has been added from J. O. Halliwell, *The Nursery Rhymes of England*, 5th ed., 1853.

57 Hangèd I Shall Be
Sung by 'Shepherd' Taylor, Hickling, Norfolk; collected by E. J. Moeran, October, 1921 (JFS VII, 1922, p. 23). Harry Cox can be heard singing a very similar version of this song on the record, *Harry Cox, English Folk Singer* (EFDSS LP 1004, 1965), under the title of 'The 'Prentice Boy'.

58 The False-hearted Knight
Sung by William ('Jumbo') Brightwell (b. 1900), railwayman, Leiston, Suffolk, on the record, *Songs from the Eel's Foot* (Topic 12TS261, 1975); recorded by Tony Engle. The singer was previously recorded in 1947 at the same time as John Salmond (see no. 25).

59 It's of a Farmer
Sung by an unnamed singer, Poolend, Ashperton, Hertfordshire; collected by Ralph Vaughan Williams, September, 1913 (MS 8vo E 5).

60 The Prickle Holly Bush
Sung by Bill Whiting (b. 1891), Longcot, Berkshire; collected by Mike Yates, 2.9.1972.

61 Maria Marten
Sung by Mr George Hall, Hooton Roberts, Yorks.; collected by R. A. Gatty, 1907 (MS no. 661164 in Birmingham Reference Library). The tune given here was sung for the second verse. The singer learnt his songs in Huntingdonshire.

IV ONCE I LOVED A LASS: COURTSHIP

62 As I Was A-walking
Sung by Henry Burstow (for whom, see no. 13); tune collected by Lucy Broadwood, 2.5.1893; words sent on later by Burstow (Broadwood Papers).

63 Green Bushes
Sung by Mr and Mrs Ratford, Ingrave, Essex; collected by Ralph Vaughan Williams, 15.4.1904 (MS II 43). Only the tune was taken down, so the text has been supplied here from a broadside printed by Wright of Birmingham, c. 1820–7, under the title of 'The False Lovers' (Birmingham Reference Library).

64 Lovely Joan
Sung by Mr Christopher Jay, Acle, Norfolk; collected by Ralph Vaughan Williams, 18.4.1908 (MS 4to I 32 (2).) The song was published (in part) in JFS IV, 1910, p. 90, and in Vaughan Williams and Lloyd, p. 64.

65 Broomfield Hill
As no. 36.

66 The Crockery Ware
Sung by Fred Cottingham, Warbrook Farm, Chiddingstone, Kent; collected by Mike Yates, 6.6.1976.

67 Three Maids A-milking
Sung by Roger Hannaford, Lower Widdecombe, Devon; collected by S. Baring-Gould, 1890. The tune was published in *Songs of the West* (edition of 1899–92), with a rewritten text. The original is here supplied from Baring-Gould's MSS (Plymouth Central Library). A modern performance by Cyril Tawney can be heard on the record, *Down Among the Barley Straw* (Leader LER 2095, 1976).

68 The Spotted Cow
Sung by Frank Hinchliffe on the record, *In Sheffield Park* (Topic 12TS308, 1977); recorded by Mike Yates, and Ruairidh and Alvina Greig, 1976. The singer was 'the son of a carter who later became a small farmer himself until 1968 when . . . he went to work for the local water Authority' (A. E. Green, article on Frank Hinchliffe in *Traditional Music*, no. 6, 1977, pp. 20–2). He should not be confused with his homonym from Holme Valley (no. 19).

69 The Mower
Baring-Gould, *Minstrelsie*, no. XXXIX, pp. 84–5. Since Baring-Gould noted that 'I have . . . entirely rewritten the song', the text has been restored from a typescript copy, entitled 'Mow the Meadows Down' (Shrewsbury City Library). Some minor adaptations have been necessary in order to marry the text to the tune.

70 The Ploughman's Glory
Sung by Mr Thompson, Flamborough, Yorks.; collected by Frank Kidson (F. Kidson, *Traditional Tunes*, 1891, p. 145). The singer had only two verses, so the remainder of the text has been supplied from a broadside printed by J. Kendrew, Colliergate, York (BL 1870 c.2, p. 144). The title of the broadside has been adopted, instead of Mr Thompson's original 'Pretty Ploughboy' in order to avoid confusion with no. 98.

71 The Barley Rakings
As no. 67.

72 The Nutting Girl
Sung by Cyril Poacher (b. 1910), farm worker, Blaxhall, Suffolk, on the record, *The Broomfield Wager* (Topic 12TS252, 1975); recorded by Tony Engle, 1974. The tune printed is as sung for the second verse.

73 The Thrashing Machine
Sung by William Nott, Meshaw, Devon; collected by Cecil Sharp, 9.1.1904 (MS).

74 The Miller's Song

Sung by George Dunn (for details of whom, see no. 50); collected by Roy Palmer, 27.1.1975. The first four verses were previously published in *Songs of the Midlands*, p. 44, and can be heard on the record, LEE 4042.

75 Oh, Once I Loved A Lass
Sung by Robert Barrett, carter, Piddletown, Dorset; collected by H. E. D. Hammond, 1905 (J. Brocklebank and B. Kindersley, *A Dorset Book of Folk Songs*, EFDSS, 1966, p. 7; first published, 1948).

76 The Knife in the Window
As for no. 60.

77 Seventeen Come Sunday
Communicated by Walter Pardon (for whom, see no. 36), August, 1978. One verse has been added from a broadside printed by Such of London (author's collection).

78 The Cuckoo
Barrett, no. 47, p. 81.

79 The Banks of Sweet Primroses
Sung by Walter Gales at the Eel's Foot (cf. no. 25). The singer's title was 'As I Walked Out One Bright May Morning'.

80 Fare Thee Well, Cold Winter
Sung by George ('Tom') Newman (b. 1882), Clanfield, Bampton, Oxfordshire; collected by Mike Yates, 13.8.1972. Previously published, though with tune transcribed

very differently from the notation given here, in *Traditional Music*, no. 1, 1975, p. 13.

81 The Water of Tyne
J. C. Bruce and J. Stokoe, *Northumbrian Minstrelsy*, 1882, p. 89.

82 The Brisk Young Sailor
Sung by James Bayliff (b. 1839), Barbon, Westmorland; collected by Anne Gilchrist, June, 1909 (A. G. Gilchrist, article quoted above, pp. 7 and 13). In the article, line 3 of verse 1 reads: 'My liberty, with my right goodwill', but I have substituted the version noted in Anne Gilchrist's original MS (Gilchrist Papers).

83 Sheepcrook and Black Dog
Sung by Mr Stacey, Holycombe, Sussex; collected by Ralph Vaughan Williams, 28.5.1904 (MS II 168). In the MS, F in the second bar is marked sharp, with a natural sign in brackets. There is some discrepancy between the words beneath the music and those in the MS text. I have followed the latter.

84 The Seeds of Love
Sung by John England, gardener, Hambridge, Somerset; collected by Cecil Sharp, September, 1903, and first published in 1904 (M. Karpeles; *Cecil Sharp's Collection of English Folk Songs*, Oxford, 2 vols, 1974; vol. 1, no. 153 D, p. 581).

V THE CHARMING BRIDE: MARRIAGE

85 The Ensilver Song
J. Sutcliffe Smith, *The Music of the Yorkshire Dales*, Leeds, n.d., p. 43. There is a modern recording by David Hillery on the record, *Transpennine* (Topic 12TS215, 1971).

86 Tuesday Morning
Sung by F. Bailey, Combe Bissett, Wilts.; collected by Ralph Vaughan Williams, 2.11.1904 (MS II 238). The singer had only three verses, which have been very slightly amended, and completed by three more verses from a broadside entitled 'I Shall Be Married on Monday Morning', published by Williamson of Newcastle

(Birmingham Reference Library).

87 Bonny Blue Handkerchief
Sung by Harry Upton, Balcombe, Sussex; collected by Mike Yates, 23.11.1974. Mr Upton, who learned the song from his father, a shepherd on the downs above Brighton, can be heard singing it on the record, *Why Can't It Always Be Saturday?* (Topic SP104, 1978). See also the article by Mike Yates on Upton in *Traditional Music*, no. 10, 1978. The singer had only three verses, of which the first is given here as verse 1, the second as v. 5, and the third as v. 2. The remainder of the text has

been supplied from a broadside printed by W. S. Fortey of Seven Dials (Bradford Public Library).

88 When Shall We Get Married, John?
Sung by Alice Green (b. 1895), Bampton, Oxon; collected by Mike Yates, 24.4.1973.

89 Three Weeks Before Easter
Sung by Ted Nevill, Little Burstead, Essex; collected by Ralph Vaughan Williams, 16.4.1904 (MS II 47).

90 The Charming Bride
Sung by Mr W. Clark, Barrow-on-Humber, Lincs.; collected by Percy Grainger, 26.7.1906 (MS no. 261). The last half of the penultimate bar of the music is conjectural, because of the faintness of the copy.

91 The Cuckoo's Nest
Text: communicated by Mr Bob Whitlock of Cheshunt, Herts., who writes 'My version . . . was obtained orally from an ex-Oxford man whose name, alas, I do not know. Its reputed source is a manuscript – presumably a field collection, but writer unknown – found in the Bodleian' (private communication, 1968). I took it that the reference was to the Manning Collection (Bodleian MS Top. Oxon. d. 200), but the only version of the song there is a fragment on p. 99 from Charles Tanner of Bampton with one verse (approximating to verse 3 here) and chorus (similar to this but not identical). The mystery therefore remains. Versions of the tune, however, abound, since it was frequently used for Morris dancing. Mr Whitlock suggests the Sherborne version, but I have preferred the tune from the manuscript of the poet, John Clare (Northampton Public Library). Alfred Williams collected it from the Tanner family at Bampton, and it may be that there is a full text of 'The Cuckoo's Nest' in his unpublished papers at Swindon Public Library.

92 Raking the Hay
Sung by Sam Larner (1878–1965), fisherman, Winterton, Norfolk, on the record, *A Garland for Sam* (Topic 12T244, 1974); recorded by Philip Donnellan, 1958/9.

93 The Foggy Dew
Tune: learned by me in the early 1950s. Text: broadside published by J. Russell of Birmingham (author's collection).

94 The Pretty Ploughboy
Sung by Walter Pardon (for whom, see no. 36) on the record, *Our Side of the Baulk* (Leader LED 2111, 1977); recorded by Bill Leader.

95 The Bonny Labouring Boy
As no. 61.

96 The Dumb Maid
Sung by Mrs Freda Palmer, Whitney, Oxon.; collected by Mike Yates, 1.5.1975.

97 Come All You Young Ladies and Gentlemen
Sung by Mr Seers or Shears, Winterslow, Wilts.; collected by Ralph Vaughan Williams, 1.9.1904 (MS II 224). Note added: 'now in Salisbury Union'.

98 Willie Went to Westerdale
As no. 38.

99 Oh, It Was My Cruel Parents
Sung by George Dunn (for whom, see no. 50); collected by Roy Palmer, 7.6.1971. The singer remembered only the last line of verse 5, but he immediately recognized the remainder when I showed him a broadside version, 'Sally's Love for a Young Man' (without imprint; John Johnson Collection, Bodleian Library). His original version is in *Songs of the Midlands* (p. 41) and can be heard on the record, LEE 4042.

100 Hey Down Derry
Sung by Charlotte Few (b. *c.* 1857), servant, Cottenham, Cambridgeshire; collected by Miss E. Bull, 1904 (Broadwood Papers).

101 The Parson with the Wooden Leg
Sung by Mr Hubert Bradley (b. 1913), Mamble, Worcs.; collected by Roy Palmer, 26.7.1972 (*English Dance and Song,* Vol. XXXV, no. 3, Autumn, 1973, p. 99). The singer learned the song from his grand-

father, who was born in Worcestershire (c. 1860), but brought up in Staffordshire.

102 It's of an Old Couple
Sung by Mrs Verrall, Horsham, Sussex; collected by Ralph Vaughan Williams, 6.9.1906 (MS I 261).

103 Coming Home Late
Sung by Alfred Welfare (b. 1917), North Chailey, Lewes, Sussex; collected by Mike Yates, 23.1.1977.

104 The Mole Catcher
Sung by Mr Christopher Jay, Bridge Inn, Acle, Norfolk; collected by Ralph Vaughan Williams, 18.4.1908 (MS 4to I 37). Although the music provides for a refrain, no words for it were noted. I have therefore borrowed the refrain from another version collected by Vaughan Williams (JFS IV, p. 87).

105 The Groggy Old Tailor
Sung by Mr Charlie Clittleborough, Sutton, Norfolk; collected by E. J. Moeran, 1927 (JFS VIII, 1929, p. 274).

106 The Grey Hawk
Sung by Bob Roberts (b. 1909), retired skipper, formerly of Suffolk, now of the Isle of Wight, on the record, *Songs from the Sailing Barges* (Topic 12TS361, 1978); recorded by Tony Engle, August, 1977.

107 The Trees They Do Grow High
As for no. 51.

108 The Dark-Eyed Sailor
Sung by a singer identified only as Jack at the Eel's Foot, 1947 (cf. no. 25). One verse had been added from a broadside without imprint (Bradford Public Library).

VI UP TO THE RIGS: SPORT AND DIVERSION

110 I'm a Young Man from the Country
As no. 72. Tune as sung for last verse.

111 Rotherham Statutes
Frank Kidson, 'Old Airs and Songs: Melodies Once Popular in Yorkshire', series of articles contributed to the *Leeds Mercury*, 1890–1; no. XVIII.

112 Sedgefield Fair
As no. 38.

113 Strawberry Fair
Sung by James Masters, Broadstone, Devon; collected by S. Baring-Gould, 1891. The tune is in *Songs of the West* (no. 68, 1905 edition), with the note: 'We have been forced to re-write the words, which were very indelicate.' The original text has been supplied from the Baring-Gould MSS (Plymouth Central Library). See details of a modern recording under no. 67.

114 Home from the Fair
Sung by Mrs Ruth Robinson (1860–1976), Winteringham, Scunthorpe, Lincs.; collected by Maurice Ogg, 1971. Mrs Robinson learned the song from her mother when she was twelve.

115 I Went to Market
Sung by Derek and Dorothy Elliott (see no. 20). The song comes from the grandfather of John and Hazel Browell of Bradford.

116 John Barleycorn
Sung by Bob Blake, Broadbridge Heath, Horsham, Sussex; collected by Mike Yates, 11.12.1974.

117 When Jones's Ale Was New
Sung by Mr Hilton, S. Walsham, Norfolk; collected by Ralph Vaughan Williams, 11.4.1908 (MS I 140).

118 The Barley Mow
Text: Dixon, pp. 178–82 (slightly amended). Tune: Chappell, p. 745.

119 The Punch Ladle
Barrett, no. 40, p. 70.

120 Good English Ale
Sung by the Cantwell family, Standlake, Oxon.; collected by Mike Yates, 21.6.1964.

121 Mowing Match Song
Sung by Becket Whitehead, Delph, Oldham, Lancs.; recorded by Seamus Ennis, 24.5.1952 (BBC Sound Archive). Collated with text printed in

A. Wrigley, *Songs of a Moorland Parish,* Saddleworth, 1912, pp. 140 ff.

122 Wa'ney Cockfeightin' Sang
Sung by John Collinson (b. 1862), blacksmith, Casterton, Kirky Lonsdale, Westmorland, at the Westmorland Musical Festival, 1905 (Barrow-in-Furness County Library, file no. Z. 2497).

123 The Bell Ringing
Sung by William George Kerswell, Two Bridges, Dartmoor (*Songs of the West,* no. 82).

124 I'Anson's Racehorse
Noted in 1888 by T. C. Smith and communicated to Frank Kidson (JFS II, 1906, p. 266). Further verses have been added from a broadside printed by H. Such of London, under the title of 'The Little Dun Mare' (private collection).

125 Hare Hunting Song
Sung by Mr Cropper at the Westmorland Musical Festival; collected by Frank Kidson, 10.4.1902 (MS, Mitchell Library, Glasgow).

126 The Huntsman
As no. 36.

127 We'll All Go A-hunting Today
As no. 38.

VII THE LIFE OF A MAN: SEASONS AND CEREMONIES

128 The Seasons
Barrett, no. 22.

129 What's the Life of a Man?
Sung by Mr J. W. Wright, Coombe Bissett, Wilts.; collected by Ralph Vaughan Williams, 2.9.1904 (MS II 240).

130 Apple Tree Wassail
Sung by C. Ash (b. 1845), Crowcombe, Somerset; collected by Cecil Sharp, 15.9.1908 (Karpeles, no. 373 M, pp. 529–30).

131 Shrove Tuesday Song
Under the heading, 'Baldon Shrove Tuesday Song 1840' in the Manning Collection, MSS Top. Oxon. d.200, p. 110 (Bodleian Library).

132 Pace Egging Song
Sung by Mr Arthur Hulme (b. 1886), Marple, Cheshire; collected by Venetia Newall, 1966 (*An Egg at Easter, A Folklore Study,* Routledge, 1971, p. 367). The text only was published and, unfortunately, the tune has been mislaid. I have therefore added a Cheshire tune for the same song (Barrett, no. 5, pp. 8–9).

133 Swinton May Song
Chambers' *Book of Days,* vol. I, 1862, pp. 547–8.

134 Peterborough May Song
Charles Dack, *Weather and Folklore of Peterborough and District,* 2nd ed., 1911 (not paginated). The song was taken down in 1904.

135 Helston Furry Dance
W. Crotch, G. A. Macfarren and J. A. Wade, *A Collection of English National Airs* (ed. W. Chappell), 1838, no. 205.

136 Bell Tune
Folklore, vol. 47, 1936, pp. 395–6. After verse 4 occurs the comment: 'One verse missing'. There are further notes on the song *ibid,* vol. 49, 1938, pp. 217–8.

137 The Mallard
Sung to W. G. Arkwright in 1907 by his wife's uncle, Rev. Maunsell Bacon, vicar of Swallowfield, Berkshire (Arkwright MSS, Broadwood Papers).

138 Herrings' Heads
Sung by Johnny Doughty (b. 1903), fisherman, Brighton, Sussex, on the record, *Round Rye Bay for more* (Topic 12TS324, 1977); recorded by Mike Yates, 1976.

139 Souling Song
R. Holland, *A Glossary of Words Used in the County of Chester,* 1886, pp. 508 (text, from Middlewich) and 509 (tune, from Mobberley). A soulers' play text is *ibid,* pp. 510–3.

140 The Old Horse
Mason, pp. 49–50. There is a modern recording by Roy Harris on *The Bitter and the Sweet* (Topic 12TS217, 1972).

141 Six Jolly Miners

Sung by Mr I. H. Baxter and the company at the Black Bull, Ecclesfield, Yorks., on the record, *A People's Carol* (Leader LEE 4065, 1974); recorded by Bill Leader and David Bland, 6.12.73.

142 The Fleecy Care
Communicated by the Rev. Peter Macken of Napton, Warwickshire.

143 Hunting the Wren
Sung by Edmund Hawkins, Adderbury, Oxon.; transmitted via his daughter to Mrs Dorothy Blunt, who in turn sent the song to Lucy Broadwood (letters of 17th May and 6th June, 1907, in Broadwood Papers).

144 The Grampound Wassail
Sung by Michael Nancarow, Grampound, Cornwall; collected by Mr J. J. Mountford of Truro (Baring-Gould, *Minstrelsie,* no. XX, p. 45).

145 The Derby Tup
Sung by Grace Brooks (b. 1931), Gordon Brooks (b. 1929) and Bob Moon (b. 1931) of Leicester; learned in childhood from parents in Derbyshire. Communicated to Roy Palmer, 1973, and published in *English Dance and Song,* vol. XXXVII, no. 2, Summer, 1975. Some amendments have now been made after checking with the informants.

146 One, O
Sung by Mr Dykes, near Weobley, Herefs.; collected by Ralph Vaughan Williams, September, 1912 (MS 8vo D 20).

147 The Tree in the Wood
Sung by Mrs Gloria Day, Birmingham; collected by Roy Palmer, 1969. The singer learned the song from her father, a Warwickshire man.

ACKNOWLEDGMENTS

I should like to thank all the collectors (or their executors) listed under Sources and Notes for permission to use material, though I must especially mention the generosity of Mike Yates and Mrs Ursula Vaughan Williams. 'The Rest of the Day's Your Own' © 1915 is reproduced by permission of Francis Day & Hunter, Ltd, 130–140 Charing Cross Road, London WC2H 0LD. The words of 'A Lincolnshire Shepherd' are reprinted by kind permission of Mrs K. M. Baggaley. I am grateful to Tony Engle of Topic Records, and Bill Leader of Leader Records, for permission to publish for the first time a number of items which have appeared on their records. I should like to thank the English Folk Dance and Song Society for permission to include nos. 13, 17, 31, 33, 43, 46, 56, 62, 75, 82, 100, 137, and 143. In a few cases, notably the late E. J. Moeran, I have been unable to trace copyright holders, and would be grateful for information leading to their whereabouts.

In addition to the many archivists and librarians listed, I should like to thank Major A. D. Parsons, Duke of Edinburgh's Royal Regiment, W. H. G. Gilmour, South Yorkshire County Council Archive Service, J. R. Elliott, West Devon Area Librarian, Plymouth, R. Caldicott, Amenities Officer, Worthing Borough Council, and last, but also the most, Mrs Theresa Thom, Librarian of the English Folk Dance and Song Society.

I am grateful for advice and assistance to Paul Adams, A. E. Green, A. L. Lloyd, Pat Palmer, Ian Russell and Mike Yates, and, for her invaluable transcriptions of music from tapes and records, Katharine Thomson.

Above all, I am deeply indebted to the singers, and here I must single out the help and friendship of Walter Pardon.

INDEX OF TITLES AND FIRST LINES

252

253